Table of Contents

The Corporate View

If you are on the eve of entering the workforce or are studying business as you prepare for a career, the *Corporate View Orientation* is for you.

Corporate View is a workplace simulation designed to help you become effective and successful in an online, interactive workplace. The *Corporate View Orientation* consists of a textbook and an Intranet—a communications system created using technology from the World Wide Web. This Intranet is typical of those used in corporations around the world. You will access the Intranet to communicate with coworkers, research information about Corporate View, and follow hyperlinks to the World Wide Web to learn about other companies and products. You will also learn about the mission-critical functions or departments of a typical corporation, the types of jobs found in various departments, and how these departments work together via the Intranet. As an intern at Corporate View, you will develop teamwork, technical, and communications skills as you complete activities and projects in several departments.

Three Know-How Skills

You must master three categories of skills to be effective in the online world of business. First, you must grasp the many ways employees, workgroups, departments, and specialized corporate teams work together. We call this *workplace know-how*. Second, you must become expert in the use of the corporate Intranet and the World Wide Web as essential tools to help you gather, organize, and share information. We call this *online know-how*. Third, you must master the methods of gathering, sharing, and organizing information in this online workplace. We call this *technical communications know-how*. These three categories of skills are blended into each chapter.

The Corporate View Series

The *Corporate View Orientation* is the first in a series of books planned to teach workplace, online, and technical communications skills in an in-depth way. The series will allow you to follow career paths in

- Corporate Communications
- Marketing, Sales, and Customer Support

- Finance and Accounting
- Human Resources and Management
- Legal Services
- Information Technology
- Research and Development

This text is the gateway to these career paths, which other books in the series will explore in more detail. Additionally, supplemental seminars can enhance your *Corporate View* experience. A seminar is a short course, approximately ten hours in duration, which focuses on a unique aspect of business. There are two seminar categories: hard business skills and soft business skills. Here are a few examples from each category:

Seminar Categories

T a b l e   1

Hard Business Skills	*Soft Business Skills*
Composing at the Keyboard	Business Ethics
Corporate Proofreading	Customer Relations
Electronic File Management	Human Relations/Team Building
Job Search and Online Resumes	Project Management
Power Business Reading	Time Management
Speech-Recognition Technology	Work Ethic

Corporate View Orientation: *Features*

The *Corporate View Orientation* is divided into three sections and 12 chapters. *Section 1* introduces you to the simulation, Corporate View, and its corporate Intranet. *Section 2* allows you to explore the mission-critical functions of a corporation as you rotate through the departments as a student intern. In *Section 3*, you will take your online skills to the Web and search for job opportunities in the online world of work.

Each chapter includes an introduction, activities, special feature boxes, and chapter review summary and exercises.

- *Introductions* describe the mission-critical functions that all businesses, large and small, must have, and how these functions work together to be successful.

- *Activities* teach basic business skills in a step-by-step way. An overview introduces each concept. Then, the spirit of modern corporate training programs is reflected in the ***Just-in-Time Training*** exercise. In this approach, you learn just in time how to get the job done in just the right way. Activity ***Debriefings*** extend the Just-in-Time Training exercise a little further, challenging you to think and write about the workplace using online and technical communications skills.

- *Feature boxes* contain three types of information that enhance the chapter concepts and activities. The feature box themes include *The Least You Should Know About...* to build understanding of new concepts, *Business Milestones* to deepen understanding of the corporate world, and *Technical Communications* to strengthen communications skills.

- *Chapter review* provides a summary of the concepts covered in the chapter and opportunities to apply your skills in a variety of ways through a series of exercises. You will build proficiency with many kinds of technical communications, work in teams to refine what you have studied, access the Web to expand what you have learned with information from cyberspace, and apply the lessons of Corporate View to small, medium-sized, large, and start-up businesses of all kinds.

About the Corporate View Intranet

In today's businesses, much of what you need to read and a great deal of the data you need to get your job done can't be found in books or in traditional forms of printed media. Instead, it is available online on the corporate Intranet.

F i g u r e   1
The Corporate View Intranet

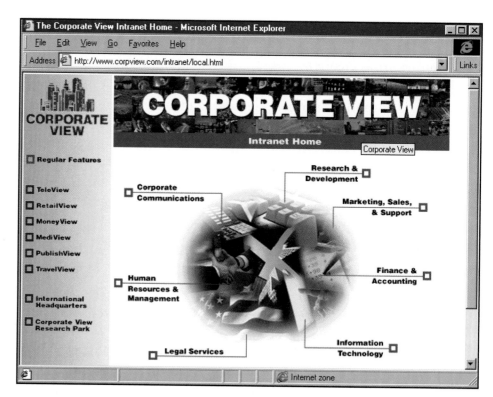

You may access the Corporate View Intranet via the Internet at **www.corpview.com** or from a local network or computer. Use the Web site to complete specific Web-based exercises, such as accessing stock quotes for an Overtime exercise or completing the online tests. Use the local Intranet site when you cannot access the Internet or when your Internet connection is slow or otherwise inconvenient to use. You will be able to complete most of the critical learning activities from your local Intranet site.

The Intranet provides information about Corporate View's strategic business units and the various functions and departments at Corporate View. Biographies of Corporate View employees, answers to frequently asked questions, a communications style guide, product testing reports, job postings, and links to related Web sites represent a sample of the information found on the Intranet.

For the Instructor

Corporate View Orientation is appropriate for students in high school and beyond in any course where understanding how a business functions in an online world and where teamwork, technical, and communications skills are emphasized. The course may be adapted for completion in a quarter or a semester by omitting or including selected activities or end-of-chapter projects and exercises. Students should be comfortable with the basic features of their word processing software and Web browsers to be used for the course.

Instructor's Guide: An Instructor's Guide is available to accompany the *Corporate View Orientation*. This guide contains an overview of the course, teaching suggestions, and sample solutions to the activities and projects in this student text.

Tests: Chapter tests, two section tests, and a final exam are available in two formats. Testing software on CD-ROM (Windows and Macintosh) allows the teacher to customize and print tests from a testbank of questions for each chapter. The **_Online Tests_** link on the Corporate View Intranet allows students to access the tests from the Web site. Students complete the tests online and receive instant feedback, while the teacher receives the students' scores via email. All grading and reporting is done by the testing system.

Corporate View: The New Face of 21st Century Business

Without warning, the World Wide Web changed business from the outside in and from the inside out.

First, from without ...

As the Web became popular, new ways of advertising, ordering, buying, and distributing products were created. By clicking a few hyperlinks you can order everything from computers to pizza. You can select your new car, pay for it with an online loan, and have it delivered to your doorstep on your day off. You can update your computer's software or buy a best-selling book. Computer banking and stock trading are commonplace. You can even download tax forms or complete them online.

... then, from within.

As Web technologies were perfected, businesses quickly discovered that the Web's greatest value might not be to entertain customers with the latest graphics, sound, and video options but to inform employees about every possible aspect of their jobs. The corporate Intranet, created from Web technologies, can help employees do their jobs more effectively:

- *Human Resources recruitment officers* can place job descriptions on the Web and attract high-quality employees from around the world.
- *Corporate Communications specialists* can post press releases online, not just to the media, but to fellow employees, shareholders, and customers.
- *Research and Development engineers* can research the latest scientific developments, share new product designs, and receive input from colleagues around the globe.
- *Marketing managers* can have the latest world-wide marketing campaign pushed to the sales force in a matter of seconds.
- *Sales representatives* can obtain the latest sale price on a product via the corporate Net, reply to a prospective customer with an email, and place a large order for an important account.
- *Finance and Accounting workgroups* can post the quarterly reports on the Intranet or track the performance of the corporate stock investment portfolio with a few hyperlinks.
- *Legal Services attorneys* can simultaneously inform the Human Resources and Accounting Departments of a major change in IRS rules.
- *Information Technology managers* can train employees in the latest software with Web pages and online step-by-step tutorials from the corporate Intranet FAQs pages.

Business has changed. It's online, interactive, and more efficient than ever before. Learn how you can be effective in business by gaining a Corporate View.

Section 1

South-Western

CORPORATE VIEW

Orientation

Karl
Technolog
Prov

Micha
Christa Mc
Brigham Yo

VISIT US
WWW.

South-Western Educational Publishing
an International Thomson Publishing company I(T)P®

www.thomson.com

Cincinnati • Albany, NY • Belmont, CA • Bonn • Boston • Detroit • Johannesburg • London • Madrid
Melbourne • Mexico City • New York • Paris • Singapore • Tokyo • Toronto • Washington

Team Leader: Karen Schmohe
Project Manager: Marilyn Hornsby
Consulting Developmental Editor: Dianne S. Rankin
Editor: Kimberlee Kusnerak
Technology Editor: Steven Ray
Production Coordinator: Jane Congdon
Manufacturing Coordinator: Carol Chase
Marketing Manager: Tim Gleim

Marketing Coordinator: Lisa Barto
Art/Design Coordinator: Michelle Kunkler
Cover/Internal Design: Ann Small, a small design studio
Cover Image: Rob Silvers, Runaway Technology, Inc.
Cover Photos: © 1998 PhotoDisc, Inc., © 1998 Digital Stock, © 1998 Digital Vision
Production: A.W. Kingston Publishing Services
Web Development: Knowlton & Associates, Inc.

I(T)P®

International Thomson Publishing

South-Western Educational Publishing is a division of International Thomson Publishing Inc. The ITP logo is a registered trademark used herein under license by South-Western Educational Publishing.

5 6 7   D4   02 01 00
Printed in the United States of America

Library of Congress Cataloging-In-Publication Data

Barksdale, Karl.

    Corporate View : Orientation / Karl Barksdale, Michael Rutter.
      p.   cm.

Includes index.

Intranet employee logon at http://www.corpview.com.

    Summary: Presents Internet/Intranet based activities that enable interns to experience work environments in various departments within an organization including human resources, management, finance and accounting, and legal.

ISBN 0-538-68471-2 (alk. paper)

    1. Intranets (Computer networks)--Study and teaching. 2. Employee orientation. 3. Business students. 4. Internship programs. [1. Intranets (Computer networks) 2. Employee orientation. 3. Internship programs.]   I. Rutter, Michael. II. Title.

HD30.385.B368 1998

658--dc21

98-31405 CIP

The spectacular Photomosaic™ image of the Cincinnati skyline on the front cover was created by Rob Silvers expressly for South-Western Educational Publishing. Photomosaic is a trademark of Runaway Technology, Inc. of Cambridge, MA. To see more fascinating photomosaics, visit **_www.photomosaic.com_**.

Table of Contents

Table of Contents

Starting Out

In Section 1, you will learn how to survive the first few days on the job. As an intern in a corporate workgroup, you will learn how a business functions and will soon be making valuable contributions as an important member of the Corporate View team.

The Corporate View Intranet is a tool you will use often to complete jobs successfully. You will explore the two levels of the corporate Intranet: the local Intranet for day-to-day functions and the Corporate View, a Web site that contains updated information direct from corporate headquarters at **www.corpview.com**.

You will learn about seven critical elements that are necessary for every business, large or small, to run successfully. At Corporate View, we refer to these as *mission-critical functions*.

You will explore how Corporate View and its TeleView division communicate and learn about how the people responsible for different company functions work together.

This section will also introduce you to the skills corporations are looking for in their employees. You will see how corporate managers organize resources and manage complex projects. You will learn how corporations fill the "training gap" by offering their employees on-the-job training seminars and courses.

Chapter 1

A View from Ground Zero

1. Explore the mission and goals of a typical corporation
2. Manipulate the corporate Intranet to find information
3. Find technical answers on the Intranet
4. Send an email and receive a reply
5. Identify key people via the Intranet
6. Begin to create a corporate portfolio
7. Apply the lessons of the corporation to small business

Technical Communications

- Think and write about business trends
- Write effectively about yourself to your colleagues
- Plan and write effective email

Welcome to TeleView, a Division of Corporate View

"Hi. My name is Melissa Kim. I'm a manager in the Human Resources Department. We call it 'HR' for short. One of my jobs is to coordinate the activities of student interns. So if you have any questions or concerns, my office door is always open. Or you can drop me an email. I'd like to get to know you.

"Now, let's get down to business. It's your first day on the job here at Corporate View. We're a large *multinational corporation* with several unique and successful *strategic business units* or *SBUs*. A business unit focuses on a unique aspect of a corporation's business. For example, one *division* might develop a line of sports products and related apparel. Another division might create and market high-tech *telecommunications* equipment and electronics. Each SBU has its own business goals that contribute to the profitability of the whole corporation.

"Business units are often called divisions or *subsidiaries*. Although Corporate View has several business units, the major link between each division is a commitment to create quality products that can compete successfully in the marketplace.

"You are assigned to TeleView, the fastest growing division of Corporate View. It designs, develops, and sells quality digital telephones and other high-tech electronic devices. TeleView will give you a variety of on-the-job experiences. This will be a perfect opportunity for you to see firsthand the world of business. This experience will give you a 'corporate view.'

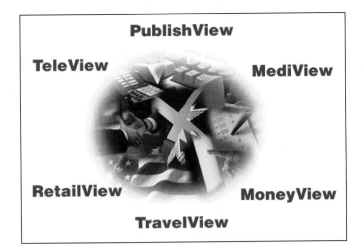

Figure 1-1
Corporate View's Strategic Business Units

PublishView

TeleView   MediView

RetailView   MoneyView

TravelView

"TeleView has become one of the largest telecommunications providers in the world. We are a leading developer of digital phones and **telephony** services for business and home consumers.

"At TeleView, we're proud of our products and services. One of the great advantages of working for TeleView is that every employee receives a free digital phone, and all our business-related calls are free. We also take pride in our people. That's why we're pleased you are with us. We believe that our employees are our greatest asset. When we hire, we look for the most qualified folks we can find. Interns are no exception.

"Even though we hire the best, we don't expect you to know everything. There might be some areas or skills you need to improve. We're more than happy to help you get up to speed. The **Intranet** will be a great help. It's not unusual to feel there's a gap between your existing skills and the skills you will need to perform your new job.

"Let me assure you, no one feels totally prepared. There's always a flood of terms that apply specifically to any new job, words that seem to exist nowhere else on the planet. The commotion of these first few days can rattle your confidence a little. When I was sitting where you are now, I said to myself, 'Did I make the right decision in coming to this company?'

"I started as an intern when I was in school, just like you. Later, I was hired for a full-time position. I can tell you, I did make the right choice—even if I was nervous at the time.

"You're going to love working here. As I said, Corporate View is a people-centered company from the top down. It lives up to its **mission statement**, which is printed on the Intranet. We'll look it up in a second.

> ### The Mission of Corporate View
> *The mission of Corporate View is to design, develop, and deliver quality products and solutions for its customers and to make a profit for its stockholders. Effective and creative employees are the keys to customer satisfaction and stockholder earnings. To enhance employee effectiveness, Corporate View will encourage teamwork and cooperation at all levels, increase the technical skills of its employees, and enhance communications among Corporate View business units and workgroups.*

"In this orientation, you will learn how to access the company resources that will be at your disposal both on the local Intranet and the Corporate View *Web site*."

Activity Overviews

In this chapter, you will take a careful look at several online business activities that will expand your ***technical communications*** skills. In the corporate world, most professionals spend about 20 percent of their workday preparing some form of written communications. Most of this time is spent in front of a computer. To help prepare you for your new job, consider the following activities.

Activity 1-1 All About Corporate View will take you to the local Corporate View Intranet and into the information center of the company.

Activity 1-2 Mirroring the Corporate Intranet will take you to the Web site to visit corporate headquarters. Activities 1-1 and 1-2 will demonstrate how backup ***mirror sites*** can protect important corporate data from a loss of Intranet service.

Activity 1-3 Help! I Think I Need a Techie will take you to a part of the Intranet where you can get a few questions answered.

Activity 1-4 An Email to the Top will acquaint you with the dominant messaging system in business today.

Activity 1-5 Who's Who at Corporate View will introduce you to the people at Corporate View who are responsible for different company functions. You will explore the concept of networking with people in a corporate environment.

Every industry and major corporation creates a vocabulary all its own. The Corporate View Intranet has a feature called ShopTalk that contains definitions for many terms related to our industry and to business in general. Terms that appear in bold italic print in this chapter are also listed below. Understanding the meanings of these terms will help you learn the concepts and develop the skills covered in the chapter. In Activity 1-3, you will learn to access the Intranet and find definitions for terms by clicking the **ShopTalk** link. After you learn to access the ShopTalk page, refer to the definitions there any time you need to find the meaning of a ShopTalk word.

Corporate ShopTalk

- Antitrust
- Browser
- Defaults
- Desktop Applications
- Division
- Downsizing
- Entrepreneurs
- Extranet
- Fortune 500
- Frequently Asked Questions (FAQs)
- Home Page
- Hypertext Markup Language (HTML)
- Internet
- Intranet
- Market Share
- Mirror Site
- Mission Statement
- Multinational Corporation
- NASDAQ
- NYSE
- Push Technology
- Regulated Monopoly
- Servers
- Stock Market Ticker
- Stockholders
- Strategic Business Unit (SBU)
- Subsidiary
- Technical Communications
- Telecommunications
- Telephony
- Uniform Resource Locator (URL)
- Web Page
- Web Site
- Workgroup
- World Wide Web (WWW)

The **Least** You **Should** Know **About...**

Corporate ShopTalk

Corporations and businesses of all kinds create their own vocabularies. Some words are industry terms that all businesses in a particular industry use. For example, *telephony* (pronounced *tell + F + a + nee*) is a common term in the telecommunications industry, but isn't commonly used in the oil business, in retail sales, or in the publishing business.

Other terms are used within a specific company and won't be understood outside that company. For example, software companies sometimes use the names of cities like Memphis and Cairo to identify products under development. When you take a job at a company, you must learn its unique vocabulary and way of speaking. If you don't, it will be like trying to find your way around Egypt after only a week of learning Arabic.

Companies often provide definitions for commonly used corporate words, and it is no different at Corporate View. The people who are successful are those who know and use the corporate shop talk effectively. When you hear or read a word you don't understand, look it up by clicking the **ShopTalk** link on the Corporate View Intranet or by using a dictionary.

Activity 1-1   *All About Corporate View*

It's your first day on the job, and you're about to learn how to find information about the corporation. You will begin by learning more about the mission of Corporate View and how one of its business units, TeleView, fits into the scheme of things.

A good place to look for information and answers is on the corporate Intranet, not to be confused with the **Internet** or **World Wide Web (WWW)**. This is a common misconception because the same technologies are used for Intranets, the Internet, and the World Wide Web. The differences are their respective audiences and purposes.

The Internet is a public, worldwide computer network made up of smaller, interconnected networks. A popular portion of the Internet is called the World Wide Web, WWW, or simply the Web. The audience includes everyone who wants to surf (look for information on) the Web. An Intranet is like a mini-Internet or a small Web a company creates for its employees. It's not open to the public. It's just for company personnel. Unlike the public Internet and Web, only authorized people are allowed to access private corporate Intranets.

The Intranet at Corporate View is an important communications link between corporate headquarters and its various business units. Without the Intranet, employees in divisions and offices around the world might not have any real contact with the leaders and officers of the corporation. Without the Intranet, employees might not learn about new corporate directions, changing goals, product improvements, changing product pricing, and new employee benefits. The Intranet keeps the corporate team members informed and working together effectively.

F i g u r e   1 - 2
The Corporate View Intranet

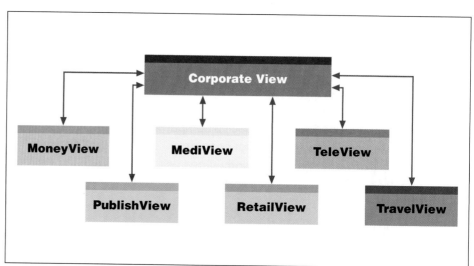

When two or more companies wish to share information together on a project, they create an *Extranet*. An Extranet opens relevant parts of each company's Intranet to all project participants so they can work together effectively, share files, route email, compare research, draw up common plans and production schedules, and share financial information. Extranets are often temporary, disappearing as soon as the work among the different corporations has been completed. With Extranets, only selected information is shared. Other, more sensitive information is reserved for the private, corporate Intranet.

Figure 1-3
An Extranet allows partnering companies to share information and resources.

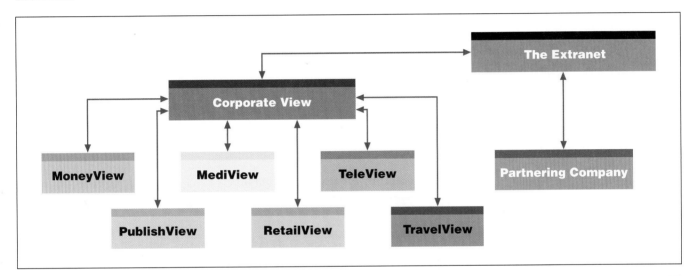

Learning to use the Intranet is easy. It acts just like the World Wide Web. If you have surfed the Web, you'll feel right at home. All you need to know is how to use a Web *browser*. A browser is a program that allows you to view *Web pages* and online information. Microsoft's Internet Explorer and Netscape's Navigator are popular Web browsers.

In this first Just-in-Time Training exercise, you will access the local corporate Intranet by using your Web browser.

The **Least** You **Should** Know **About...**

Intranets

An Intranet is a localized business Web. Business discovered and embraced the World Wide Web in 1995. The Web changed the way information was shared with customers and helped define how business will be conducted into the next decade. Business and consumers alike discovered that Web technologies are easy to use.

The Intranet became an important business tool in 1997. By the end of 1998, most *Fortune 500* companies and tens of thousands of smaller companies were already using Intranets. Intranets have replaced other, more expensive networking schemes because they are easy to use and less expensive to implement. They soon became a standard way to communicate within the modern business world.

Just-in-Time Training

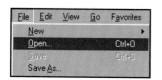

Access the Corporate View Local Intranet Site

1. Open your Web browser.

2. Open the *local.html* file from your local Intranet. (Your instructor will provide information on where the *local.html* file is stored on your local network or stand-alone computer. This information can be accessed live on the Web at ***www.corpview.com***. See Activity 1-2, page 15.) Locate and follow the directions for using your Web browser below. When you have opened the file, go to step 3 of this training exercise.

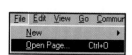

Figure 1-4
*Select **File, Open** in Internet Explorer.*

Figure 1-5
Browse to the local *file in the Intranet folder.*

Internet Explorer Instructions

- Select **Open** from the File menu.
- Browse to choose the *Intranet* folder.
- Select and open the *local.html* file.

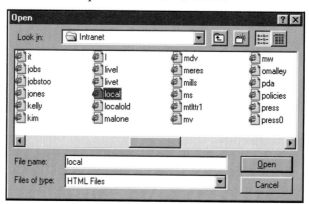

Figure 1-6
*Choose **File, Open Page** in Netscape.*

Netscape 4.0 Instructions

- Select **Open Page** from the File menu.
- Click the **Choose File** button and browse to choose the *Intranet* folder.
- Select and open the *local.html* file.

Netscape 2.0 and 3.0 Instructions

- Select **Open File** from the File menu.
- Browse to choose the *Intranet* folder.
- Select the *local.html* file.

Filename Extensions

Depending on your system settings, and whether you are using a Windows or Macintosh computer, you might or might not see filename extensions. The filename might appear as *local.html* or *local.htm*. Don't be confused, this is the correct file to choose to access the local Intranet.

Extensions designate the type of file. For example, Word documents typically have a *.doc* file extension, while WordPerfect documents usually use *.wpd*. Web and Intranet documents written in **Hypertext Markup Language (HTML)** are denoted by the *.html* or *.htm* extension.

3. When you open *local.html* (step 2), the Corporate View Intranet Home page appears. On this page you have access to information about Corporate View's mission-critical functions, such as Corporate Communications, by choosing the appropriate link. Information about Corporate View's strategic business units may be accessed by clicking the SBU name at the left of the screen. Also at the left, you will find links to ***International Headquarters***, the ***Corporate View Research Park***, and the ***Regular Features*** pages. You will explore all these areas of the Intranet during your internship at Corporate View.

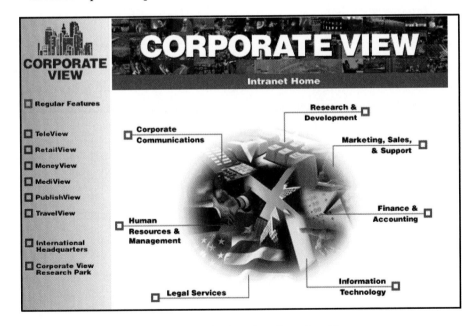

Figure 1-7
The Corporate View Intranet Home page

4. Click the ***Regular Features*** link. The Regular Features page contains links to valuable information that you will use often as you complete your work for TeleView. To begin, click the link and read ***Update from the CEO***, Madeline Tucker.

Think and write about the following:

5. Madeline Tucker describes the purpose of the corporate Intranet. Why is the Intranet important to her as the CEO of a major multinational corporation?

_____

_____

6. She chooses her words very carefully. In the beginning, she uses the term *semi-independent* to describe the business units she later describes as once being *very independent*. What meaning does this subtle change in wording convey? Could she be trying to remedy a problem by implementing the Intranet corporate-wide? What might the problem be? Explain.

_____

_____

_____

_____

7. The slogan "Designing, Developing, and Delivering Quality Products for People" in the CEO's message is an attempt to define in a single phrase Corporate View's business goals. In your own words, what do you think Corporate View's primary business goals are?

_____

_____

8. Does the slogan match those goals? Is it a good slogan? What kind of company image does it portray? Can you think of a better slogan for Corporate View?

_____

_____

_____

_____

9. In terms of its stock performance, how is Corporate View doing these days?

_____

10. What are the most pressing human resource issues this week?

_____

_____

11. Click the ***Regular Features*** link, then select the ***All About Corporate View*** hypertext link and review the messages. There is a lot to digest here. Spend 10 to 15 minutes reviewing the following:

- ***Mission Statement***
- ***News from the Corporate Officers and Business Units***
- ***Corporate Causes and Charities***

12. What other business units does Corporate View have in addition to TeleView?

_____

_____

13. What is Corporate View's policy on contributing to charities?

_____

_____

14. Return to the Corporate View Intranet Home page and visit the TeleView business unit by clicking on the link. How does TeleView contribute to the success of Corporate View?

_____

_____

_____

_____

_____

Debriefing

Corporations are a bit like countries in that they conjure up images all their own. Even strategic business units within the same corporation can take on unique characteristics. The image a business portrays is a reflection of its unique corporate culture made up of the beliefs, customs, and practices of the corporation.

Just as Greece has a different culture from Spain or England, IBM has a different culture from Microsoft or General Motors. Each of these companies has a different corporate culture. The same can be said for sports franchises. What adjectives come to your mind when you think of the Green Bay Packers, the Dallas Cowboys, or the Denver Broncos? A professional sports team is a corporation that creates an image and markets it to its fans. Most companies want to present an image of being honest and providing quality goods or services.

Think and write about the following:

1. Given what you have learned about Corporate View and TeleView through the Intranet, what kind of image and working environment is this company trying to create for its employees through its Intranet?

_____

_____

_____

2. What kind of information can a corporation provide on its Intranet so that each employee has a clear idea of the corporate culture, its beliefs, goals, direction, and attitudes?

_____

_____

_____

3. What kind of corporate culture does a successful company need to create if it wants to attract the best employees?

_____

_____

_____

4. How does an Intranet help in developing a successful, high-performance corporate culture?

_____

_____

_____

The **Least** You
Should Know
About...

Stock Market Tickers

Many people in the business world keep an eye on the stock market and the prices of corporate stocks—and for good reason, as they are *stockholders* who have money invested in the stock market. Some invest through their company's 401(k) investment plan or have stock-related retirement programs. Others invest their surplus cash or bonus money in stocks.

You will see a *stock market ticker* symbol for most companies mentioned in this book. The first part of the symbol indicates the stock exchange where the stock is traded. For example,

the New York Stock Exchange is abbreviated *NYSE*. The *NASDAQ* is another exchange. The second part of the symbol is an alphabetic code for the particular company. For example, Microsoft, the maker of the Internet Explorer browser, has the ticker symbol MSFT. Netscape Communications Corporation, the maker of the Netscape browser, once had the ticker symbol NSCP. Digital Equipment Corporation, a computer manufacturer, uses the ticker symbol DEC.

To look up a stock, go to the **Regular Features**, **Stock Watcher Links** on the Intranet, select a stock search system, and enter a ticker symbol as instructed.

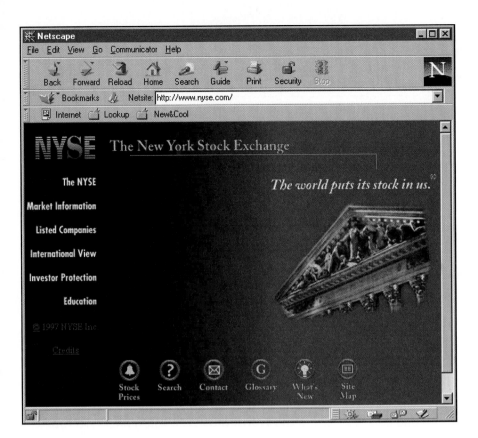

Figure 1-8
*The New York Stock
Exchange on the Web*

Activity 1-2 *Mirroring the Corporate Intranet*

As a NASCAR racing team always has a spare set of tires, a passenger jet has more than one engine, and a student carries more than one pencil to an ACT or SAT exam, a corporation has backup Intranets to support its employees.

Intranets are the backbones of corporate communications systems. Companies can't afford to have their Intranets down for long. For this reason, Intranet Web sites are often duplicated, creating *mirror sites*. In a large company with divisions scattered around the world, each major division may maintain a mirror of the main "live" Intranet site.

At Corporate View, you can access the local mirror site by opening the *local* file from your local system (as you did in Activity 1-1). To access the Corporate View main site, you must have a live connection to the World Wide Web. The address to the live site is ***www.corpview.com***.

Obviously, the local mirror site and live site will look and feel very much the same. Remember, a mirror site is a backup, a duplicate, a site to maintain important business activity in the likelihood the Internet or Web connections break down somewhere between Corporate View headquarters and its local business units.

It's a good idea to check the primary Corporate View Web site from time to time. Why? For one thing, the main site is likely to be updated more frequently. Plus, a few services are always only available through corporate headquarters. For example, to maintain security, employee testing and evaluation systems are safely maintained on the Corporate View Web site at ***www.corpview.com***.

If you do not have access to the World Wide Web, don't panic! That is why the local Intranet mirror site exists. If you do have a live Web connection, however, all the better.

In the Just-in-Time Training exercise, you will visit the main Web site and see some information and links available only here.

Business Milestones

Netscape Communications Corporation

Netscape, more than any other company, is responsible for the birth of the modern corporate Intranet. By popularizing the World Wide Web with its Navigator browser, it unleashed a wave of innovative technologies that made Intranets possible.

Netscape's place in computing history is secure. When Netscape's stock went public in its *IPO* (initial public offering), it set the computer industry on its ear. Netscape Communications Corporation went from a private company to a company that traded stock publicly on the NASDAQ stock exchange. (NASDAQ:NSCP)

Netscape's rise gave a needed shot of adrenaline to an industry becoming complacent manufacturing ***desktop applications***. Netscape made itself a major force in the market by giving away copies of its Navigator Web browser to millions of Web users and by emphasizing the need to develop Web-ready software applications.

Netscape's rise in 1994–95 started a race for control of cyberspace (that is, the Internet or the Web). The stakes are high. As businesses discovered the Web in 1995, they also discovered how Intranets can help keep their employees informed. They began to buy thousands of Web ***servers*** to provide this Intranet service for their corporations. With billions of dollars to be made selling Intranet servers and services, Netscape gave birth to the multibillion-dollar Intranet industry.

1. Launch your Web browser.

2. Access the Corporate View Web site at **_www.corpview.com_**. Locate and follow the directions below for your Web browser. (If you do not have access to the Web, open the *local* Intranet page from your local Intranet as you did in Activity 1-1. You will be able to complete much of your work. When you get a chance to go live to the Web, you can return to and finish the balance of this exercise.) Once you have accessed the Web site, go to step 3 of this exercise.

Internet Explorer Instructions

- Enter the Web address **_www.corpview.com_**, which is called a **_URL (Uniform Resource Locator)_**, into the address/location window as shown in Figure 1-9.

- Press **Enter** or **Return**.

F i g u r e   1 - 9
Entering a URL in Internet Explorer

Netscape Navigator Instructions

- Enter the Web address **_www.corpview.com_**, which is called a **_URL (Uniform Resource Locator)_**, into the address/location window as shown in Figure 1-10.

- Press **Enter** or **Return**.

F i g u r e   1 - 1 0
Entering a URL in Netscape

3. Click the **_Intranet Employee Login_** link. The Intranet Employee Login page appears.

F i g u r e   1 - 1 1
The Employee Login page

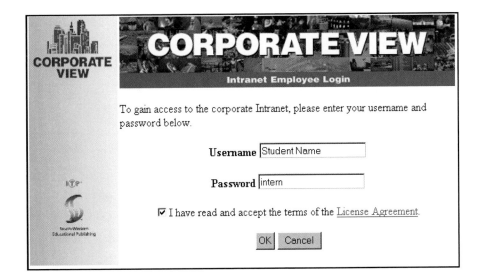

4. Key your name in the Username textbox. Key **intern** in the Password textbox. Click **OK**. (If you wish to abandon the login procedure, click **Cancel** to exit.)

5. When you have successfully completed the login, the employee portfolio page appears. Click the ***Corporate View Orientation Intranet*** link. Click the ***Regular Features*** link on the Corporate View Intranet Home page.

6. Select the ***Intranet FAQs*** link. (***FAQs*** stands for *Frequently Asked Questions*.)

7. Select the first link on Intranet FAQs ***Using the Intranet @ Corporate View*** and read the explanation that appears.

8. Why does an Intranet improve communications among employees within the corporation?

   _____

   _____

9. What team maintains the corporate Intranet?

   _____

Basic Intranet Skills

10. Scroll down to the bottom of the Using the Intranet at Corporate View page. Find and click on ***Ten Basic Intranet and Web Skills***. Read and follow the instructions to view the slide show. List the 10 basic skills that all employees need in using the Intranet and Web effectively.

    _____
    _____
    _____
    _____
    _____
    _____
    _____
    _____
    _____
    _____
    _____

Stock Links

Business people are stock watchers! Many have money in stocks. If you work for a company that trades stock on one of the major stock exchanges, you should watch the stock price to get a feel for how your company is doing. One service that Intranets often provide is a live link to various stock-watching services. To use one of these services, you need a live connection to the Web, because stock prices are updated every few minutes throughout the trading day.

11. Access the **_Regular Features_** page on the Corporate View Web site and click the **_Stock Watcher Links_**. Follow the instructions online and investigate how to look up a stock to check on its performance by using a stock ticker. In the Online Business Trends section at the end of each chapter, you will look up the stock price for various companies. Practice by looking up the current stock price for two or three of the following tickers:

Stock Ticker	List the Current Price	Name This Corporation
T	_____	_____
MSFT	_____	_____
FON	_____	_____
NSCP	_____	_____

Online Testing

The Corporate View Web site hosts the corporate training and evaluation site. Employees who attend training can prove their knowledge and abilities by taking and passing examinations there. You will learn more about Corporate View's employee training and testing program in Chapter 3. To get a feel of the online testing system:

12. Access the **_Regular Features_** page on the Corporate View Web site and select the **_Employee Training and Evaluations_** link. Click the **_Online Tests_** link, followed by the **_Sample Test_** link. Follow the instructions and complete the sample test as shown in Figure 1-12.

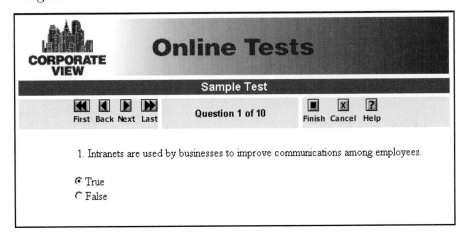

Figure 1-12
Sample Test from the
Corporate View Web site

The Breakup of AT&T

On December 31, 1993, AT&T (NYSE: T) was the biggest company in the world. A day later, on January 1, 1994, it was broken up by the U.S. Department of Justice. AT&T was a *regulated monopoly*. An *antitrust* action forced the company to release its control over the telephone system. More than a million employees were distributed among seven independent regional phone companies. The new smaller AT&T was pushed into the competitive long-distance and telephony markets.

AT&T found itself competing hard with Sprint (NYSE:FON), MCI, and other emerging telephone service carriers. Still, with aggressive research and development being provided by AT&T's Bell Labs, outstanding marketing and sales, and a reputation for quality, the company has held on to its *market share*.

The breakup of AT&T opened the telecommunications industry to new competition. Many new corporations moved into the market. Most of these telecommunications companies were soon to benefit from the rise of the Internet and World Wide Web. Companies like AT&T, MCI, and Sprint are all involved in providing Internet services to business. Corporations will often use the communications services provided by these telecommunications giants to support their corporate Intranet efforts.

Debriefing

Intranets are popular for several reasons. Intranets are easy to use because they work just like the World Wide Web. A great deal of money is saved training employees, because many have already used the Web at school or at home and require little additional training to use a corporate Intranet. Most important, Intranets help company employees communicate effectively.

Think and write about the following:

1. How extensively have you used the Web?

   _____

2. What differences do you see between the average Web site and an Intranet site?

   _____

   _____

3. What similarities do you see between the Web and a corporate Intranet?

   _____

   _____

4. The Intranet at Corporate View is a rich resource for its employees. It is the repository of sensitive information the corporation does not want to be accessible to its competitors. What do you think is the role of the employee regarding the safekeeping of this inside information? What kinds of information should employees be careful sharing with the outside world?

_____

_____

_____

Activity 1-3   *Help! I Think I Need a Techie*

Lost on the network? Don't know how to do something? Do others make it look simple? Hear a term you don't understand while drinking some juice in the break room? Does a process sound terribly technical? Check the Intranet for help.

It's not surprising that almost all Fortune 500 corporations and thousands of smaller businesses have Intranets. It makes good sense. It's good business to keep employees informed with up-to-date information and online help.

When you have a question, it's likely you're not the first to ask it. Most questions have been raised by other employees and are easily answered on the Intranet.

The team responsible for keeping the Corporate View Intranet up and running is the IT (Information Technology) Department. In some companies, it might be called *MIS* for Management of Information Services or *IS* for Information Systems. Whatever the team is called, it keeps all the technical bits and pieces connected and working. You can bet these techie-gurus hear many of the same questions over and over.

Because its members can't always be available to answer questions immediately, the IT team compiles frequently asked questions, called *FAQs* for short. These questions and their answers are posted on the Intranet. Before you contact the folks at IT with a question, see whether you can solve the problem yourself by reading the Intranet FAQs.

Business **Milestones**

The Fortune 500

Each year, *Fortune* magazine compiles the business list to end all business lists. It is called the Fortune 500. The list showcases the biggest and most successful corporations and ranks them by how much they earned in the previous year.

You will find perennial Fortune 500 corporations with household names like General Motors, Ford, Apple Computer, AT&T, PepsiCo, and Microsoft. Some you might not have heard about, such as E. I. du Pont de Nemours and Company, American International Group, Dayton Hudson Corporation,

and ConAgra, also make billions of dollars each year.

Throughout this text, you will read Business Milestones reports that feature top corporations from around the world. The ticker symbol and the appropriate stock exchange will be given for each of these corporations when they are introduced. For example, in the name *NYSE:GM*, NYSE is short for the New York Stock Exchange, where GM stock is traded (bought and sold). GM is short for General Motors, which led the Fortune 500 list in 1998 with over $168 billion in reported earnings for the previous year. That is more money than the entire gross national product of some small countries!

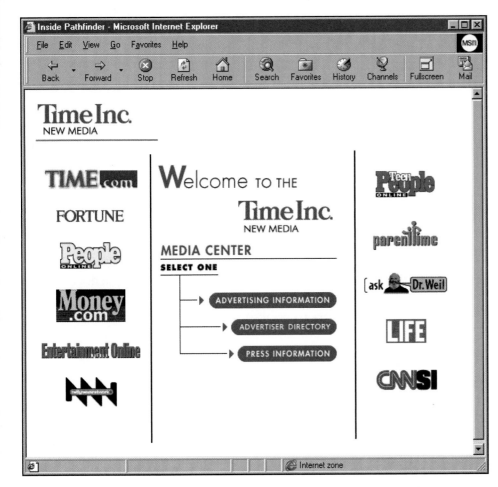

Figure 1-13
Fortune *magazine, a strategic business unit of Time Warner, publishes the official Fortune 500 list every year.*

Another good source of information is the ShopTalk page on the Intranet. Here you will find definitions of terms related to the telecommunications industry and to business in general. You will learn to access the Intranet FAQs and ShopTalk in the following Just-in-Time Training exercise.

Just-in-Time Training

Finding Help on the Intranet

1. Access your local Intranet or the Corporate View Web site. Refer to Activities 1-1 and 1-2 if you need a few reminders on how to do this.

Intranet FAQs

2. Click the ***Intranet FAQs*** link on the ***Regular Features*** list.

3. Select the ***Netiquette on the Corporate View Intranet*** link. What does the term *netiquette* mean?

_____

_____

4. Select the **_Intranet Netiquette_** link. Summarize the eight Intranet netiquette rules briefly in your own words.

_____
_____
_____
_____
_____
_____
_____
_____

5. Return to the Corporate View **_Regular Features_** page and select the **_Intranet FAQs_** link again. Select the **_Bookmarking and Making Favorites Lists_** link. Read the information on this page.

6. Why is it a good idea to bookmark your corporate Intranet site?

_____

7. List the steps you would follow to create a bookmark or a favorites list by using your browser.

_____
_____
_____

8. Return to the Intranet FAQs page and select the link, **_Setting the Corporate View Intranet as Your Default Home Page_**, which explains setting **defaults** for the **home page** on your browser. Read the information on this page.

9. What is **push technology**?

_____
_____

10. Why does the company want its employees to set the Corporate View Web page as their default home page?

_____

11. Why does Corporate View have both a "live" Web site and a local Intranet site?

_____
_____

ShopTalk

12. Return to the **_Regular Features_** page and select the **_ShopTalk_** link.

13. Locate the following ShopTalk terms by clicking on the first letter of the word under Choose a Letter. Scroll through the entries for that letter. For example, to find *stock market ticker*, click on **S** and scroll down. Record the meaning of each term in your own words.

Stock Market Ticker

_____

Technical Communications

_____

14. Read the ShopTalk entry for *telephony*. Why is telephony a key term in the TeleView strategic business unit?

_____

_____

Debriefing

The Intranet at Corporate View is meant to be a rich resource for its employees. Many departments contribute information. For example, the IT Department provides FAQs to help employees use the Intranet effectively. The Corporate Communications Department provides the ShopTalk definitions as a service to the employees of Corporate View.

Think and write about the following:

1. Nearly every Fortune 500 company has an active Intranet. What other services do you think might typically be provided (or should be provided) over a corporate Intranet? List three or four ideas.

_____

_____

_____

_____

2. Return to the ShopTalk page near the beginning of this chapter and scan the list of vocabulary terms. Identify any terms you don't currently understand and find their meanings on the ShopTalk Intranet page. List the terms and record their definitions in your own words here.

_____

_____

_____

_____

3. If you have already accumulated several bookmarks of favorite Web pages, take time to organize them now. List your bookmarks or favorites and then group them into logical categories. Create a folder for each category and place the bookmarks or favorites inside the proper folders. Review this procedure in the Intranet FAQs if needed.

_____

_____

_____

_____

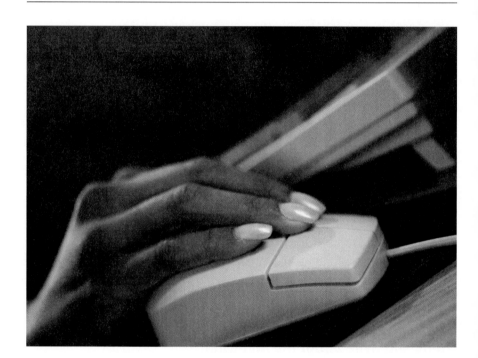

An Email to the Top   **Activity 1-4**

In an office, people communicate in many ways:

- Talking face to face

- Memos and notes

- Telephone conversations

- Email

- Voice mail

- Video conferencing

- FAX messages

These forms of communications are either *synchronous* or *asynchronous*. With synchronous communications, you communicate directly with someone in an immediate, two-way exchange. With asynchronous communications, you leave a message the individual can act on when he or she has the time. Both types of communications are important.

Business
Milestones

The Road Ahead

Bill Gates, co-founder, Chairman and CEO of Microsoft Corporation (NASDAQ:MSFT) wrote a great book on the past, present, and future of the computer industry called *The Road Ahead*. In 1995, Gates discussed the merger of synchronous and asynchronous business communications in this way:

Very soon you'll check your PC, wallet, or television set—the informational appliance of your choice—for email, including bills. When a bill comes in, the device will show your payment history. If you want to inquire about the bill, you'll do it asynchronously, at your convenience, by sending email: "Hey how come this charge is so high?"

Within a few years there will be hybrid communications systems that combine ele-ments of synchronous and asynchronous communications…

…It will work this way: when companies post information about their products on the Internet, part of that information will include instructions for how a customer can connect synchronously with a sales representative who will be able to answer questions through a voice-data connection. (Gates, pp. 145-146)*

In his book, Gates also predicted a computer OS (operating system) that is voice activated using speech recognition like the computers on the Starship Enterprise, an Internet gold rush by businesses, and spatial navigation of cyberspace. Years later, how many of his predictions have come true? What might his predictions mean for the TeleView division?

*Gates, B. (1995). *The Road Ahead*. New York: Viking Penguin.

Email has become the asynchronous communications system of choice in business. Email is electronic mail or electronic messaging. Email can be a much faster way to communicate than a regular telephone voice-mail system. If you leave a voice message on an answering machine, it may take quite some time to get a reply message or even longer actually to speak with the other person. For example, when you place a call, the person you need to talk with is picking up supplies. By the time you get a minute to call again, it's lunch time and no one is there. When the return call arrives, you are at lunch. In the afternoon, you phone again but the other person is running an errand. Finally, after several hours or even days of phone tag, you manage to make contact. (By the way, don't forget to delete all the messages left on your voice mail.)

Figure 1-14
The Microsoft Homepage

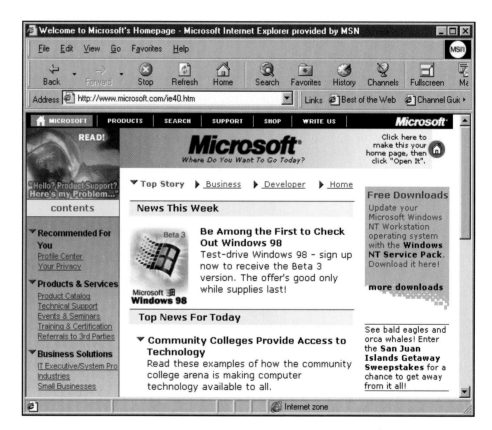

With email, however, a message can be answered in as little as a minute. Email, because it is asynchronous, has certain advantages over the telephone. You can even leave the message, "Call me at 4:30. My meeting should be finished by then." Or you can ask a question and get an answer quickly with an email reply. Another advantage is that you have an electronic record of the message that you can print and refer to later. Although email is not the best choice for every situation, it is the workhorse of the business communications world because it is so fast and effective.

Email does have its disadvantages, however, and it can be abused. Later in this activity, you will learn proper email netiquette. Primarily, email is an important tool. It should help you get your job done—or help you help others get their jobs done.

Some personal email via the company's network is appropriate if the privilege is not abused. Many employees leave email messages for their children at school or at home or send personal messages to colleagues. For example, an email message about a job well done, a birthday greeting, or a get-well wish is in good taste. Just remember that you are at work to work, not to write lengthy personal messages.

As a cost-saving measure, employees at Corporate View are encouraged to use email whenever possible, rather than using memos and letters to communicate. There was a time when interoffice memos would pile up on each employee's desk, sometimes 10, 20, or 30 each day. With email, a similar number of messages might arrive, but they are neatly organized in an electronic inbox. Some employees review hundreds of messages every day.

At Corporate View, every new employee is asked to email the President and CEO of the company about a work-related question. Ms. Tucker does not have time to answer every message from every employee, so an automatic reply system has been set up to provide up-to-date information on key issues. Ms. Tucker's administrative assistant reviews her email and passes on key messages to the CEO. In the following Just-in-Time Training exercise, you will learn about email netiquette and "go to the top" by sending an email to the president.

Just-in-Time Training

Sending Email

1. Access your local Intranet or the Corporate View Web site.
2. Select the **_Intranet FAQs_** link from the **_Regular Features_** list.
3. Click the **_Netiquette on the Corporate View Intranet_** link.
4. Click the **_Email Netiquette_** link. Summarize the eight email netiquette rules briefly in your own words.

_____

_____

_____

_____

_____

_____

_____

_____

_____

5. Launch your email software. (If you don't have email, visit **_Email Services_** under **_Intranet FAQs_**. There you will learn about various free email options available to the public on the Internet and instructions for sending and receiving email.)

6. Write an email to Madeline Tucker, the CEO of Corporate View. Think about what you are going to say. Keep the message short. Enter Madeline Tucker's email address in the To field as shown in Figure 1-15. Her address is **_mtucker@corpview.com_**. (Note that the period that appears at the end of the previous sentence is not part of the email address.)

Figure 1-15
A typical email form

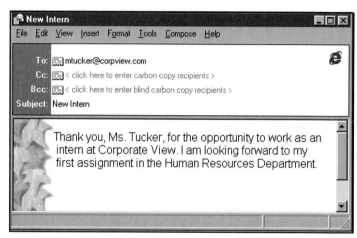

7. Place a descriptive title in the Subject field as shown in Figure 1-15.

8. Write a short note to the CEO. Let her know you are pleased to be a new intern at Corporate View and are looking forward to your first work assignment. Include any questions or comments you have about your internship, the company, or its products.

The **Least** You **Should** Know About...

Free Internet Email

Do you need a quick and easy email account, one you can take with you anywhere you work, live, or play? The Internet offers a host of free email accounts to which you can subscribe. Nothing is ever really "free," however. There is a catch. You must provide consumer-related information about yourself. This information is turned into an advertising profile that is used to sell advertising that supports the system financially.

The best free email providers will not ask you for your home telephone number or address. You will only receive advertisements via your email account. Never provide credit card or bank account numbers or other information you wish to remain private. Read the subscription requirements thoroughly before opening an email account. If you look around the Internet, you will be able to find many email services by typing the words *free email* into a search engine. Some of the more popular email providers can be found on the Intranet on the **_Intranet FAQs_** link. Click the **_Email Services_** link.

9. Review and spell-check your email message; then send it.

10. Check your email periodically for a reply. The reply can take a few minutes or a few days, depending on many factors, including how your email system operates. If you want an answer right away, open **_President Madeline Tucker's New Employee Reply_** in the **_Corporate View Archive_** on the Intranet's **_Regular Features_** list.

Debriefing

In this activity, you reviewed Corporate View's email netiquette rules, sent an email message to the CEO of the company, and received a reply. Like many other companies, Corporate View has messages prepared via email for new employees. This means information can be directed immediately to new employees and interns.

As Intern Coordinator, Melissa Kim has a standard email message for new interns. Send an email to Melissa, thanking her for making you feel comfortable and welcome at Corporate View. Her address is **_mkim@corpview.com_**.

Summarize her reply below.

_____

_____

_____

_____

_____

_____

_____

_____

Activity 1-5   *Who's Who at Corporate View*

In this activity, you will learn about some of your coworkers via the corporate Intranet. At Corporate View, employees often prepare profiles that are posted on the Intranet. These corporate profiles list professional goals, titles, and experiences and provide some personal information. Because these profiles are accessed only by other employees, they are less formal than they would be on an Extranet or on the Web, where they might be viewed by customers.

The Least You Should Know About...

Sharing Information on the Intranet

If someone on the Net asks you for personal information, he or she has a reason. The reason might be valid, or it might not. Never place any information on the Net that you are uncomfortable sharing with the entire world. Share those things you think are appropriate, and no more.

Many Netizens (citizens of the Internet) make it a rule never to give their phone numbers, addresses, or credit card numbers over the Web. Think about the information you should and shouldn't share with the millions of people and companies in cyberspace. Make a list of the types of information you feel comfortable sharing, such as your email address, and another list of information you do not want to share.

There is a reason for sharing personal information with the rest of your team. The more appropriate information team members know about one another, the more likely it is that the team will be able to work together effectively. Sharing common interests is a big help in getting conversations going within teams, also called *workgroups*. Eventually, personal chitchat will turn to shop talk, and new ideas on how to improve work will surface. For example, when conducting a study of their technical field service representatives (tech reps), Xerox found that the tech reps often stood around the watercooler and swapped business "war stories" on breaks. At these informal get-togethers, the reps would also share solutions to problems. The watercooler became an important training center.

The better employees know each other, the more they share solutions or brainstorm about common problems. Informal sharing of ideas can often lead to improved productivity and customer service.

Corporate View is a large multinational company with offices scattered around the world. In this far-flung virtual world, the "watercooler" is the corporate Intranet. Intranets are excellent tools for exchanging ideas and keeping employees up to date on new developments. Some corporations ask their employees to post pages so that they can look up people they are working with, start a conversation, and jump-start the flow of ideas.

You should get to know some key people at Corporate View. They can't all come to speak with you, but you can get to know them by dropping in on the Corporate View Intranet "watercooler."

In a later chapter, you will learn how to post information about yourself on the Intranet. In the following Just-in-Time Training activity, you will read a few personal biographies (also called bios), prepare a bio of your own, and save it in a special folder for safekeeping.

Just-in-Time Training

Accessing Employee Online Bios

1. Open your local Intranet or access the Corporate View Web site.

Employee Profiles

2. Select the **Employee Contacts** link on the **Regular Features** page.

3. Find and read the bios for the following employees. Write each person's title beside his or her name.

   - Madeline Tucker _____

   - James Brown _____

   - Melissa Kim _____

   Think about what each person does and what his or her bio is about.

4. What can you learn about the company by looking at bios of some of the top-level employees?

   _____

   _____

5. Would you want to work for these people? Explain why or why not.

   _____

   _____

6. Which of these people do you think are well suited to their jobs? Do you think any are misplaced?

   _____

   _____

7. When writing about themselves to the entire company, did any one of the three get carried away and actually detract from his or her online bio?

   _____

   _____

Technical Communications

You have reviewed three employee profiles on the Intranet. You probably found a bio you liked and perhaps even one you didn't. Now it's time to create one of your own.

This will be a widely read piece of technical communications. In writing your bio, stick to the facts. In any online communications, you have only about three seconds to gain the reader's attention and to interest him or her in reading more.

Wording a bio carefully is especially important for an intern. If a department is hiring, its staff might become interested in hiring you through reading your online bio. What you write could lead to a full-time job or advancement.

Portray yourself honestly, stating your skills and abilities. Provide a quick, clear snapshot of who you are and why you are qualified for the job you now have. Project the idea that you want to expand your skills into new areas and that you are able to get along with others. As you write, think, What do I want another employee to know about me, especially a TeleView employee who could become a future member of my workgroup team?

8. Create your own bio in a word processing document. Use the questions in this activity as a guide to the content you wish to include.

   - What is your name?
   - Where are you from?
   - What does *technology* mean to you?
   - What is your experience with Intranets?
   - Have you ever used the Internet? For what purposes?
   - When was the last time you emailed someone, and whom do you email most often?
   - Have you ever worked in a group? What groups have you been a part of?
   - How did you work with that group?
   - What was your role in that group?
   - What cartoon do you read first in the funny pages?
   - What software are you familiar with? Word? WordPerfect? Netscape? Internet Explorer?
   - What software programs do you know extremely well?
   - What computer software programs are you shaky with?
   - If you were going to contribute five hours per week in the community, where would you spend your time?
   - What are your professional goals?

- What do you expect to learn from this internship with TeleView? (This might be hard to answer; that's okay.) What do you want to learn from this experience?

- What are your other interests and hobbies?

9. Create a folder (directory) in which to save your work. (If you need help, click on the ***Intranet FAQs*** link on the ***Regular Features*** page, and select the option ***Creating Saving Folders***.) Name your folder *CV* (for Corporate View) and your name or initials. For example: *CVKarl* or *CVMR*. Place in this folder all writing assignments and Corporate View documents you create.

10. Save your bio in a word processing format for now. In a later activity, you can turn it into an HTML document. Use the filename *mybio* as indicated by the Save As icon on this page. In future activities look for the Save As icon and use the filename shown there to save your work in the folder you created for Corporate View documents.

11. Proofread your profile carefully and correct all errors.

12. Print your bio and give the hard copy to your supervisor (your instructor) or email it to this person.

MYBIO

Almost everyone agrees that the employees make a business work. Knowing a little about the company managers and your coworkers will help you communicate and fit in more quickly. It will also help you be more sensitive to the individuals you come into contact with at work.

Think and write about the following:

1. Do you find it easier to communicate via telephone or email with someone you have met in person or someone you have not met in person? Why?

   _____

   _____

2. Do you like writing about yourself? Why or why not?

   _____

   _____

3. What is appropriate and what is inappropriate to include in an online biography? List several examples of each.

   _____

   _____

   _____

4. From the biographies that you read earlier, choose the one you liked the least. Proofread the bio and critique it according to the criteria listed in the Technical Communications report on page 35.

   - *Audience:* Who is the audience for this online biography? Does this biography connect with this audience? Describe how it does or doesn't connect.

     _____

     _____

   - *Purpose:* What is the intended purpose of this online bio? How is that purpose accomplished, or why is that purpose not accomplished?

     _____

     _____

   - *Personality:* What personality is portrayed in this bio? Is this bio effective in portraying a "personality"?

     _____

     _____

- *Length:* Is this bio too long, too short, or an appropriate length? If it is too long, what parts of it could you cut without taking away from the bio?

_____

_____

_____

Writing for an Online World

What sets technical communications apart from other forms of writing such as the short story, historical writing, or fiction? Why should it be studied and learned independently? Consider the following situation that involves technical writing.

If your washing machine started to make strange sounds and leak buckets of dirty water, you would probably call a repairperson. Before beginning work, she would want to know about the problem. So, over the telephone or in a note on the kitchen counter, you'd explain what was happening. In that way, she would have an idea of how to fix it. Your description of the problem would be a piece of technical communications: direct and to the point.

Your objective would be to describe the problem in succinct, precise terms; you'd say only what was needed to fix the problem. You wouldn't talk about the weather or about what you had for dinner last night. You wouldn't write a poem or tell her how having a broken appliance makes you feel. You'd stick to the facts and present them in the clearest logical order. This is typical of technical communications.

When you prepare technical communications such as an email or your online biography, consider the following:

- Be aware of your *audience.* Don't write anything that might be offensive to your reader.

- Focus on your *purpose.* Why are you writing this message? Make sure your writing fits the intended purpose.

- In some writing situations, it's in good taste to interject a little of your own unique *personality.* A little personality goes a long way, however. Don't overdo it.

- Consider the *length.* Short and sweet is usually better than long and dry. Most technical communications should be concise and direct.

- One last bit of advice... *proofread.* Then proofread again! No correlation exists between spelling and intelligence. Nevertheless, like it or not, we're still judged by our spelling and punctuation skills.

Chapter Review

Executive Summary

As in most corporations, the Corporate View Intranet is the information center of the company. It's a catalogue of critical data. It includes, among other things, the company's mission statement and goals, answers to technical questions, a listing of contacts, and online biographies. It is a place to learn about the different strategic business units, divisions, departments, and groups within the company.

The Intranet is mirrored, or copied locally, so that divisions of the large corporation can continue to function even if one part of the corporate Intranet is down.

The Intranet is divided into two parts: the local Intranet site where you do your work and the Corporate View main Web site where you can go for the most current information.

The Intranet is like a mini-World Wide Web for use by Corporate View employees only. It provides email messaging and communicates important information to and from the various employees within the company. It is also where employees discuss day-to-day issues and work together in virtual teams. The Intranet is the lifeblood of the organization and helps Corporate View run smoothly.

Intranets can often be confused with the Internet because the same technology is used in both. The Internet (which includes the World Wide Web) is a huge interconnected, public network of the world's computer systems; it is also the world's biggest repository of business information.

The Intranet is a much smaller web of computers used by a business—in this case, Corporate View—to network its business units, workgroups, teams, and employees.

An Extranet is that part of an Intranet shared with other companies doing business together.

The many ways that employees communicate fall into two categories: synchronous (personal exchange, face-to-face or voice communications) and asynchronous (email, voice mail—no "live" personal exchange).

The Intranet can provide you with all sorts of information about the company and its mission and goals. Learning about the people, teams, or workgroups you will be working with can be very important. It will help you interact more smoothly with others in the corporation.

The Intranet's FAQs section can help you find answers to technical questions. Definitions for business terms can be found in the ShopTalk section of the Intranet.

Technical Communications

When you are writing, consider the intended audience of the message, your purpose for writing, whether it is appropriate for your personality to be revealed, and an appropriate length for the message.

Proofreading and correcting errors is very important because you will be judged by the spelling, punctuation, and grammar skills exhibited in your writing.

The Corporate Inbox

Corporations get lots of questions through telephone calls, FAXes, and email. Even a letter or two will come in loaded with questions. Questions come from customers, employees, and other interested people. Here are some messages that need to be answered by someone in Human Resources—perhaps an intern like you.

Answer these messages with the help of the Corporate View Intranet and your own best judgment to arrive at a logical answer. If you need help preparing these documents, use the corporate Style Guide. The Style Guide helps employees prepare email, FAXes, letters, phone scripts, and other documents. The Corporate Communications Department maintains this service. Look for **Style Guide** under the **Corporate Communications** link.

Save As:

Inbox1A

TO: Intern
FROM: *mkim@corpview.com*
SUBJECT: Job Applicant
MESSAGE:

A letter arrived from Miguel Cervantes of Monterey, Mexico. He is interested in applying to our new Mexico City office. He has a background as a telephone repair technician. He wants to know which Corporate View business unit he should investigate. We need help in this new office and would like this prospective employee to apply.

Please write a letter selling him on the idea of applying to Corporate View and describing an SBU he would most likely want to join. Have your draft of the letter on my desk in the morning. Miguel's address is:

   Mr. Miguel Cervantes
   120 Hidalgo
   Monterey, Mexico

Melissa

Hi, this is Melissa. An email came in from an aide working in Senator Jackson's office. They want us to provide information on antitrust legislation. We need to reply today on how the breakup of AT&T allowed Corporate View to compete in the telecommunications market. The message will be forwarded to Sandy Workman. Please send the email to me for review, and I will pass it along to Sandy. Send it to **mkim@corpview.com**.

Thanks, Bye.

Save As:

Inbox1B

Note

Do not actually send these two emails to Melissa Kim. Since these emails do not require a reply from Melissa, please submit them to your instructor.

CORPORATE VIEW

From the Desk of Melissa Kim...

Dear Intern:

We have been getting a ton of calls by our own employees asking what the difference is between the Intranet, Extranet, the Internet, and WWW. Write a phone script we can send to our helpdesk people that explains the differences and gently emphasizes why sensitive corporate data shouldn't be shared on the Extranet or WWW. Email your script to me, please. (mkim@corpview.com)

Thanks,
Melissa

Save As:

Inbox1C

CORPORATE VIEW FAX

TO: Melissa Kim
FROM: James Baker
DATE: Current
RE: Push Technology

As a new employee, I have been hearing a lot about push technology. Could you please give me some information on what this technology involves or how it is applied?

Thanks for your help.

Intern:

This new employee obviously doesn't know about the ShopTalk link on the Intranet. Please prepare a FAX for me that I can send to James Baker in our London office. Include information on how to use the Intranet and to set the defaults so that the Corporate View page appears every time James starts his computer. Give me the FAX so that I can proof it and send it along.

Thanks,
Melissa

Save As:

Inbox1D

Online Business Trends

Access the Corporate View Web site. (A live Web connection is needed to check stock quotes. If you do not have access to a live Web connection, move on to the second part of this exercise under When a Few Words Will Do.) Click the **_Stock Watcher Links_** and follow the instructions. Identify the following ticker symbols and learn how each of these companies did in the stock market today.

Current Date _____

Ticker	Exchange	Company Name	Current Price
T	NYSE	_____	_____
FON	NYSE	_____	_____
IBM	NYSE	_____	_____
MSFT	NASDAQ	_____	_____
NSCP	NASDAQ	_____	_____
GM	NYSE	_____	_____

When a Few Words Will Do

Answer the following questions using what you have learned reading the Business Milestones and The Least You Should Know About… reports. Use 25 to 50 words to write your answers in a word processing document.

1. Why was Netscape so important in the history of cyberbusiness and the development of Intranets?

2. Explain why the breakup of AT&T was such a pivotal event in the history of telecommunications and telephony.

3. Bill Gates makes a distinction between synchronous and asynchronous business communications. Explain these differences with examples. What are the advantages and disadvantages of each type?

4. What is the Fortune 500, and why is it valuable? Why is it good for other businesses to know about the top corporations?

Save As:

Online1

Portfolio-Building Project

Requesting a Letter of Recommendation

Portfolios are personal expressions of who you are and what you can do. Portfolios let you showcase your technical communications skills and illustrate your marketability. A good portfolio can help you find a job or advance up the corporate ladder.

A personal portfolio requires thinking and careful planning to display your skills and detail your experience in the best possible light. A personal portfolio can contain samples of your work, awards or other recognitions, certificates or degrees related to training or education, and letters or recommendations.

To begin your portfolio, write a block-style letter to a key person in your academic education, asking for a letter of reference you can use in your job search after your internship is over.

1. Before you begin keying this letter with your word processor, review block-style letters on the Intranet. Click on the **_Corporate Communications_**, **_Style Guide_**, **_Letters_** links.

2. In preparation for writing the letter, review the technical communications tips shown on page 35.

3. Spell-check and proofread your letter before you print.

Save As:

Pfolio1

High-Performance Workgroup Project

Many projects turn out better when a team collaborates. This is especially true in writing for the online world. Before you post your online bio for others to see, proofread it carefully and let a few trusted colleagues review it for content, audience appeal, and readability.

1. Print three or four copies of the online bio you created in Activity 1-5.

2. Share your online biography with a team of three or four reviewers. Ask the team to read your bio, make corrective marks, and add comments on the back about the audience, purpose, personality, and length of your bio.

3. Return to your online bio file and make changes and corrections based on the feedback you received from the reviewers.

4. Print a revised copy of the bio and save it, using a new filename.

Save As:

HP1

Thinking and Writing About Your Business

On the basis of what you have learned in this chapter, answer seven of the following questions in your own words. Write answers of 25 to 50 words using a word processor.

1. Why has the use of Intranets increased in recent years, and why do businesses come to depend on them?

2. When you think about technical communications, what ideas come to your mind? What are technical communications, and why are they so important in business today?

3. Describe how Intranets can improve employee performance on the job.

4. Describe the corporate culture of Corporate View. What kind of image does the company hope to portray for its employees?

5. Describe telephony and how it is expanding into the world of the Internet.

6. What are the advantages and disadvantages of using email?

7. How can you get access to free email via the Internet?

8. Why do companies like Corporate View encourage their employees to share information about themselves over the Intranet.

9. Why are business people "stock watchers"?

10. What points should you remember when you write about yourself on a corporate Intranet?

Think1

Overtime

Visit the Competition

You can learn a lot about a company by looking at the companies to which it compares itself. Marketing, Sales, and Support provides a link on the Intranet to information about other companies. Read the information about some of TeleView's competitors.

1. Access the Corporate View Web site. (A live Web connection is needed to complete this exercise.)

2. Choose the ***Marketing, Sales, & Support*** link. Navigate to the ***Sizing Up the Competition*** page under the ***TeleView*** link.

3. Select three competitors and visit their sites by clicking on the appropriate links. Remember that you can use the Back button to return to the Sizing Up the Competition page to choose a different competitor's site.

4. In a word processing file, list the competitors whose sites you visited. Discuss three strengths of each of the competitors.

5. Explain what have you learned about TeleView's goals in the marketplace from looking at its major competitors.

Otime1

Applications to Small Business

Telecommuting

William Bridges in his book, *JobShift: How to Prosper in a Workplace Without Jobs*, states that nearly everyone will be an independent contractor in the future. The "cradle-to-grave" employment mentality, epitomized by IBM during the 1950s, 1960s, and 1970s, is no longer a reality. People who work for Fortune 500 companies may find themselves leaving one day, taking the skills they learned in big business with them. These skills will become valuable as they begin their own "start-up" businesses.

Many of the *downsizing* efforts of the early nineties produced a new wave of *entrepreneurs* who took the skills they learned from corporate America and began applying them to new home-based businesses of their own. Within hours of leaving an employer, you can have a virtual office established in your home office. You can begin telecommuting almost instantly with a personal computer, a printer, a FAX, and a connection to the Internet.

Think and write about the following:

1. What kinds of businesses do you think people can establish in their own home offices?

2. What skills from the Corporate View do you think can be applied by people establishing home-based or virtual businesses online?

3. The TeleView business unit has a group dedicated to helping small and start-up businesses become successful. From what you know about the company, what kind of support do you think TeleView can give small entrepreneurial businesses?

Save As:

ASB1

Online Evaluation

Access the Corporate View Web site and take the Online Evaluation for this chapter.

1. Click on the *Employee Training and Evaluations* link on the *Regular Features* page.

2. Select the *Online Tests* link and click the *Register* link. You must be a registered user to access the online tests. Follow the instructions on the screen to complete the registration process. After registering, click the *Online Tests* link to return to the Online Tests page.

3. Choose the *Chapter 1 A View from Ground Zero* link on the Online Tests page.

4. Enter the username and password you selected when you registered. (You will be required to enter this username and password each time you access a test.)

5. Take the test. Click the **First**, **Back, Next,** and **Last** buttons to navigate through the questions. Click the **Finish** button to submit your test for grading. If you wish to close the test without submitting it for grading, click the **Cancel** button. Any answers you have entered will be lost if you cancel the test.

Chapter 2

A View of the Mission-Critical Functions

CHAPTER OBJECTIVES

1. Learn how the mission-critical functions work together, interact, and support each other
2. Analyze product data from a variety of sources
3. Organize to solve a problem
4. Identify key workgroup members
5. Evaluate various sources of information from the Intranet
6. Expand your portfolio
7. Measure the strengths and weaknesses of competitive products

Technical Communications

- Research and write a product performance report
- Use email or memos to request information and analyze and solve problems
- Create a written agenda for action

Generating Synergy

"Welcome back. I want to introduce Corporate View in a little more detail. You're here to have a corporate experience, and that's what we're going to give you.

"At Corporate View, you'll jump into the action with both feet. As our interns, we want you to be players, not benchwarmers. Before we send you off to your first assignment, though, I want you to become a little more familiar with our departments, the *mission-critical functions*. We want you to have a better handle on how each department or function performs. In this exercise, you'll have a chance to see how each of these areas works.

"We want you to see firsthand how managers work. We coordinate manager training through *Human Resources (HR)* and *Management*. You'll also get a bird's-eye view of *Corporate Communications*, *Research and Development (R&D)*, *Marketing and Sales*, *Customer Support*, *Finance and Accounting*, *Legal Services*, *Information Technology*, *Manufacturing*, and *Warehousing*.

"We want you to have a big picture, an overview, of how a corporation operates. To do this, we are going to put you through a teamwork and leadership training exercise. By the time you're finished, you'll have a better idea about how Corporate View works from the outside in and the inside out.

"I ought to tell you that this training exercise, along with department rotation, is part of our standard training for every new employee. It doesn't matter whether you have an MBA from Harvard, are hired with 20 years of experience, are a new intern, or are transferring from another division. Every person needs to know how Corporate View works because we don't work in a vacuum. We work as a team.

"We often refer to our teams as workgroups. We feel these workgroups are a major reason we've been so successful. To borrow a cliché, at Corporate View one hand knows what the other hand is up to at any given moment.

"Part of being an effective team player is understanding something about what the other person, team, or department does. Working through the CF4000/SE training scenario not only gives our employees and interns a big picture, but also gives them a *we*- not a *me*- perspective. This then filters through in their interaction with other employees and departments.

"Our motto is: *Don't look for blame, look for solutions!* There's a **synergy**, or a creative power, when we pull together. Negative thinking or finding fault drains our creative energy and is a waste of time.

"Let me explain further about what we are going to do. We're going to simulate a situation and let you help the team solve the problem. I want you to look closely at what is required to handle a crisis and how the team members come up with suggestions and solutions that are good for the customer and good for Corporate View.

"Good luck!"

Business
Milestones

GM—Atop the Fortune 500

When *Fortune* magazine releases its list of the top 500 companies each year, you can rest assured that General Motors (NYSE:GM) will be at or near the number-one position. It has been for years. A company like GM doesn't reach the top without knowing how to get the highest performance out of its divisions and subsidiaries. GM has several famous divisions you're likely familiar with. These include Buick, Chevrolet, Oldsmobile, GMC trucks, and Cadillac.

Did you know that Saturn is a part of the GM family, too? Saturn is not a typical division of GM, like Chevrolet or Buick. Instead, it's a wholly owned subsidiary. This means Saturn operates more like an independent company.

Saturn is free to develop its own corporate culture, conduct research and development, and pursue its own mission and philosophies. The core of Saturn's philosophy revolves around teamwork:

We, the Saturn Team, in concert with the UAW and General Motors, believe that meeting the needs of Customers, Saturn Team Members, Suppliers, Retailers and Neighbors is fundamental to fulfilling our mission.*

This philosophy extends to every part of the business, even to its recruiting of new employees. As seen in Figure 2-1, Saturn looks for team members who enjoy contributing to the future of the company.

Just remember, we're not looking for employees, we're looking for team members. That means strong communications and problem-solving skills and a desire to think creatively and act decisively.**

*Saturn Corporation. *Saturn, Let's Talk*. Online. Available: **www.saturn.com/communication/index.html**. March 26, 1998.
Saturn. *Saturn, Online Recruiting*. Online. Available: **www.saturn.com/company/recruiting/index2.html. March 26, 1998.

Figure 2-1
Saturn is a wholly owned subsidiary of General Motors.

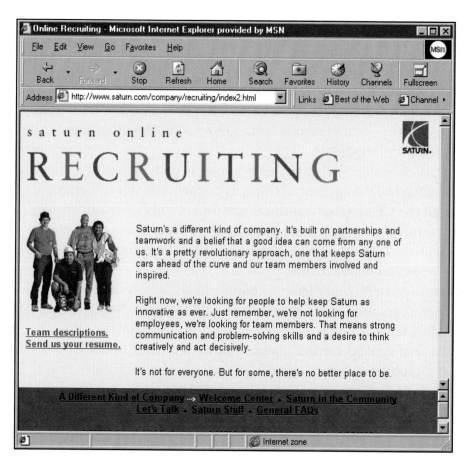

Activity Overviews

In this chapter, we will take a close look at *product workgroups* (sometimes called product teams). A product workgroup, as the name implies, is the group responsible for taking a product from R&D to market.

Members of each major department or function make up a product workgroup. In this training exercise, you will see how each department contributes to the solution of a problem. Such contributions allow the corporation to run smoothly. Each workgroup team member is ready to do his or her part to correct the problem.

Learning about the different departments or functions will give you a glimpse into how a corporation works.

Activity 2-1 Researching a Product on the Intranet will put you into the corporate learning center as a member of an existing product workgroup. You move into a position vacated by another employee and need to come up to speed fast on the product, what it is, what it does, and what your responsibilities are.

Activity 2-2 Product Performance Report will have you reporting on a product that is doing quite well. Sales figures are very good; the support problems seem to be minimal. You are new on the job. How will you present your data?

Activity 2-3 Agenda for Action will put you in a leadership role as a problem is identified and a plan of action is formulated. You must get to the bottom of the problem and find a solution without alienating the people who have worked so hard to bring the product to market.

Activity 2-4 Your Solution, Our Solution will give you a chance to resolve the problem, count the cost, and administer a remedy. You can then compare your solution to ones suggested by others.

Understanding the meanings of these terms will help you learn the concepts and develop the skills covered in the chapter. In preparation for completing the chapter activities, access the Intranet and find the definition for each of these terms by clicking the **ShopTalk** link on the **Regular Features** page.

Corporate **ShopTalk**

- Bundle
- Corporate Communications
- Customer Support
- Finance and Accounting
- Human Resources

- Information Technology
- Legal Services
- Management
- Manufacturing
- Marketing and Sales
- Problem-Solving Workgroups

- Product Workgroups
- Research and Development (R&D)
- Revenue
- Shipping
- Synergy
- Warehousing
- Win-Win

Activity 2-1   *Researching a Product on the Intranet*

In this teamwork and leadership training exercise, you will learn about each department or function at Corporate View. (In Section 2 Getting Down to Business, you will be rotated into each department for a more in-depth look at how each department functions.)

You will also learn about teams (or workgroups) and how they work—specifically, how teams "synergize" at Corporate View. The *team* concept is a fundamental principle; it drives how business is done in our company. The team is stronger as a unit than any individual team member.

In this scenario, you are a new employee in a product workgroup in Corporate View's TeleView division. TeleView specializes in high-tech electronics and makes most of its money from digital phones and long-distance services. You have inherited the CF4000/SE phone product from your predecessor, who has taken a job at another company.

You don't know much about the CF4000/SE. It has been explained to you that the product has been **shipping** for a year and is doing rather well in this new "student" market. You know the product is a **bundle**, which is a combination of a phone customized for students and a long-distance pricing plan geared to student budgets. The bundle is being marketed on 100 college campuses around the country. You don't really know much about the phone or the bundle, so you had better access the Intranet and find out a little more.

One of your jobs is to monitor how the product is doing from a customer perspective. Spend a half hour reading the Customer Support phone reports and related email messages from customers as directed in the Just-in-Time Training.

Business Milestones

C o v e y   L e a d e r s h i p

Synergy is a word that has floated around university circles for decades. Essentially, it means that the whole is more than the sum of the parts. Stephen R. Covey, a former college professor teaching human relations, popularized the word for millions of business managers in his blockbuster book, *The 7 Habits of Highly Effective People*. Covey adroitly explained that 1+1 really can equal 3 if you bring people together to solve problems in a *win-win* way. Popularizing concepts like *the emotional bank account, principle-centered management*, and the idea that employers should treat their employees like their "best customers," the book launched a new era in business management.

Covey went on to form a highly influential business management training company and became one of the most sought-after business speakers in the world. His company merged with another planning and management giant, Franklin Quest, in the mid-1990s to form Franklin Covey Co. (NYSE:FC).

Something to consider as you proceed through this chapter comes from the Franklin Covey Web page: "With the right information, success is at your fingertips."*

*Franklin Covey Co. *Franklin Covey Co. Corporate Information*. Online. Available: ***www.franklincovey.com/fcinfo/***. March 26, 1998.

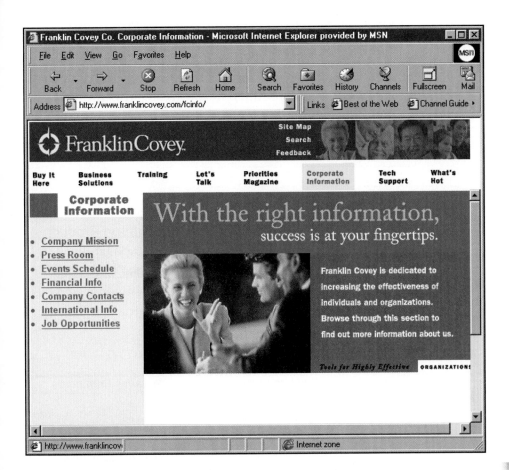

Just-in-Time Training

Researching a Product on the Intranet

1. Access your local Intranet or the Corporate View Web site.

2. Access the ***Marketing, Sales, and Support*** page. Select the ***TeleView*** link, and then choose the ***Products, Promotions, & Pricing*** link.

3. Learn all you can about your product by clicking the ***CF4000/SE (Student Edition)*** link.

4. As you read, create a table, spreadsheet, or chart listing the main features of the CF4000/SE. Make your list as if you were a customer, listing all the features and prices that are promised in the product description as in this brief sample in Table 2-1.

CF4000/SE Product Promises

Table 2-1

Feature or Promotion	Positive Comments	Negative Comments
5 cents a minute for all calls home		
3 friends @ 5 cents a minute		

---

5. After you have finished reading and have your chart ready, access the **_Research and Development_** page. Click the **_TeleView_** link. Choose and read the **_CF4000/SE Bug Report_**. Did you learn anything new about your product? What makes this product different from previous TeleView phones?

_____

_____

_____

6. Return to the **_Marketing, Sales, and Support_** page. Click the **_TeleView_** link. Read the **_CF4000/SE Customer Support Product Reports_**. This is where you will need the table or chart you created earlier. As you read **_Phone Calls_** and **_Email Messages_**, indicate the number of positive and negative comments on your chart. Jot down a few of the comments if you think they are important, as shown in shown in Table 2-2.

T a b l e   2 - 2   **CF4000/SE Product Promises**

Feature or Promotion	Positive Comments	Negative Comments
5 cents a minute for all calls home	✔✔✔ Love the pricing	✔
3 friends @ 5 cents a minute	✔✔	✔✔ Want to add more friends to list

7. Proofread your chart carefully and correct all errors before printing your chart.

Debriefing

One important task a workgroup must do is check the performance of a product after it has gone to market. In this training exercise, you were looking for positive results as well as potential problems with the product. How did you do? You probably had some positive feedback about the product and perhaps even a few negative comments.

Think and write about the following:

1. From how many other groups or functions in the company did you pull information? List them here.

_____

2. What people, teams, or groups actually posted the information on the Intranet for you to find? Name them here.

_____

3. How many mission-critical functions were involved in making your job of learning about your new product possible? List them here.

_____

4. What single resource was the most helpful to you? Explain why this resource was the most helpful.

_____

Activity 2-2 *Product Performance Report*

A responsible company doesn't create a product and turn its back once the product has gone to market. Marketing a product is a never-ending process. At TeleView, tracing a product's market performance is standard procedure. It's also good business. The company needs to know how a product is doing at all times and how customers view the product they've purchased.

If customers are having a problem with the product, TeleView needs to know about it right away. If the customer is happy, the division wants to know that, too—and why. TeleView wants to serve its customers' communications needs. TeleView can only do this if customers are satisfied.

In this activity, you will continue the teamwork and leadership training exercise you began in Activity 2-1. In this exercise, you're a member of the product team in charge of the CF4000/SE cell phone product. You and the other team members are TeleView's experts on this product. Any internal (inside-the-company) or external (outside-the-company) questions or concerns, will be addressed to you. It's your job to track this product in the market and deal with customer concerns.

Your job is to assess how the CF4000/SE is doing in the market, so you'll be looking closely at the marketing data. You'll also look closely at customer calls and email. You'll examine the data and prepare a product performance memo, a report created on a quarterly basis, in the Just-in-Time Training.

Technical **Communications**

Writing Product Performance Memos

When creating a product performance report in memo form, make your writing clear, crisp, and to the point. Include this information in your report:

- A brief description of the product
- Sales and *revenue* trends
- Pluses (positive feedback or results)
- Minuses (negative feedback or results)
- Brief summary in the form of a conclusion

Remember your audience (upper management), the purpose of the report (to assess the performance of the product), personality (how you want the message to portray you as a person), and the report length (around 500 words). You may want to include a table (like Table 2-2) or create a chart or graph to make your report easy to follow.

Just-in-Time Training

Writing a Product Performance Report Memo

1. Access your local Intranet or the Corporate View Web site.
2. Check the sales data for the CF4000/SE in preparation for writing your report. Click on the ***TeleView*** link on the ***Marketing,***

**Sales, & Support** page. Check the _**CF4000/SE Sales and Revenue Summaries**_.

3. Access the _**Corporate Communications**_ link and select the _**Style Guide**_. Read the tips and review the proper format for completing _**Memos**_.

4. Read the Technical Communications feature Writing Product Performance Memos before you begin writing.

5. Summarize your findings in a memo to your supervisor about the performance of the CF4000/SE. Include a summary of the information you placed in your table or chart from Activity 2-1.

6. Proofread, spell-check your memo, and correct all errors. Send your memo to your supervisor (your teacher) in printed form or via email.

Save As:

SEMemo

The **Least** You **Should** Know About...

Copying from the Intranet

To copy text from the Intranet, select the text to be copied in your Web browser as you would in your word processor. Then choose **Copy** from the Edit menu. Move to your word processing document and select **Paste** from the Edit menu. (See the _**Regular Features**_, _**Intranet FAQs**_, _**Copying and Pasting Information from the Web and the Intranet**_ links.)

To copy a picture from the Intranet, point to the image (called a *graphic*). In Windows, click your right mouse button. For Macintosh, click and hold down your mouse button. Then choose the **Save Image As** or **Save Picture As** option (wording varies). Save the picture in your personal *CVFolder*. Open your picture in your word processing software as you would open other images from a file. (See the _**Intranet FAQs**_ link, _**Copying and Pasting from the Web or Intranet**_.)

Debriefing

Every product report you write is important and should reflect your best efforts. If you write a poor report, people will lose confidence in your writing, thinking, communicating, and reporting abilities.

A product performance report memo should be short and to the point. More words do not necessarily make the information clearer. A few carefully selected graphs, charts, tables, or other attachments may get your point across a lot more efficiently than wordy descriptions.

Make sure your paragraphing is logical and no words are misspelled. After you're done writing, read over the memo a few times. Is it clear and easy to read? Is the information complete and accurate?

Think and write about the following:

1. How might an unclear report waste the valuable time of other employees?

   _____

   _____

2. What are some possible consequences of including incomplete or inaccurate information in a product report?

   _____

   _____

   _____

   _____

In this phase of your teamwork and leadership training, you will assume the role of team leader for the CF4000/SE product group. As you review customer email on the CF4000/SE, an alarming trend starts to appear. There's a problem with the phone. As you look at more email, the same problem keeps coming up. The written mail and comments from the phone lines confirm the problem.

To make matters worse, an advance copy of *Technophobia* magazine has just been delivered to your desk. It gives a less-than-favorable review of the phone. The review confirms what your consumers have suggested: The phone's email and Web connections are hard to figure out—"if they work at all." Your boss also sent you a note.

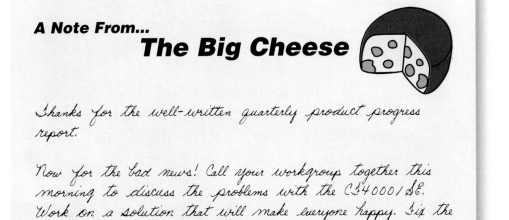

A Note From...
The Big Cheese

Thanks for the well-written quarterly product progress report.

Now for the bad news! Call your workgroup together this morning to discuss the problems with the CF4000/SE. Work on a solution that will make everyone happy. Fix the problem and keep me informed.

Your boss has also enclosed his copy of the *Technophobia* review with a paragraph circled (see page 56).

Your job is to identify the problem and propose possible solutions—a course of action. And you must get the job done as soon as possible. In a real situation, the first thing you might do is get on the phone and talk with the reviewer who wrote the article. You should thank her for her honesty and inform her that steps will be taken to correct the problem. You would probably send her an updated phone for another review as soon as the problem is fixed.

The phone gets high marks for its pricing (five stars), but the retractable antenna is temperamental (two stars), while the Web and email features are laughable (no stars).

Just-in-Time Training

Creating an Action Agenda

Stop for a second and think: What are the steps you need to follow to isolate and overcome this problem? Yes, you are in a hurry. Yes, the problem has become urgent. During a crisis, however, you *must* take time to plan, even if just for a few minutes. Read The Least You Should Know About... Planning Through Problems before following the steps below.

Planning Through Problems

A good way to begin solving a problem is to break it down into small parts. The first thing to remember about solving a problem is to relax, sit down for a few minutes, and create a step-by-step *agenda for action.*

In a word processing document, make two lists. In the first list, include the names of everyone you may need to contact during the crisis. Put the letter *A* next to the names of the people you *must* contact or who will definitely have a say in the solution of the problem. Put a *B* by those you may need to contact and a *C* by those you probably won't need to contact at this time. Sort your list by the A, B, C ranking. Then, rank the people in each group by the order in which you need to contact them by placing a number next to each person's name. Sort each group again by number.

Do the same with all the steps you need to follow to solve the problem. In this scenario, you need to determine exactly what is wrong. To do so, you need to write a short email and a memo

asking all the members of the workgroup to check their part of the product development process to find out exactly where the problem lies. Your list might look like this partial list:

			Agenda for Action
✔	1	A	Write a brief description of the problem
✔	2	A	Email workgroup members and ask for their help and immediate feed-back
	3	A	Ask IT to create a newsgroup posting of the replies
	1	B	Contact (Name of workgroup member)
	2	B	Contact (Name of supervisor)
	1	C	Contact supplier of keypad used in manufacturing the phone

Make the steps as detailed and specific as possible. You might wish to add a column to the list for checking off steps as they are completed.

1. In a word processing file, make a list of all the people you may need to communicate with during this crisis. You can add additional names as you go along. Include everyone you think could be of any help. The Intranet can help. Select the **_Employee Contacts_** link from the **_Regular Features_** page. Select **_Contacts for Interns and New Employees_** to see a list of team members for your CF4000/SE training exercise.

2. Create a second list to include the steps you need to follow to solve this crisis. Once again, you can add steps as you go along as needed, but an initial list will help you get started and control events and the use of your time.

3. Send a copy of your lists to your supervisor (instructor) via email or hard copy.

4. Prepare a short memo (or email) to the CF4000/SE workgroup members and others on your list of those who may help solve the problem. Explain the problem to the best of your knowledge. Ask for help in pinning down the problem and welcome any

Save As:

CrisList

Figure 2-3
Lotus gave birth to workgroup software and promoted the workgroup collaborative mindset.

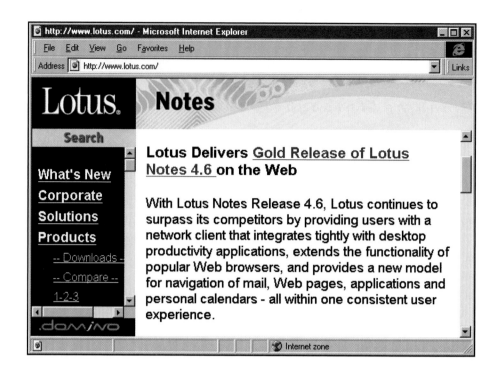

The **Least** You **Should** Know About...

Workgroups

Lotus popularized the concept of *workgroups* in the tech world. It created Lotus Notes, software that allows employees to work together to solve problems. This new generation of workgroup software became very popular in high-performance organizations. It soon became the structure for many Intranet software solutions. The workgroup idea is so essential to business that IBM bought Lotus Development Corp. as part of its workgroup software strategy for business customers. Lotus continues as a strategic business unit of IBM.

As important as workgroup software is, the concept of organizing employees into workgroups is even more important. There are essentially two kinds of workgroups: *product workgroups* and ***problem-solving workgroups***. A product workgroup takes a new product from R&D through Manufacturing, Marketing, and Sales. Problem-solving workgroups solve specific problems. If a problem is long-term, a permanent workgroup will be formed. If the need for action is only temporary, like planning a party for the division, then a temporary group can be formed.

Intranet software helps product and problem-solving workgroups communicate and work together effectively. Lotus pioneered this kind of teamwork-enabling software.

HelpSE

suggestions for a possible solution. Set a deadline of 24 hours for responses. In the communication, ask Information Technology (IT) to create a newsgroup-like posting of the replies. Remember, be polite. People usually respond to trouble, but they have other assignments that might be even more urgent. They are also judging your handling of the situation. In a real situation (rather than a training exercise), once you get to the bottom of an issue, send thank-you notes to all those who helped out.

5. Give a copy of the memo to your supervisor (instructor) for input before you send it out.

In your quarterly product report/memo you wrote for upper management, you discussed your findings in a crisp, factual manner. You included sales figures and related data. How was your writing different in the email you just created for your workgroup peers? In some ways, it should be the same in that the problem, as well as the pluses and minuses of the product, should be outlined. You don't want to discourage everyone or make the problem sound bigger than it is.

In such "pressure" writing, it is essential to be clear about your request for help—what you need your workgroup members to do. Your request for help must be clear if you are to expect any assistance. You must also be sensitive to people's time and to their feelings about the product. Remember, you are new to the group. This is an established team with a proven track record.

Think and write about the following:

Read the unclear sentences shown below. Rewrite each sentence to make the request clearer or more concrete.

Unclear Get back to me on this in a few days.

Better Please send me the answers to these questions in an email no later than next Friday.

1. **Unclear** The problem can only be identified by a complete team effort, harnessing our resources to our fullest potential.

   Better _____

2. **Unclear** We are at a crossroads in our product implementation. The crisis can be contained by unleashing our creativity, energy, effort, and skills! We are counting on each and every one of you in this concerted effort. Carry on!

   Better _____

   _____

3. **Unclear** Relate the issues in your corresponding reply as you have encountered them while considering all the relevant aspects of the problem.

   Better _____

   _____

4. **Unclear** It is a pleasure being on this highly organized and professional workgroup team, and I know I can count on each and every one of you to give this problem your 100 percent fullest attention.

   Better _____

   _____

Activity 2-4   *Your Solution, Our Solution*

In this activity, you will complete your teamwork and leadership training exercise by considering the input from other team members and departments. Team members will help you formulate a solution to the problem with CF4000/SE phone.

It's not easy being responsible for a product. You often have to make difficult decisions. Sometimes a clear direction is hard to identify. This is one reason why employees work in teams at TeleView. Many heads are better than one, and the synergy that comes from a group focused on a common goal can be very effective in solving problems.

In your assumed role as the team leader, your goal is to guide the team to a win-win solution.

Some of the most difficult work has already been done. You may have already pinpointed the problem on your own. If not, you soon will with the help of the reports that will come from the product workgroup. This is a positive step. Sometimes it takes a lot of valuable time just to identify the cause of a problem.

Go to the Intranet and see whether your workgroup has come up with any answers you can use to solve this problem.

Just-in-Time Training

Formulating a Problem Solution

1. Access your local Intranet or the Corporate View Web site.

2. Choose **_Corporate View Archive_** from the **_Regular Features_** list. Click on **_CF4000/SE Workgroup Postings_**.

3. Read the information. Read, read, read, and think, think, think. What exactly is the problem, and what do you suggest doing about it?

4. Write another memo (or email) to your direct supervisor, stating the problem clearly. Brainstorm possible solutions to the problem as well and recommend the ones you think are best. In the memo, include answers to these questions:

   • What exactly, in clear, simple terms, is the problem?

   • How can TeleView ensure that phones shipped in the future will not have this problem?

- How can we fix all the phones that have been shipped so that the consumers have a product that meets their expectations?

- How can we rebuild customer loyalty? To counteract any ill will this faulty product might have created, what can we do for customers who have purchased a defective phone? (This goes beyond repairing or replacing the product.)

5. Print your memo and send a hard copy or an email version to your supervisor.

Save As:

SeSol

Debriefing

In the final phase of your training exercise, you carried out the steps you planned for solving the problem in your agenda for action. You stated the problem clearly, considered suggestions from other team members and departments, brainstormed solutions, and made your recommendation to management. But you weren't alone. Think about how many people assisted you in solving this problem. Think about how the different departments assumed a part of the total responsibility. What did they do, say, think, or contribute to your solution?

Think and write about the following:

1. Which departments or functions were most helpful in determining exactly what the problem was?

_____

2. Which departments, functions, or people recommended similar solutions?

_____

3. Were there any team members or departments you did not receive a response from? If so, which ones?

_____

4. Review your agenda for action. What steps, if any, did you not complete and why?

_____

Chapter Review

Executive Summary

In this chapter, you learned how the mission-critical functions of the corporation work together to solve problems. In a teamwork and leadership training exercise, you assumed the role of a team leader, learning about a new product and the workgroup or team assigned to a product—in this case, the CF4000/SE phone.

In this training exercise scenario, there was a problem with the product. Problems such as this one are commonplace in the corporate world. This exercise gave you a sense of how many people from different parts of Corporate View were required to find a solution to a potentially costly mistake.

In the course of solving a potentially costly problem, you saw how a corporation shares information among departments and people in different areas of the company.

By accessing the Intranet, you were able to locate your team or workgroup. You were also able to learn specific details about your product bundle. While investigating the performance of your product, you were able to assess bug reports and analyze Customer Support product reports based on phone calls and email messages from customers.

In performing a routine monitoring task, you uncovered a problem with potentially catastrophic implications. You were asked to brainstorm a solution. To do so, you needed help from your workgroup. Suggestions and information came from many departments. By taking suggestions from other members of the workgroup, you saw a range of options that included everything from a total recall of the product to more practical solutions.

The important lessons you should have learned in this scenario were how to plan a systematic approach to a problem and how to share information in a complex working environment. You also learned how to use the Intranet to research the problem and find the people who could help you solve it. By making a list of key contacts and people who could help you and by listing the steps you needed to follow to solve the problem, you were able to plan and organize your time. By thinking through a step-by-step process, you simplified the problem.

Essentially, two kinds of workgroups are found in a corporation. Some are long-term. These include product workgroups whose responsibility is to see a new product from R&D through Manufacturing, Marketing, and Sales. This group is also responsible for maintaining the product once it is on the market. A problem-solving workgroup works on an ad hoc basis and solves a specific problem; then the group usually disbands.

Technical Communications

In a fast-moving business, long and detailed documents often go unread and can be highly unproductive. For this reason, your technical communications should be clear, crisp, and to the point. In the training exercise, you were forced to stick to the facts about the product, its pluses and minuses, and to propose complete solutions in just a few words. You used a memo report format, which by its very nature is short. In today's world, a memo is usually emailed, but sometimes it is printed and distributed in hard copy form. This is especially true for meetings, where memos make sharing information convenient.

The Corporate Inbox

Corporations get lots of questions from phone calls, FAXes, and email. Even a letter or two will come in loaded with questions. Questions come from customers, employees, and other interested people. Here are some messages that need to be answered by a product manager for the CF4000/SE.

Answer these messages with the help of the Intranet and your own best judgment to arrive at a logical answer. If you need help preparing these documents, access the **Style Guide** from the **Corporate Communications** page.

Note

Remember to save your work in your CVFolder.

MegaElectronics Inc.

800 Elm Hill Pike, Suite A
Nashville, TN 37210-2850

Current Date

Ms. Casey Jones
Director of Marketing and Sales
One Corporate View Drive
Boulder, CO 80303-0103

Dear Ms. Jones

Thank you for your product announcement regarding release of the CF4000/SE bundle. Our company is a major distributor of telecommunications equipment with 20 stores along the East Coast, all near college campuses. I was planning to contact you regarding carrying this product in our stores when I saw the article in *Technophobia* magazine.

Are the problems with the CF4000/SE bundle as serious as this article implies? We are worried about the bad publicity as well as actual problems with the product. Please let me know how serious the problems really are and what your company plans to do to restore customer confidence in this product.

Sincerely

Lee Merrit, Jr.

Lee Merrit, Jr.
Product Acquisition Coordinator

Intern
Please write a reply to this letter from Mr. Merrit. If you clarify the issues and present the revenue picture to him in a win-win manner, I am sure his company will still carry the CF4000/SE bundle. Please give me your first draft of the letter before we send it along. I would like my signature on the letter.

Thanks,
Casey

Save As:

Inbox2A

From the Desk of Charles Cooper...

CORPORATE VIEW

Dear Intern:

An email came in from a lawyer at the FCC, wondering whether we were going to recall the CJ4000/SE phone and whether the phone was defective. He suggested "legal implications."

Please create a reply for me, stating only the facts of the problem and what we are doing about the problem. I will add whatever legal jargon is needed. Send it to your supervisor first for sign off, and then email it to me so that I can critique it here in Legal.

Thanks,
Charles
ccooper@corpview.com

Voice Mail

Hi, this is Melissa Kim. How are you doing now that you have completed your leadership training? Please evaluate your experience and send me an email letting me know how the training went for you. This is just an informal evaluation, something I like to do after interns and new employees complete the teamwork and leadership training exercise. This is how we make the training exercise even better for future employees.

Please list the things you learned and the things you would add to the training to make the exercise more effective. Put "Leadership Training" in the subject line.

Thanks. My email is __mkim@corpview.com__.

Inbox2D

TO: Intern
FROM: *Ldelgado@corpview.com*
SUBJECT: Email Addresses
MESSAGE:

A technician in IT says the email is down at his mirror site in Dallas, Texas, and they can't forward any email. He has several email messages that look urgent. He can FAX copies of the messages to the appropriate people, but he first needs to know names for the following employees. Because of a network server failure, all he has are their email addresses. Use the Intranet to find out who these people are. I think they are all part of the CF4000/SE workgroup team.

mbravo@corpview.com
smalone@corpview.com
mkim@corpview.com
rmills@corpview.com
dwu@corpview.com
cjones@corpview.com
ccooper@corpview.com
lomalley@corpview.com
sfrank@corpview.com

Can you put this into a FAX format so that I can send it along? Thanks, I really appreciate this.

Luis

Online Business Trends

Access the Corporate View Web site. (You will need a live Web connection to check stock quotes. If you do not have access to a Web connection, move on to the second part of this exercise under When a Few Words Will Do.) Click ***Stock Watcher Links*** on the ***Regular Features*** page and follow the instructions. Identify the following ticker symbols and learn how each of these companies did in the stock market today.

Current Date _____

Ticker	Exchange	Company Name	Current Price
GM	NYSE	_____	_____
FC	NYSE	_____	_____

When a Few Words Will Do

Answer the following questions using what you have learned reading the Business Milestones and The Least You Should Know About... reports. Use 25 to 50 words to write your answers in a word processing document.

1. What is GM and what is GM's business? Why is this company at or near the top of the Fortune 500 every year?

2. What is Saturn, and what makes it unique?

3. Who is Stephen R. Covey, and why has he been influential in business management?

Save As:

Online 2

Portfolio-Building Project

Writing Memos for an Online World

Memorandums, or "memos," were a mainstay in business communications for over a century. Email, however, has largely replaced the typed and printed memo. Email is faster, easier to distribute, doesn't require printing, and is less costly to distribute to many people.

Nevertheless, there is a time and a place for the traditional memo. For example, in a meeting, a memo is a great communications tool. All the people at a meeting can quickly see the information without using their portable computers to check their email. So don't count hard copy memos out in today's electronic world.

If printed memos are not commonly used in an organization, they can offer a refreshing change of pace. A well-constructed memo placed on a manager's desk (followed by an email with a copy of the memo as an email attachment) can be a good communications combination and shows a high level of professionalism.

Demonstrate your technical communications skills by creating a great looking and well-written memo for your portfolio.

1. Before you begin keying this memo in your word processor, review proper memo formats. Click on the **_Corporate Communications_**, **_Style Guide_**, **_Memos_** links on the Intranet. Use the format shown there to create your memo.

2. In a memo to your supervisor (instructor), outline the steps you followed as you solved the problem posed to you in Activities 2-1, 2-2, 2-3, and

2-4. Give a full accounting of your thoughts and actions, what you did and why, and what you think you accomplished and why.

- In the first paragraph, briefly describe the problem.

- In the second paragraph, explain the steps you followed to resolve the problem. You might wish to use a numbered list to walk your reader step-by-step through the process you used to resolve the problem.

- In the third paragraph, document the resources you relied on to solve the problem.

Generally, memos are kept to one page, but in this case, you have the liberty to extend the memo to two pages.

3. As you write, remember your **audience** (your supervisor), your **purpose** (explain the process), your **personality** (make it reflect *you* and who you are), and the **length** (limit it to two pages).

4. Proofread and spell-check your memo before you print. Give the memo to your supervisor as hard copy or via email as an attachment.

Pfolio2

High-Performance Workgroup Project

Perhaps you are wondering why Activity 2-4 was called Your Solution, Our Solution. Collaboration can beget controversy. Often, when you propose a solution to a problem, another person will have a different idea and propose something else. This is especially true in a crisis. To turn "your" solution into "our" solution, discussion, debate, and compromise are usually required. Practice this process in the following workgroup exercise.

1. Share the solution you invented in Activity 2-4 Your Solution, Our Solution with a team of three or four other employees.

2. Discuss the various solutions each of you came up with in the training exercise. Clarify your various definitions of what the problem was or might have been.

3. Finally, brainstorm a group solution to the problem. Have one person act as the scribe, and together draft a team proposal addressing the delicate problem of keeping your new student customers happy with the CF4000/SE bundle.

HP2

4. Present your combined solution to your supervisor by sending an email with your memo as an attachment, or print and deliver it as hard copy.

On the basis of what you have learned in this chapter while re-solving the problem of the CF4000/SE, think and write about the following questions. Record your answers of 25 to 50 words in a word processing document.

1. What resources on the Intranet helped you learn the most about the CF4000/SE?

2. In solving the problem of the CF4000/SE, what was your role? Describe the importance of your role and how it differed from the role of other workgroup members in the scenario.

Some mission-critical functions were more helpful than others in helping you solve the problem of the CF4000/SE. Complete five of the following descriptions or comparisons. Revisit the Intranet if you need help recalling their roles.

3. Describe the role played by Customer Support in the scenario.

4. Describe the role played by Marketing and Sales.

5. Describe the role played by Finance and Accounting.

6. Describe the role played by Information Technology.

7. Describe the role played by Manufacturing and Warehousing.

8. Describe the role played by Corporate Communications.

9. Describe the role played by R&D.

10. Compare the most helpful group or function to the least helpful group in solving the problem of the CF4000/SE.

Save As:

Think2

Overtime

Comparing the Competition

How does the CF4000/SE stack up against its competition? You're about to find out.

1. Access the Corporate View Web site. (A live Web connection is needed to complete this exercise.)

2. Under the *TeleView* link, on the **Marketing, Sales, & Support** page, you will find a link called **Sizing Up the Competition**. Select two companies from the Electronics Manufacturers list. Search for information about their digital phones on their Internet sites.

3. Compare the CF4000/SE by TeleView with *similar* phones made by these two other companies. Select phones that would be attractive to students. Do not include phones geared toward older customers because the target market for the CF4000/SE consists of college-age students.

4. Write a memo or an email to the CF4000/SE product team, comparing the CF4000/SE to two other phones. Provide the name and model and a description of each competitor's phone. Explain features that the CF4000/SE has in common with the competitors and note also the features that are different.

Otime2

Applications to Small Business

Solving Problems

In small businesses, owners and employees often wear several hats. A single employee may be the marketing manager and the entire sales force for a product. It is not uncommon to have the R&D leader also handle Customer Support calls and customer emails, as well as manage the company's Internet and Intranet sites.

Think and write about the following:

1. In what ways is it easier to solve a problem (like the one described in this chapter with the CF4000/SE) in a small business as opposed to a large corporation?

2. Is a corporation better equipped to handle a problem such as this, or would a small business be more efficient in dealing with this kind of problem? Why?

3. In any problem scenario, methods and steps can be followed to solve the problem. Do small businesses and corporations need to use the same problem-solving techniques and procedures to resolve issues that threaten their business? Explain your answer.

ASB2

Access the Corporate View Web site and take the Online Evaluation for this chapter.

1. Click on the ***Employee Training and Evaluations*** link on the ***Regular Features*** page.

2. Select the ***Online Tests*** link. (You must be a registered user to access the online tests. If you are not a registered user, click the ***Register*** link and follow the instructions on the screen. Then click the ***Online Tests*** link to return to the Online Tests page.)

3. Choose the ***Chapter 2 A View of the Mission-Critical Functions*** link on the Online Tests page.

4. Enter the username and password you selected when you registered.

5. Take the test. Click the **First**, **Back**, **Next**, and **Last** buttons to navigate through the questions. Click the **Finish** button to submit your test for grading. If you wish to close the test without submitting it for grading, click the **Cancel** button. Any answers you have entered will be lost if you cancel the test.

Chapter 3

A View of Corporate Planning and Training

Planning for High-Performance Teamwork

"In the previous session, we put you into a leadership and teamwork training exercise. This simple experience gave you a valuable frame of reference—that is, a shared experience that will help you in the days to come. In this session, we explore some planning tools that can help you in similar situations in the future.

"This will be our last formal meeting together. You're a great group of interns, and I appreciate your cooperation. When your internship is done, you might consider looking into one of our part-time jobs until you're out of school. Internships and part-time jobs often lead to great full-time employment.

"As you've already learned, at Corporate View we work in teams. A team is a support system. Few things are done solo in corporations. That's because the nature of doing business today is so complex. No one person can know it all—or do everything it takes to bring a product to market. Only when people pull together is it possible to get things accomplished in a professional way.

"The scenario of the CF4000/SE is similar to situations that occur daily in the corporate world. And it was mitigated by teamwork. I hope you've learned something about how a business works. But more important, I hope you've learned something about problem solving in corporations.

"Stop for a minute and review what happened in the CF4000/SE scenario. You were thrown into a new situation with a new product you knew nothing about, and immediately the product hit a snag that could cost the company millions. Because a team was in place, you were able to resolve the situation. How would this situation have turned out if people had not been willing to work together?

"You learned about the wealth of information on the corporate Intranet and about the synergy that comes from teamwork.

"I've been a part of many workgroups, and I've learned one lesson again and again. For me, at least, being a part of an effective team means I have a practical perspective about how the situation can be handled. It means I can view the problem from a *we-* not a *me*-position.

"As you know, a workgroup is created to solve a problem or create and market a product. Let me give you an example of how a product workgroup functions.

"Several years ago, I worked for a major software development company. To develop and promote our next software product, a workgroup was assembled. Members of this team included representatives from every vital function of the company, including Research and Development; Marketing, Sales, and Customer Support; Finance and Accounting; Human Resources; Legal; Information Technology; and Manufacturing, Warehousing, and Shipping.

"The person responsible for managing the entire operation was the product marketing manager. Sound familiar? This was not unlike the hypothetical role you just assumed in the training exercise with the CF4000/SE.

"The manager organized every aspect from designing the software to getting the software package to market. This included product development, testing, pricing, licensing, building, packaging, and shipping the product. Everything was planned well in advance. For example, the advertising campaign was planned a year in advance.

"To keep things coordinated, *flowcharts* were created. **Todo lists** as long as your arm were generated for team members from each part of the corporation that had a mission-critical function to perform. Some snags were hit, and adjustments had to be made.

"Each group worked with clocklike precision to meet the product deadline, and it paid off. The outcome of our workgroup's effort was success. It was the hardest I have ever worked. But do you know what? It was fun because were doing something important. We made a difference. Although I left to join Corporate View shortly after, I still email members of my old workgroup just to see how they are doing.

"*Fortune* magazine, besides tracking the Fortune 500, follows important business trends. In the January 12, 1998 issue, *Fortune* listed the top 100 companies to work for in the USA. Southwest Airlines won top honors for 1998. Enjoying work and feeling part of the team are reasons employees often give for choosing to work at a particular company."

Figure 3-1
Southwest Airlines uses email and the Internet to reach its customers in a highly competitive industry.

Southwest Airlines Home Gate
The Home of Southwest Airlines on the World Wide Web

Figure 3-2
Southwest Airlines was listed as the best company to work for in 1998, as this article on its Web site proclaims.

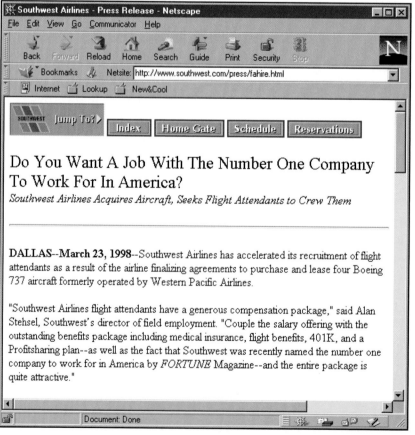

Activity Overviews

In this chapter, you will learn about high-performance workgroup planning and employee training. You will use the Intranet and the World Wide Web to expand your understanding of this topic.

High-performance workgroups are built upon three components:

- Time management and project planning
- Workgroup coordination with the timely flow of information to workgroup members
- Ongoing preparation and continuous training

If individual members of a workgroup are disorganized, the entire workgroup will be fragmented, disorganized, and incomplete. Individuals must organize their own work before they can organize and help their workgroups.

Workgroups must also be connected by something more substantial than just a name and a meeting every now and then. A continuous, accurate, and timely flow of information must be maintained via the Intranet to keep the members working together as a group and moving toward completing the group's goals and assignments.

Finally, members of the group must be constantly learning and developing professionally. No one comes into a job with all the skills he or she needs. To be effective, employees must add new skills on a regular basis.

Activity 3-1 Personal Planning with PIMs, Planners, and PDAs will explore how personal planning by all members of the team will enhance team efficiency.

Activity 3-2 Managing the Flow of Information will demonstrate planning and management tools that help coordinate the actions of project and product teams and workgroups.

Activity 3-3 Ongoing Training and Preparation will look at the way corporations help improve workgroup performance through ongoing training and professional development.

"Corporate ShopTalk"

Understanding the meanings of these terms will help you learn the concepts and develop the skills presented in this chapter. In preparation for completing the chapter activities, access the Intranet and find the definition for each of these terms by clicking the ***ShopTalk*** link on the ***Regular Features*** page.

- Acronym
- Administrative Assistant (AA)
- Bonus
- Critical Path
- Flowchart
- Freeware
- Gantt Chart
- Groupware
- Outsourcing
- PDA (Personal Digital Assistant)
- Personal Planner
- PERT Chart
- PIM (Personal Information Management)
- Profit
- Project Planning Software
- Seminar
- Shareware
- Stipend
- Todo List

In a recent meeting of industry experts, skills were identified that corporations expect new employees to have. They include:

- Problem-solving skills

- Technical communications skills

- Flexibility

- Drive

- Interpersonal skills

- Project management skills

- Teamwork skills

All of these skills are important. In solving the problem of the CF4000/SE, you showed your problem-solving abilities. You also shared your technical communications skills in how well you communicated technical information in your email and memos during the CF4000/SE crisis. In solving the problem, you had a chance to test your flexibility, drive, teamwork, and leadership skills. Although it was only a training exercise, it allowed you to improve your abilities in each of the skills listed above. In the next few weeks, you will have plenty of chances to improve and develop these skills even further.

No Pod Is an Island

Remember that you are never alone; help is always available in the many nearby pods and cubicles in your office. You've seen pods or cubicles, those temporary offices in the Dilbert© cartoons. Many friendly people work in those cubicles. Don't be afraid to ask some of them for assistance. Most employees are very happy to help if they are approached in a positive way. If you work in a virtual office, or from home, you can still ask for help by using your Intranet email system or by picking up the phone and calling someone who works in your industry.

In business, no one works in isolation. Whether large or small, a business is dependent on the efficiency of others. Consider, for example, FedEx, UPS, and the U.S. Postal Service. If they didn't deliver correspondence, packages, and products on schedule, many other businesses would be disrupted, their customers would be upset, and sales would slump. Business depends on complete efficiency.

Efficiency depends on planning. Every person on the team must be organized to contribute to a high-efficiency workplace. Your success is based on the success of many others. In the CF4000/SE simulation, nearly a dozen busy people stopped doing whatever was important for them to help you solve *your* problem.

How were these busy executives able to find the time to be helpful? For starters, they were extremely organized people. Each knew where and when he or she would have a few minutes to address your concerns and answer your pleas for help.

High-performance workgroups are built upon the foundation of personal planning. Giving help and assistance takes time and, as they say in business, "Time is money." Any kind of group involvement takes precious time from the duties of busy people.

Before a team can be effective, individuals on the workgroup team must make effective use of their time. Personal time management is the first step to high-performance teamwork. You can manage your time and tasks effectively in several ways.

Paper, PC, or Plastic

Effective business people develop their own unique ways to plan and organize their time. First, there is the paper-based group; those individuals who carry around *personal planners*, usually in leather binders, containing paper calendars, todo lists, notes, addresses, and appointments.

Then there is the PC group—personal computer users. These people use *PIM (Personal Information Management)* software to organize their time and tasks. They have this software on their desktop computers or their portable computers. Examples of PIM software include:

- Notes (Lotus Development Corporation: A business unit of IBM: ***www.lotus.com***)

- Outlook (Microsoft Corporation: ***www.microsoft.com***)

- GroupWise (Novell Corporation: ***www.novell.com***)

PIM software designed for use by groups is called *groupware*. Intranets often make groupware and PIM software features available to employees.

Finally, there is the plastic group. Members of this group carry small, palm-sized computers or *PDAs (Personal Digital Assistants)*. These handheld computers go by names such as:

- Newton (Apple Computer Corporation: ***www.apple.com***)

- HP620 LX Series (Hewlett-Packard: ***www.hp.com***)

- PSION (Psion: ***www.psion.com***)

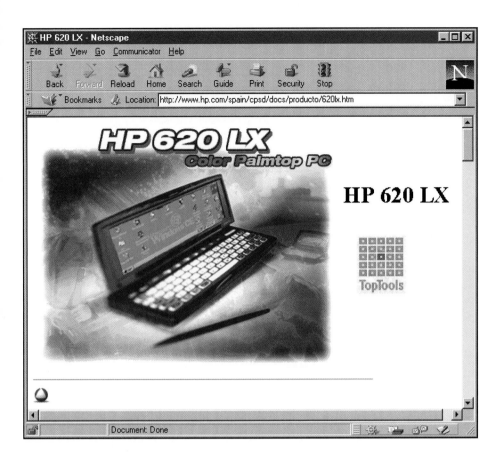

There are many ways to get organized. One of the easiest is to use a PIM on your personal computer. Nearly every new PC has one. In the Just-in-Time Training exercise, you will explore a popular PIM program, Outlook by Microsoft. You will also compare a paper-based personal planner page with the PIM screen and learn more about PDAs via the Intranet.

Business
Milestones

The Franklin Covey Company

Franklin Covey Co. (formerly Franklin Quest Co, NYSE:FC) is a time-management training company. It makes the world-famous Franklin Day Planner. The planner is part of a personal planning system. Franklin trains tens of thousands of business people every year in its system of personal time management. The company also markets a PIM software package called ASCEND.

Clients include corporations such as Intel, Chrysler, General Electric, General Motors, Honda, Hughes, and Merrill Lynch, to name a few. When Franklin Quest and Covey Leadership Center merged, they formed the dominant personal planning corporation in America. Here is a key quote from the company's mission statement on the FC Web site:

Franklin Covey offers tools and strategies for improving individual and organizational effectiveness through proven principles. We provide a broad range of products and training programs to help people achieve personal fulfillment and career satisfaction, and help institutions build highly skilled, high trust, high performance cultures. Above all, Franklin Covey supports individuals, families, and organizations in accomplishing what matters most to them.*

*Franklin Covey Co. *Corporate Information.* Online. Available: **www.franklincovey.com/fcinfo/fcmission.html**. March 28, 1998.

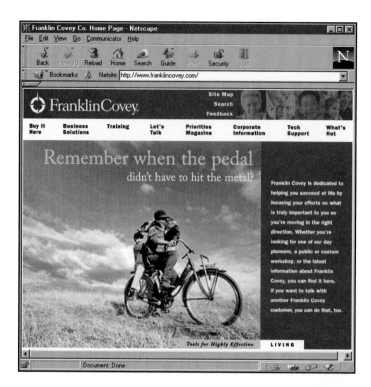

Just-in-Time Training

A Good Outlook on Planning

Microsoft Outlook

Figure 3-5
The Outlook icon

If you have Outlook, which is part of the Microsoft Professional Office Suite, follow the steps below to launch and explore it. If you don't have Outlook, read the steps and refer to the pictures; or open your PIM and see what features the two products have in common.

1. Launch Outlook by clicking or double-clicking on the Outlook icon.

2. Every PIM has several features. If you are using Outlook, select each of the icons listed below to learn about the program's features. If you are using another PIM, see whether you can locate similar features in that program:

   - Inbox (for email)
   - Calendar
   - Contacts List or Address Book
   - Task or "Todo" List
   - Personal Journal
   - Notes

3. If you have Outlook or another PIM, use the calendar feature to plan your day. Print a hard copy of your plan for the day.

4. Many people still prefer using a paper-based planner, rather than an electronic one. Look at the planner page shown in Figure 3-7 (page 82). How does it compare with the PIM screen shown in

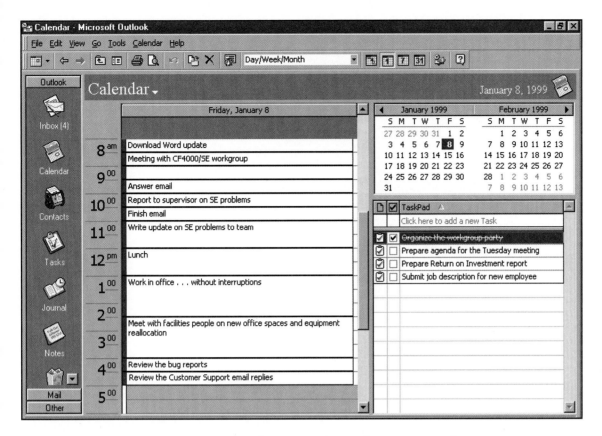

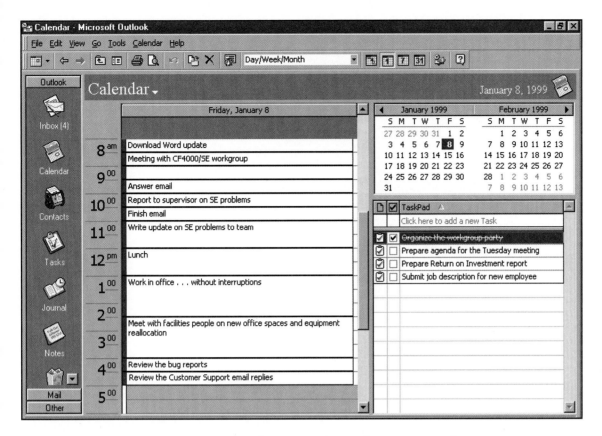
```
Calendar - Microsoft Outlook                                              _ 🗗 ✕
File  Edit  View  Go  Tools  Calendar  Help
⊞ ▾  ⇐ ⇒  🔁 ▦  🖨 🔍  ↺  🗗 ✕  🔳  Day/Week/Month  ▾  🔳🔳🔳🔳  ⮨  🔲

Outlook    Calendar ▾                                       January 8, 1999

Inbox (4)                 Friday, January 8          ▲    ◄  January 1999      February 1999  ►
                                                         S  M  T  W  T  F  S   S  M  T  W  T  F  S
                8 am   Download Word update              27 28 29 30 31  1  2        1  2  3  4  5  6
                       Meeting with CF4000/SE workgroup   3  4  5  6  7 [8] 9    7  8  9 10 11 12 13
Calendar        9 00                                     10 11 12 13 14 15 16  14 15 16 17 18 19 20
                       Answer email                      17 18 19 20 21 22 23  21 22 23 24 25 26 27
                10 00  Report to supervisor on SE problems 24 25 26 27 28 29 30  28  1  2  3  4  5  6
Contacts               Finish email                      31                     7  8  9 10 11 12 13
                11 00  Write update on SE problems to team
                                                         🗋 ☑ TaskPad  △              ▲
Tasks           12 pm  Lunch                                Click here to add a new Task
                                                         ☑ ☑  Organize the workgroup party
                1 00   Work in office . . . without interruptions  ☑ ☐  Prepare agenda for the Tuesday meeting
Journal                                                  ☑ ☐  Prepare Return on Investment report
                2 00                                     ☑ ☐  Submit job description for new employee
                       Meet with facilities people on new office spaces and equipment
                3 00   reallocation
Notes
                4 00   Review the bug reports
                       Review the Customer Support email replies
Mail
Other           5 00                                  ▼                              ▼
```

Figure 3-6 or with your PIM software? What information is the same?

Figure 3-6
Microsoft Outlook's planning calendar

_____

_____

5. What features of the PIM and the paper planner are different?

_____

_____

6. Close your PIM software.

7. Access the Corporate View Web site. (You will need to be on the Web for this part of this activity.)

8. Access the links on the Intranet to see what PDAs can do. Click on the ***Marketing, Sales, & Support*** link. Select the ***TeleView*** link and choose ***Product Promotions and Pricing***.

9. Learn all you can about PDAs by selecting the ***Personal Digital Assistants (PDAs) and Hand-held Computers*** link. Select the links and evaluate the various PDAs, making notes for the table you will create in the next step.

10. Create a table, spreadsheet, or chart listing the main features of three PDAs. Make your list as if you were a customer, listing all the features and prices that are promised as in this sample in Table 3-1 (page 82).

11. Proofread your table carefully and print a hard copy.

Save As:

PDAs

Figure 3-7
Page from a Franklin Day Planner

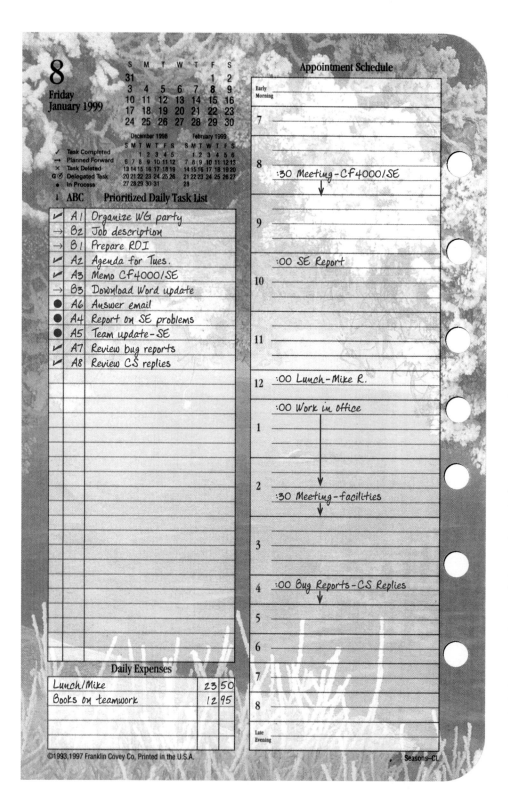

Table 3-1   **Popular PDAs**

HP Palmtops	PSION	Apple Newton
List features...	List features...	List features...

You can use many tools to help you plan your day. It isn't important which of these options you use. For that matter, you can use an established system or invent a system all your own. What matters is that you plan your time. When you receive an assignment, add it to your todo list. When you have a meeting, plan time to prepare for the meeting, time to attend the meeting itself, and time after the meeting to complete any assignments or tasks as needed.

Think and write about the following:

1. What are the advantages and disadvantages of PIM software?

   _____
   _____
   _____

2. What are the advantages and disadvantages of PDA devices?

   _____
   _____

3. What are the advantages and disadvantages of a paper-based personal planner?

   _____
   _____

4. Which one of these personal planning systems would have helped you organize more efficiently your agenda for action in the CF4000/SE training exercise in Activity 2-3?

   _____
   _____

Business
Milestones

A P D A I s A - O K a y

A Personal Digital Assistant, or PDA, is really a hand-held computer. The Apple Newton first made PDAs popular. PDAs have the same planning features you can find in your PIM but in a small, economical package. A PDA can cost between $100 and $800.

Several companies build and market PDAs. Hewlett-Packard (NYSE: HWP) produced the first major line of PDAs with color screens. The New-

ton from Apple (NASDAQ:AAPL) set the standard for handheld computer devices with a penlike instrument that allows you to write as you would on a notepad. The Newton then interprets the letters and turns your writing into text. PSION (L:PON—the L is for the London Stock Exchange) is one of the world's leaders in PDA development, selling its quality line of PDAs around the world. Visit the links on the Corporate View Web site to see what these PDAs can do.

Once you have organized your time and tasks, you are prepared to help your team. You will need to set aside time to attend workgroup meetings, complete group assignments, work with others, and communicate with your team—either synchronously in meetings, face-to-face, or on the phone; or asynchronously through email.

Remember the list of skills employers expect employees to have?

- Problem-solving skills
- Technical communications skills
- Flexibility
- Drive
- Interpersonal skills
- Project management skills
- Teamwork skills

Think about these skills in more detail. Good personal organization and planning will give you more flexibility in your day. If you know what you have to do and how much time you have to do it in, you can juggle your schedule to meet the needs of others and better help the team. If you aren't organized and work in a frantic or haphazard way, you will become frazzled and frustrated at the pace of your job.

Team organization is even more complex than personal organization, particularly when you are asked to organize a project or product. This kind of planning requires strong problem-solving skills and a great deal of flexibility and drive. In other words, it isn't easy.

Imagine having to plan every detail of a project and manage the time of dozens of other employees. At corporations such as Corporate View and many others, that is exactly what individuals must do.

To keep all the complex details straight, the workgroup and managers responsible for a product must plan extensively. Many workgroups use project-planning software to help them organize the details. They create work flowcharts or diagrams that help them calculate the ***critical path***, or the shortest time between the beginning of the project and the end of the project.

Using a flowchart isn't difficult. Each of us, at one time or another, will have to either prepare a flowchart or interpret a flowchart.

As an example, consider the steps you must take to write a research report. For the initial list, don't worry about placing the steps in any particular order. Simply brainstorm and list each possible step and the approximate time span required to complete it.

Step	Estimated Time Required
1. Search for sources of information on the report topic	2 days
2. Proofread and print a final copy	1/2 day
3. Choose a topic	1 day
4. Write the first draft	3 days
5. Revise based on peer reviews	1 day
6. Get peer reviews of report	1 day
7. Read information from sources	5 days
8. Format the report in the required style	1/2 day
9. Write a report outline	1 day

A chart called a **Gantt chart** (as seen in Figure 3-8) can be used to sequence the steps in a logical order and show how long it should take to perform the entire task or project—in this case, 15 days. After entering the steps, the user indicates which step should come first, second, and so on. This order is then reflected on the chart. Notice that the process starts with step 3, goes to step 1, and so on until the final step in the process is completed. The width of each bar on the charts represents the amount of time needed to complete that step. Notice that the bar for *Read information from sources*, which takes five days, is much longer than the bar for *Choose a topic*, which takes one day. More detailed charts might label each bar with the appropriate time.

Gantt charts are great at showing how long it takes to complete a process or project. The longest path on a project's Gantt chart is the critical path.

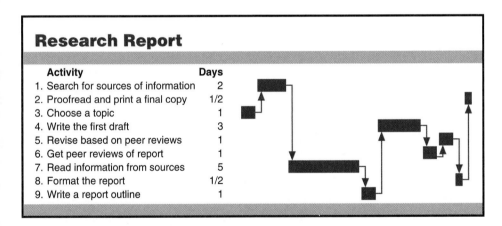

Research Report

Activity	Days
1. Search for sources of information	2
2. Proofread and print a final copy	1/2
3. Choose a topic	1
4. Write the first draft	3
5. Revise based on peer reviews	1
6. Get peer reviews of report	1
7. Read information from sources	5
8. Format the report	1/2
9. Write a report outline	1

Figure 3-8
A Gantt chart

Another way to demonstrate the relationships among events in a project or process is with a **PERT chart**, as shown in Figure 3-9. A PERT chart uses boxes to show the relationships among activities. Sometimes a PERT chart is easier to use than a Gantt chart when organizing a project and identifying its steps.

Figure 3-9
A PERT chart

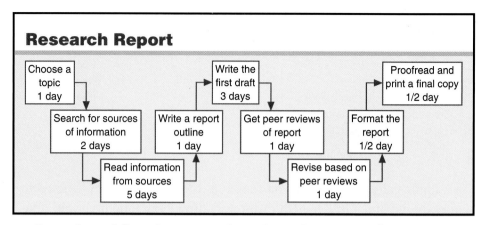

Several good flowcharting and *project planning software* programs are on the market, such as Microsoft Project. Some are free on the Intranet (*freeware*). Others are *shareware*, which means you can try the software for a trial period, and if you like it you can keep it by paying a small fee to the creators of the program.

If you do not have a flowcharting program, you can always create a chart with the simple drawing tools found in your word processing program. For that matter, you can use paper and pencil to create your first flowchart. Flowcharting is easy and will help you plan your critical paths in the corporate world. You will practice creating a flowchart in the Just-in-Time Training for this activity.

The **Least** You
Should Know
About...

Administrative Assistants

For many years, one of the key employees in any company has been the secretary. In days past, the secretary was usually a personal assistant to one or perhaps several executives or other company managers. Secretaries would handle the correspondence and take care of routine support tasks to assist managers. Some corporations still employ "secretaries," but most have taken the position to a new level.

Over time, secretaries gradually assumed tasks that were much more important than simply completing letters and filing papers. Many secretaries took on additional responsibilities and

became know as *Administrative Assistants (AAs)*. AAs are managers in their own right. They might be asked to monitor all the details of a project and keep a department or workgroup functioning.

Without AAs, communications would falter, and the efforts of individual group members would not be as effective or as well coordinated. The administrative assistant is an essential employee in the modern corporation.

Every major project, product, or workgroup will have an AA to manage the continuous flow of information from group member to group member. He or she will monitor deadlines, remind people of their responsibilities, and facilitate the timely and efficient completion of projects.

Creating a Flowchart

In the previous chapter, you were asked to perform tasks to research and solve a problem with the CF4000/SE phone. At times, it might have seemed as if you were simply reacting to problems, unable to stop for a second to organize. In this activity, you will reflect on the steps you took in that training exercise and create a Gantt or PERT chart as a better, more efficient path to your solution. Later, in the High-Performance Workgroup Project, you will create a flowchart with a team.

1. Launch your word processor, drawing program, or flowcharting software. If you do not have flowcharting software or are not familiar with the drawing or charting features of your word processor, you can do this project on a sheet of paper. Use a ruler and a pencil so that you can erase mistakes and move boxes around.

2. Examine the steps shown below in alphabetical order. Based on your previous experience with this problem, write an estimated time for completion by each step.

Step	Estimated Time Required
• Brainstorm possible solutions to problems with the CF4000/SE.	_____
• Create a list of CF4000/SE workgroup members.	_____
• Create a product performance memo on the CF4000/SE and submit it to a supervisor.	_____
• Examine the memo from the supervisor on problems with the CF4000/SE.	_____
• Learn all about the CF4000/SE.	_____
• List positive and negative comments from customers about the CF4000/SE.	_____
• Read the bug reports from R&D on the CF4000/SE.	_____
• Review Customer Support email reports on the CF4000/SE.	_____
• Review Customer Support phone reports on the CF4000/SE.	_____
• Review the *Technophobia* magazine review of the CF4000/SE.	_____
• Review workgroup replies and postings on the problems with the CF4000/SE.	_____
• Write email to workgroup members, asking for input on CF4000/SE problems.	_____
• Write a memo to the supervisor, summarizing the problems with the CF4000/SE.	_____

Audience of a Flowchart

The flowchart is one of the great examples of technical communications. Words, symbols, lines, and arrows show the flow of a project or a plan. Sometimes a little box will say more about what needs to be done than pages and pages of text.

The goal of a flowchart is the same as it is for every form of technical communications: to communicate clearly and concisely exactly what another person needs to know.

Even with a flowchart, you must consider your audience. A good way to think about your flow-chart is from the perspective of your supervisor. Pretend your supervisor doesn't know anything about what you are doing. You must be extremely clear to communicate all the steps and decisions that need to be made.

You must define for your reader anything in your chart that you think your supervisor will not understand. For example, if you used a technical term or *acronym*, you should define that term or acronym the first time it is used. An acronym is an abbreviation derived from a series of words. For example, *As Soon As Possible* is shortened to *ASAP*.

3. Determine an efficient sequence of events and diagram them by using either a PERT or Gantt chart. (A simple way to plan a PERT chart is to put all 13 issues on index cards, then move them around until you get the correct order of events.)

4. Estimate the time it will take to complete all 13 tasks in your chart.

5. If you are creating your chart on a computer, print a hard copy of the chart.

Save As:

Chart1

Debriefing

The flowchart is a good tool for planning projects and sharing those plans with others. Flowcharts can be created with pencil and paper, word processing or drawing programs, and project or flow-charting software.

You might not need anything as sophisticated as Microsoft Project to help plan your projects; nevertheless, this kind of software can speed up your planning and make your flowcharts and group todo lists look more professional.

Think and write about the following:

1. In the teamwork and leadership training exercise in Chapter 2, you used a simple list of tasks to plan your approach to solving a problem with the CF4000/SE (called the "agenda for action" in Activity 2-3). In Activity 3-2, you created a flowchart with the

same information. Which method of organizing information did you find more effective? Why?

_____

_____

_____

2. Give an example of a project or product for which a Gantt chart might be the most effective way to plan and organize the project. Explain why a Gantt chart is a good choice to help you plan.

_____

_____

_____

3. Give an example of a project or product for which a PERT chart might be the most effective way to plan and organize the project. Explain why a PERT chart is a good choice to help you plan.

_____

_____

_____

Activity 3-3 *Ongoing Training and Preparation*

This is the final activity in your orientation to Corporate View. You will soon begin your work with the mission-critical functions of the corporation. You will spend a week or two learning in more detail what each department does and how it contributes to the success of the corporation.

You have learned about the mechanics of personal planning and group planning. You discovered how flowcharting can help organize events and people for a project. In this activity, you will learn about other skills that are just as important as planning for high-performance workgroups—for example, interpersonal skills or your ability to work with others.

The **Least** You **Should** Know About...

People must work together. They must learn how to get along and perform their separate functions as a team. It is always much easier if the people in a workgroup like each other. This isn't always the case, however. Sometimes personalities clash. But this must be overcome by adopting a professional attitude and by sticking to the job at hand without letting personalities get in the way.

Seminars

Seminars and in-house training programs are often voluntary and exist for the benefit of both the employees and the business. Every now and then, a business will require members of a department, function, or workgroup to attend a seminar or in-house training session. For example, everyone in Manufacturing will attend safety training. It is required. Everyone in Corporate Communications will attend a seminar on technical communications. All Customer Support operators might be required to attend a seminar on telephone skills and voice control. Seminars can be targeted at a small group of employees or be expanded to include everyone in a corporation. Seminars and training programs are a way of life in the corporate world.

Human Resources usually organizes training, but sometimes other departments are involved too. For example, if HR doesn't have anyone on its team qualified to teach flowcharting, then it might

call on an employee from R&D to teach this important skill. HR could go to Customer Support to find professional operators skilled in handling difficult customer situations and have them conduct a training seminar on working with difficult situations.

For some topics, corporations will hire an outside company to provide the training. You have already learned how Franklin Covey makes a substantial living training corporate clients. When one company hires another company to do a job, this is called *outsourcing*.

Many corporations give *stipends* or *bonuses* or provide additional pay for completing training successfully. Other corporations give performance points or "bonus points" to employees who attend and meet the requirements of the training session.

At Corporate View, every training session is followed by a course evaluation. This helps ensure the quality of the training and the preparation of the participants. You may take a similar kind of online evaluation at the end of each chapter.

Corporations, including Corporate View, often organize training sessions or *seminars* to help people learn how to work better in groups and overcome the differences they might have. These seminars focus on human interactions and relationships in the workplace.

Corporate View also provides other seminars designed to improve the effectiveness of workgroups and individual employees. The seminars help people improve their planning skills, keyboarding skills, dictation skills, electronic online resume writing, verbal communications, and a variety of other work-related skills.

In this activity, you will explore the Intranet and see what additional in-house training programs are available to employees.

Just-in-Time Training

Research the Intranet for Training Seminars

1. Access your local Intranet or the Corporate View Web site.

2. Select the **_Employee Training and Evaluations_** link from the **_Regular Features_** list.

3. Browse through the list of seminars and read the descriptions of several that interest you. Choose three of the seminars and write a short note about how each of these seminars can help improve your skills.

   Seminar 1: _____
   How can this seminar help in your career?

   _____
   _____

   Seminar 2: _____
   How can this seminar help in your career?

   _____
   _____

   Seminar 3: _____
   How can this seminar help in your career?

   _____
   _____

Figure 3-10
*Intel designs its safety and
environmental training for its
employees.*

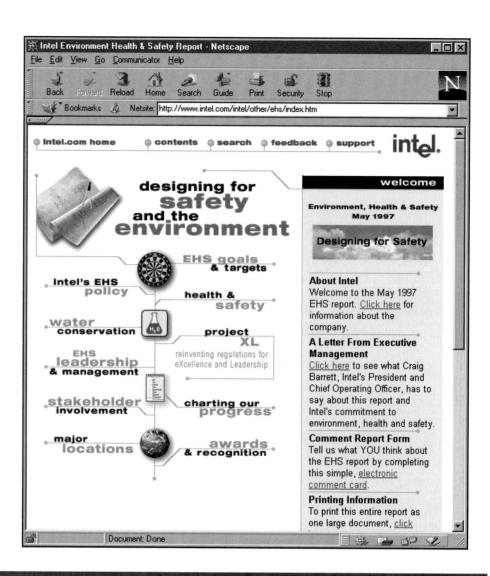

Business
Milestones

Intel Corporation's Commitment to Safety and Training

Intel (NASDAQ:INTC) is the largest maker of computer microprocessors in the world. Its corporate culture tries to involve every employee in the smooth running of the company. And it is a good thing, because many Intel employees work with some of the most sophisticated equipment in the world. Some employees must also work with hazardous chemicals in the course of making computer processors. This requires some very thoughtful and well-planned safety training programs and seminars. And the training program is working. In the three years prior to 1998, Intel reduced "the recordable injury rate 68 percent and the lost-day case rate 75 percent." Every time

Intel can prevent an injury, it saves money.

All employees involved in the manufacturing process are required to attend safety training. They are also required to prove their understanding of the training through various kinds of performance evaluations.

The Intel commitment to safety also extends to the environment. Working with the U.S. Environmental Protection Agency (EPA), Intel is pursuing a goal of "superior environmental performance" through its Project XL (eXcellence and Leadership). Employees who work with environmental issues will be trained by Intel's internal training system.*

*Intel Corporation. *Investor Information.* Online. Available: ***www.intel.com/intel/ANNUAL 96/INVESTOR.HTM***. March 29, 1998.

Working in the corporate world means you can never stand still, relying only on the skills you currently possess. You must acquire new skills, knowledge, and techniques on an ongoing basis to keep abreast of current trends and innovations in your particular field and in business in general.

Internal or in-house training in the business world is a multibillion-dollar industry. Even though students might do well in school, graduates are often lacking in the specific job skills they need to work effectively in many jobs. This means that training must be an ongoing part of business.

In this environment and with technology changing every day, it is important to adopt a flexible attitude and to be a lifelong learner.

Think and write about the following:

1. Describe three areas of general academic knowledge you plan to acquire or improve during the next two quarters.

    _____

    _____

    _____

2. Describe three technical skills you plan to acquire or improve during the next two quarters.

    _____

    _____

    _____

3. Describe one or more technical skills you have that need to be updated. For example, perhaps you learned a version of a software program that is now outdated. How can you update your skills in this area?

    _____

    _____

    _____

Chapter Review

Executive Summary

The CF4000/SE simulation demonstrated the complex interactions among the *critical functions* of a corporation. Teamwork helped mitigate a problem and resolve a difficult product issue. In this chapter, you learned how planning tools can help improve project planning and individual and workgroup performance.

Teamwork is a key component of successful corporations. It improves performance and job satisfaction. Research has shown that working in teams can be very rewarding. Many people find working in teams more satisfying than working alone.

High-performance teamwork is based on personal time management, workgroup coordination, and the timely flow of information to group members. It also depends on the ongoing preparation and training of employees so that they can continue to grow and improve in their jobs.

Individual planning is the key to group success. If individuals in a workgroup are well organized, they will be able to schedule time for group assignments, meetings, and activities.

Personal planning precedes successful group planning. Business people use a variety of tools to plan their time, projects, and products. These tools include personal digital assistants, personal information management software on computers, and paper-based day planners. All these planning tools share many similar features, such as calendars, contact or address books, task or todo lists, notes, appointments, and personal journals. Electronic planners also organize email messages, FAXes, and other electronic correspondence.

Planning software for workgroups is often called groupware. Groupware is used to coordinate team schedules, calendars, tasks, email, documents, and other team communications. Intranets include many or all of the components found in commercial groupware.

Project planning software allows managers to organize the development of products and projects. Microsoft Project is perhaps the best-known project planning software. Other project planning software tools can be found on the Internet in the form of freeware or shareware.

Flowcharts are often used to help in planning new products and business projects. Flowcharting symbols help users determine the critical path of a project and to account for all the decisions and actions required to make a project happen.

Companies are looking for employees who have problem-solving skills, technical communications skills, interpersonal skills, teamwork skills, and project management skills, as well as flexibility and drive.

No one can learn all he or she needs to know about business before leaving school. There are simply too many specific skills to learn. Therefore, corporations spend billions of dollars providing in-house training and seminars to employees on a variety of subjects. Corporations often require certain training courses, such as safety and customer service classes.

For many corporate training courses, the employee proves his or her skills by taking competency- and knowledge-based tests at the end of the training. Course evaluations are often completed by the trainees to help assess the value of the training.

Corporations often outsource part of their training to outside training companies. Outsourcing often saves time and money while providing quality training courses.

The corporate Intranet lists several seminars and training sessions that can help expand or improve your skills and knowledge.

Technical Communications

When flowcharting, remember your audience. A good technique is to put yourself in the place of a person who knows nothing about the project you are planning. Make sure each symbol you use is clear. Define every new term, acronym, or abbreviation you use.

The Corporate Inbox

Corporations get lots of questions from phone calls, FAXes, and email. Even a letter or two will come in loaded with questions. Questions come from customers, employees, and other interested people. Sometimes questions are sent to employees to answer. Here are some messages that need to be answered by someone familiar with new-employee orientation and training.

Answer these messages with the help of the Intranet and your own best judgment to arrive at a logical answer. If you need help preparing these documents, access the **_Style Guide_** under the **_Corporate Communications_** link.

Save As:

Inbox3A

TO: Intern
FROM: *ccooper@corpview.com*
SUBJECT: Job Applicant
MESSAGE:

I just got a FAX from a shareware provider offering me a 30-day free trial on a PIM. I thought we should check it out. All we need to do is FAX back information to them on the PIMs, PDAs, groupware, and planners we are most familiar with. (They say they use this information to help prepare their Marketing and Sales materials.) I know that most people in Legal still use planners.

Please prepare a FAX I can send them so that we can qualify for the 30-day trial period. The company is Great Applications Inc. and their FAX number is 1-800-555-0112.

Thanks,
Charles

Voice Mail

Hi, this is Melissa Kim. A new employee got sick during the orientation session and was unable to attend the final session. He wants to know which seminars he can participate in to qualify for his first bonus. Please give some suggestions in an email message on which seminars you think would be of value to this employee. Send it to me first, and I will add some employee benefit information before I forward it. I know you have my email address.
Thanks. Bye.

Save As:

Inbox3B

TO: Intern
FROM: *ldelgado@corpview.com*
SUBJECT: Flowcharting
MESSAGE:

Janice Robertson, our new IT manager, is struggling with the management of an Extranet between TeleView and a workgroup at MegaElectronics. I heard from Melissa that you really caught on to charting and planning.

Can you prepare a short memo outlining for Janice what you know about PERT and Gantt charts? Help explain the concept of critical-path planning, or how you can brainstorm first and then organize the sequence of events later, perhaps with the help of software. Please let Janice know about the software options available.

Project planning is a struggle. The MegaElectronics account is a big one, and we can't afford to look bad with a company as highly regarded as MegaElectronics. Your memo could do the trick. Please send it to Janice via the intercompany mail and copy me.

Thanks,
Luis

Save As:

Inbox3C

From the Desk of James Brown...

Dear Intern:
We have been approached by a Fortune 500 company that wants to partner on the development of groupware. I responded politely, but I don't know a lot about this type of software. What do you know about groupware? Please email me anything you can find about it so that I can get back to them.

James
Email: jbrown@corpview.com

Save As:

Inbox3D

Online Business Trends

Access the Corporate View Web site. (A live Web connection is needed to check stock quotes. If you do not have access to a live Web connection, move on to the second part of this exercise under When a Few Words Will Do.) Click the **_Stock Watcher Links_** on the **_Regular Features_** page and follow the instructions. Identify the following ticker symbols and learn how each of these companies did in the stock market today.

Current Date _____

Ticker	Exchange	Company Name	Current Price
AAPL	NASDAQ	_____	_____
ADBE	NASDAQ	_____	_____
HWP	NYSE	_____	_____
INTC	NASDAQ	_____	_____
TXN	NYSE	_____	_____

When a Few Words Will Do

Answer the following questions using what you have learned reading the Business Milestones and The Least You Should Know About… reports. Use 25 to 50 words to write your answers in a word processing document.

1. Is it really possible to determine the top 100 companies to work for? How would this be done? What points would you consider when choosing a great company to work for?

2. Why would a large corporation outsource its training to a business like Franklin Covey Company? What can a company like Franklin Covey offer a major corporation like Intel, Chrysler, GE, or GM?

3. Describe the role of an administrative assistant (AA). How can an AA help make workgroups more efficient?

4. What are some of the ways corporations encourage employees to attend additional training and seminars the company thinks are important?

Save As:

Online3

Portfolio-Building Project

Planning for an Online World

To become proficient at planning, you must have some experience making plans. It could take months and months of practice to develop a system that works for you. In this portfolio-building project, you will get a chance to develop that elusive perfect planning system.

1. Choose a personal planning method (PIM, paper-based planner, or PDA). Use the method to plan the use of your time for an entire week. Plan all the activities of your life: school, play, and work.

2. At the end of the week, write a report of 90 to 100 words about your experience. Think about and answer these questions as you write:

   - How did planning help you or hinder you?

   - What did you like or dislike about keeping track of all your activities?

   - Did you accomplish more by planning ahead?

   - Did you think you were using your time more or less efficiently?

Save As:

Pfolio3

3. Spell-check your report before you print or share it, and remember to proofread and correct all errors.

High-Performance Workgroup Project

Creating good flowcharts takes practice. More important, creating charts with team members takes a special kind of patience, practice, and persistence. Workgroup members often disagree on the sequence of events or the steps that need to be followed to a successful conclusion. In this activity, you will see exactly what we mean. Practice group flowcharting for this exercise.

1. Team up with three or four coworkers and brainstorm all the events and decisions required to create one of the following:

   - A new software game that will be sold at computer stores and department stores

   - A new PDA for TeleView

   - A new airline flight and vacation package from your city to Orlando, Florida, or from your city to Aspen, Colorado

   - A corporate safety or computer training seminar for new employees

2. Create a Gantt or PERT chart to illustrate the events and decisions your group agreed on. Show all the decisions and steps you as a group think are important to bring the project or product from its idea stage to a product that will make a *profit*. Remember to include an estimated time for each step and for the total project.

HP3

3. Proofread your flowchart and correct all errors. Print a hard copy if you created the chart electronically.

Thinking and Writing About Your Business

So many training programs and seminars are available to businesses today that it is often difficult to decide which ones will provide the most helpful training or be worth the money required for employees to attend. And it isn't just the cost of paying the instructor and buying the materials that go with the seminar. It is also the cost of having employees take time away from work to attend.

Review the seminar descriptions on the Intranet by revisiting the **Employee Training and Evaluations** link on the **Regular Features** page. Answer the following questions and justify attending one of these seminars. Record your answers of 25 to 50 words in a word processing document.

1. Which three seminars do you think are the most important in the development of your personal business skills? Rank the seminars in order of importance.

2. Write a memo or email to your supervisor, describing your top seminar and justifying to your boss why you need to participate in this training. Explain how what you learn will help you do your job better and why the corporation should allow you time away from your regular duties to attend the seminar. What is the win-win outcome or the benefit to both you and the corporation?

Think3a

3. Choose a topic for an additional training seminar you would like your employer to offer its employees. Identify the type of seminar; then decide how much you think a training company would charge for this course. Email your suggestions to **suggestions@corpview.com**. Include the following information in your email. (Write a memo to your supervisor if you do not have access to email.)

   • Place "Seminar Idea" in the Subject Line.

   • Name the seminar.

   • Suggest the content of the seminar.

   • Indicate what you think would be an appropriate cost for the seminar.

   • Explain what you would hope to gain from this kind of training.

Think3b

Proofread and correct all errors. Print a hard copy of the email or memo.

Comparing PDAs Online

The Web provides an unprecedented opportunity to search for business-related information. In this Overtime, you will search for personal planning systems and personal information management software. (A live Web connection is needed to complete this exercise.) Create a list of Web pages that discuss the kinds of personal management and project management tools discussed in this chapter.

There are lots of Web sites. You can't possibly click on enough hypertext links to find them all. When you need to search through lots of information, use a search tool as outlined in the steps below.

1. Launch your Web browser software and connect to the Internet.

2. Click the **Search** button in your Web browser.

3. Select one of the search tools that appears.

4. Enter search words, such as *personal digital assistant* or *palmtop computer*, and submit your request.

5. Use search tools to find 10 Web pages that discuss any or all of the following:

   - Personal digital assistants

   - Palmtop computers

   - Groupware

   - Personal planning tools

   - Project planning software

6. Create a list of the best sites you find. Include the name of the site, the Web address (URL), and a brief description of each, as in this example:

   Web Site: Hewlett-Packard

   URL: *www.hp.com*

   Description: HP has several palmtop computers or PDAs with color displays, like the 620 series. These palmtops use the Windows CE operating system.

Save As:

Otime3

Small-business owners and employees working in virtual or home offices also need training. How can these workers improve their job skills as employees often do in larger corporations?

Several resources are available to small companies. First, conferences, organizations, and government agencies such as the U. S. Small Business Administration offer training sessions. Second, universities and colleges offer classes. Third, many magazines provide technical information useful to employees. And last, but certainly not least, many training programs are offered over the Web.

Use your browser searching skills to look up answers to the following questions and record them in a word processing document.

Think and write about the following:

1. Search the Web. Use your search tools to find classes and courses available online. Make a list of three or four online courses. List the source, URL, and cost of each of these online training options.

2. Visit your local bookstore. Make a list of magazines geared toward business people. Which magazines do you think would be the most valuable to small start-up businesses?

3. Search the ads in the magazines you identified in step 2 above. Do they list any conferences that business people can attend? Make a list of two or three conferences that pertain to business people. List the cost, location, and sponsoring organization for each.

Save As:

ASB3

Access the Corporate View Web site and take the Online Evaluation for this chapter.

1. Click on the ***Employee Training and Evaluations*** link on the ***Regular Features*** page.

2. Select the ***Online Tests*** link. (You must be a registered user to access the online tests. If you are not a registered user, click the ***Register*** link and follow the instructions on the screen. Then click the ***Online Tests*** link to return to the Online Tests page.)

3. Choose the ***Chapter 3 A View of Corporate Planning and Training*** link on the Online Tests page.

4. Enter the username and password you selected when you registered.

5. Take the test. Click the **First**, **Back**, **Next**, and **Last** buttons to navigate through the questions. Click the **Finish** button to submit your test for grading. If you wish to close the test without submitting it for grading, click the **Cancel** button. Any answers you have entered will be lost if you cancel the test.

Section 2

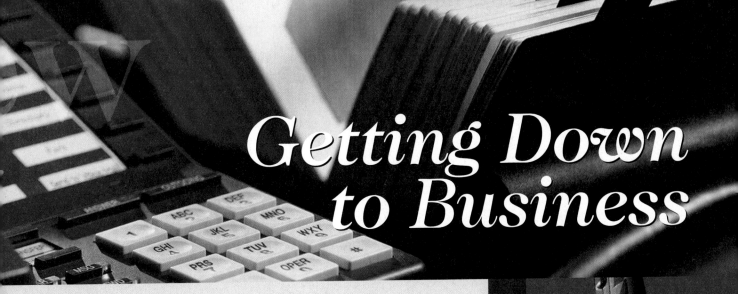

Getting Down to Business

Technology has brought us products and services previously only dreamed of in science fiction novels. Now, the average person can own a powerful laptop or palm-top computer that weighs only a few pounds or ounces—a machine that will play music or movies, a machine that will store and effectively access, in seconds, more information than a room full of books. And thanks to the Web, the world is literally at our fingertips. Because of corporate Intranets, video conferencing, email, wireless phones, and pagers, employees are more connected and have access to more information than they ever have before.

In spite of all this wonderful technology, never have people been so dependent upon each other as they are today. People skills and communication skills have never been more important. Indeed, these critical skills drive business.

In the new millennium, we have to work together to find solutions to our collective problems. Business is not an exception, since it is literally a problem-solving enterprise. A group of minds is always better than one. Working together gives the workgroup a shared sense of urgency, a shared sense of responsibility…and a shared vision. And the corporate Intranet keeps us connected and informed.

Section 2 will be a journey of discovery as you look closely at how the corporate world works. Each group and critical function must work in concert with the others if the corporation is going to be successful. In this section, you will learn a great deal about the relationships that exist between the mission-critical functions and corporate employees and workgroups at Corporate View.

Chapter 4

A View from Human Resources and Management

The Talent Search

"Hello. My name is Robin Mills. I am the Director of Human Resources at TeleView. I understand you've met Kim, who works in our department. She's wonderful, isn't she? Let me add that Kim and I were both quite impressed by your resumes, and we're delighted to have you here with us.

"It's time now for you to learn a little more about the role of Human Resources and Management at TeleView. Even though we are a subsidiary of Corporate View, we handle all our own employment and *personnel* issues. Because TeleView is Corporate View's fastest growing business unit with well over 5,000 employees, this is quite a task.

"We feel that every individual working at TeleView is a valuable resource. That's why we've named our department Human Resources, rather than the Personnel or Employment Division. We look for talented people who are willing to work *with* us, not *for* us.

"Our job at HR is to manage the services and benefits that will attract, motivate, and retain a highly talented, committed, and diverse workforce for TeleView. It is HR's job to help managers promote the fair and equitable treatment of all employees and to provide continuous training opportunities that will allow employees to move up in the company. We strive to help managers and TeleView identify and reward excellence and productivity. A big part of this task is to prepare *job descriptions* and to determine *salary ranges* for certain job categories. We also help devise bonuses and *benefits packages*.

"A job description lists the activities an employee is hired to do. A *salary schedule* shows the starting salary for a job and salaries for

The **Least** You
Should Know
About...

employees with higher levels of experience and/or skills. For example, a starting Customer Support telephone operator (a person who answers customer questions about corporate products) can earn $15 per hour when hired. That person can earn as much as $25 per hour, however, as she or he matures in the job.

"A Customer Support manager may start at $40,000 per year and advance to $70,000. The difference between a position's lowest and highest salaries is called the salary range.

"In Human Resources, we make a point to scout around and learn how much other companies are paying their employees. One of my team members spends a good part of his day gathering information and tracking trends. He uses the World Wide Web extensively, but also relies on trade journals and newspapers like *The Wall Street Journal*, as well as personal contacts with some large **headhunter firms** (companies that find qualified people for specific jobs). This information lets us know where we stand in relation to the rest of the industry. It also helps us know whether we are following trends or setting them.

"The only way we can compare salaries is to create a job description and compare it with similar jobs in other corporations. If another company starts its Customer Support manag-

Management by Objectives

Perhaps the best-known management system ever devised is called **Management by Objectives (MBO)**. MBO asks managers to set clear, specific, and measurable goals or objectives. This allows employees to know exactly what is expected from them. If the objectives are clear, employees are more likely to achieve their goals.

MBO sometimes gets a bad rap because many companies that used it in the early days did not involve their employees in the goal-setting process. Setting objectives can be a win-win situation for the employee and the manager, however, if MBO is done properly.

MBO also allows employees a great deal of autonomy, or freedom to choose how best to achieve objectives. This allows individual creativity and personal satisfaction.

The last component of MBO is probably the most important: having frequent reviews with managers and team members on how things are going. These reviews are often called **performance reviews**. HR often sets guidelines for how these reviews are conducted. When goals and objectives are being met, it is easy for a manager to give a good performance review. When objectives are not being met, the performance review provides an opportunity to get productivity back on track.

ers at $50,000 and we start at $40,000, then that company has a **competitive advantage** over us in hiring the most talented people.

"Beyond competitive salaries and benefits, our corporate strategy involves rewarding individual and team contributions with bonuses and other benefits that will make the job appealing to qualified candidates. This is also how we recognize and encourage creative thinking, innovative ideas, and a strong work ethic.

"I hope you enjoy your short stay in HR. Knowing how we work can help you get a job, keep a job, and move up in whatever business you choose."

Activity Overviews

A big part of the "business" of business is finding, hiring, improving, and keeping the best employees. This job falls to the Human Resources Department. HR fulfills one of the most critical of all functions in the corporation. Its duties include the following:

- Attracting and hiring talented employees
- Training new employees and interns so that they get off to a good start
- Continuing to train employees to provide ongoing growth opportunities
- Managing job descriptions, salaries, and benefits
- Resolving conflicts among employees
- Coordinating and publicizing changes in corporate policies and procedures
- Ensuring the fair and equitable treatment of employees

For most new employees, the HR Department is the first contact with the business. They will derive their first impression of the corporation from the way they are treated by the HR personnel they meet, interview, and train with.

Managers and team leaders must work with HR to bring the most qualified team members into their groups. Therefore, everyone can benefit from a working knowledge of how HR operates.

Activity 4-1 So Many Jobs, So Little Time allows you to explore job descriptions for positions in all of the critical departments of the corporation. This may help you decide on a career that interests you.

Activity 4-2 Writing Job Descriptions shows you how job descriptions are created. Later in this chapter, you will learn how a job description is used to determine salary ranges and benefits, and help with the evaluation of employees.

Activity 4-3 Questions for Interviews describes the process HR uses to prepare interview questions for prospective job candidates.

Activity 4-4 Evaluating Performance will illustrate how important evaluation scales are in the selection of new employees and in employee growth and development.

Understanding the meanings of these terms will help you learn the concepts and better understand the roles of Human Resources and Management covered in the chapter. In preparation for completing the chapter activities, access the Intranet and find the definition for each of these terms by clicking the **_ShopTalk_** link on the **_Regular Features_** page.

- Base Salary
- Benchmark
- Benefits Package
- Biannual
- Competitive Advantage
- Composite Score
- Headhunter Firm
- Job Description
- Job Environment
- Management by Objectives (MBO)
- Peer Evaluation
- Performance Review
- Personnel
- Post
- Salary Range
- Salary Schedule

Activity 4-1   *So Many Jobs, So Little Time*

Corporations hire thousands of people every day. In fact, some large corporations receive thousands of job applications every week. Sifting through all these applications to find the best-qualified people is the job of the Human Resources (HR) Department.

But before anyone can apply for a job, she or he must first know what the job is all about. This is where the job description comes in. A *job description* details the tasks to be performed. An effective job description will help applicants decide whether they qualify for the position being advertised. They can also decide whether the job is one they are really interested in.

In this activity, you will look at several job descriptions; later, you will write one of your own. Like almost every other document in an effective business, a job description should be short. Long, wordy job descriptions are not as effective as short, concise ones.

Think of a job description as a snapshot or photograph of what a job looks like, not a documentary movie on all the details of the position.

Business Milestones

Manpower!

When Manpower Inc. (MAN:NYSE), an employment agency, first opened its doors in 1948, few people had any idea it would become the most requested staffing service in the world.

The term *temporary* (temp) *agency* is used to describe a corporation like Manpower, but that definition is too narrow to describe Manpower's mission and impact on employment. Manpower has more than 2,800 offices in 48 countries. Manpower has employed millions of people all over the globe with a clearly defined goal: Find out what employers need, and then find and train the people to fill those jobs.

Manpower can provide temporary employees for a day, a week, a month, or longer periods of time. Many of these "temps" become full-timers in the companies they work for. Manpower can staff your office with trained people to fit almost any job description.

To help their candidates, Manpower tests their skills with an effective testing system and then provides training if necessary. This far-sighted approach gives Manpower a competitive edge. For example, the demand for personnel in the technical fields became so great that Manpower opened a new division, or business unit, called Manpower Technical. Manpower Technical will train Information Technology or Systems employees for a variety of software, networking, and other computer-related jobs. Many of these courses are offered to students over the Internet in exchange for copies of their resumes. Launch your browser and visit Manpower at **www.manpower.com** to learn more.*

*Manpower Inc. *Manpower Technical Intro.* Online. Available: **www.manpower.com/mp15.html**. February 3, 1998.

```
Manpower Global Home Page - Microsoft Internet Explorer provided by MSN    _ □ ✕
 File   Edit   View   Go   Favorites   Help                              MSN
  ←        →       ⊗       ⬜        ⌂        ⬟        ✴        🌐       🌎       ⬜
 Back    Forward   Stop   Refresh    Home     Search  Favorites History  Channels Fullscreen
 Address   http://www.manpower.com/                              ▼   Links
```

Just-in-Time Training

Evaluating Job Descriptions

1. Access the local Intranet or the Corporate View Web site.

2. Select the **_Human Resources & Management_** link from the Corporate View Intranet Home page.

3. Click the **_About Human Resources_** link and read the description of HR.

4. Write a 25-word description in your own words of what HR is all about.

_____

_____

_____

_____

_____

5. Click on the **_Current Job Openings @ TeleView_** link. These job descriptions are varied, ranging from administrative assistant to director. There are several job descriptions from each mission-critical function in the corporation. Pick five or six job descriptions and read them.

6. Which major function or department did you click on first?

_____

7. Why did you click on one mission-critical function over another?

_____

_____

8. List the five job descriptions you selected by title. Rank them in order from A to E, with A being the most interesting.

A. _____

B. _____

C. _____

D. _____

E. _____

9. Comment on the positions you noted. Why are you attracted to these particular jobs?

_____

_____

_____

_____

10. Revisit the **_Current Job Openings @ TeleView_** link. Search for a job you would not like to do. Which job sounds so boring that you cringe at the prospect of having to take the position?

_____

11. Write a 25-word response about a job you would not want to do. Explain why this job does not appeal to you.

_____

_____

_____

_____

_____

Debriefing

During the hiring phase, a job description is like an advertisement, attracting likely candidates so that they will apply for the job. Out of the 10, 20, 100, or several thousand people who apply for a position, only one can be selected. The company is hoping to find the right person. You hope that person is you.

Think and write about the following:

1. What phrases and words interest you in a job description?

    _____

    _____

    _____

2. What part of the job description do you think is the most important: the salary, the environment, the location, or the responsibilities? Which part pulls you in and makes you want to know more about the position?

    _____

    _____

    _____

3. How many of the jobs listed at TeleView are you qualified for? What do you need to do to become qualified for the position you want?

    _____

    _____

    _____

It's easy to see how important Human Resources is to TeleView. If HR doesn't do its job right, if it doesn't hire the kinds of people who can work well in this kind of corporate environment, TeleView will not survive. Its parent company, Corporate View, will suffer financially as a result. That sounds dramatic, but it's true.

One method of screening candidates is to let them screen themselves. If HR **posts** a job description on the World Wide Web for a Human Resources recruitment specialist, it must include enough information about the job so that only qualified, interested people will apply.

Job descriptions consist of several parts:

1. Job title

2. Date posted and date closed

3. Department or group name

4. Brief description of the job environment

5. Location of employment

6. Main responsibilities

7. Education, skills, and experience

   • Years of experience needed

   • Degree required or preferred

   • Skills and qualifications required

Before a job description is prepared and posted on the Web, the job must be researched. Managers and group members must be consulted so that the specifics of the job are known. A salary search must be conducted to **benchmark** the position—that is, to determine a competitive salary for the position by researching what other companies are paying for the same job.

The salary range is reviewed by Finance and Accounting to make sure the department or group has enough money in its budget to cover the expenditure. Then a head count is taken for the department. Often, the managers of the company will determine the maximum number of employees they think are needed to accomplish the work of a department. A head count is simply counting the employees in the department to see that the number does not exceed the maximum set by management.

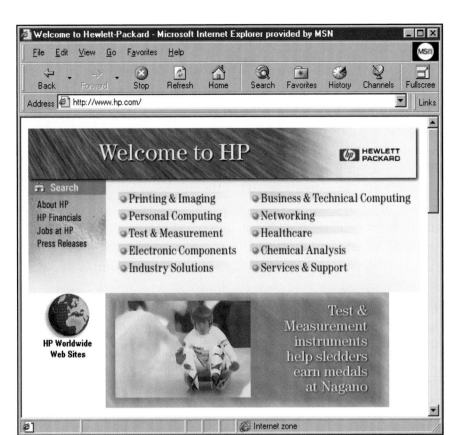

Figure 4-3
The HP Web site

Technical
Communications

Online Job Descriptions with a Style All Their Own

Most corporations list job openings on the Internet where they can be reviewed by eager job seekers from anywhere on the planet. In the Overtime for this chapter, you will visit the Web sites for some Fortune 500 companies and view job descriptions online.

Once you visit these sites, you will see that each company uses its own job description style to attract applicants. Each is trying to gain a competitive advantage by attracting the most talented people. One interesting job Web site is maintained by Hewlett-Packard (HP:NYSE). HP once posted the following on its Web site:

Why work at HP?
People: Making Our People Count
At HP, people don't become human cogs in

some gigantic corporate machine. From their first day of work here, people are given important responsibilities and are encouraged to grow.

From the very beginning, it was clear that Hewlett-Packard would develop a people-oriented corporate culture as unique as its products. One early sign: Bill Hewlett and Dave Packard insisted that they and everyone else at HP be called by their first names. This is a tradition that is still honored. *

What kind of employee is HP trying to attract? Would this persuade you to consider employment at HP? Would you expect other companies, like banks or car manufacturers, to conduct business on a first-name basis? Why might this style work for some successful corporations like HP and perhaps not for others?

*Hewlett-Packard. *People*. Online. Available: **www.jobs.hp.com/USA/why/people/**. February 25, 1998.

Hiring a new employee requires a huge financial commitment on the part of any company. Insurance and other benefits, as well as salary, must be considered in creating a total financial package for the new employee.

Melissa Kim was the former Human Resources recruitment specialist. According to her old job description, she was responsible for interns. Then the job grew. Soon she found herself spending all her time in the Internship Training Program. Thus, the decision was made to split the job into two positions. This means TeleView needs to hire another person.

Melissa interviewed Robin, her department manager, to get her perspective on the new position. Melissa considered Robin's comments, along with her own observations about the position—all part of the research process.

Based on Melissa's and Robin's notes and observations, you will write the job description for this new position. Who knows, you might be good at this and want to apply for this position yourself!

Just-in-Time Training

Writing Job Descriptions

TeleView needs to hire a recruitment specialist in HR to replace a very competent Melissa Kim. Melissa compiled this information needed to write the job description:

- First, she asked Robin (the manager this new employee will report to) to share her ideas about the job qualifications.

- Based on her experience in the position, Melissa listed the skills and traits she thinks are crucial to the job.

- Then, she talked with the workgroup managers this new person will work with and got their ideas.

Review Robin's ideas and Melissa's notes on the job (shown on pages 117, 118, and 119). Use this information to write a job description that will attract a qualified candidate for the job.

1. Create a one-page job description in an attractive format. Use the format of the job descriptions on the Intranet as a general guide. Make the job description concise but use descriptive words and phrases to make the job sound interesting and challenging. Include the seven parts of a job description listed on page 114.

2. If you would like to see sample job descriptions as you work, access the local Intranet or the Corporate View Web site. Select the ***Human Resources & Management*** link from the Corporate View Intranet Home page. Click the ***Current Job Openings @ TeleView*** link.

Save As:

Act4-2a

TO: Intern
FROM: *mkim@corpview.com*
SUBJECT: Job Description
MESSAGE:

Robin's ideas for the job description are in her email message below.

<<From Robin Mills, Forwarded by Melissa Kim>>

Melissa, our new recruitment specialist must be able to create job descriptions for each department at TeleView. This includes the usual skills. You know; the ability to research salaries, compensation, benefits—that sort of thing—for each position.

This person must be able to write job descriptions that will attract competent people. I think the person needs to come up to speed quickly and develop an understanding of how each department works, what each one does, and what its workgroups are like. I think we should find someone who is creative and can put some style into these descriptions to attract interest.

Hire a person who can help plan and organize recruitment shows at universities. These are becoming increasingly important. The person must be able to travel confidently at least once every month, set up a recruitment booth at the universities, and interview prospective job candidates. This is important in getting talented graduates to consider TeleView.

- Commitments
- Journal Entry
- Thoughts & Ideas
- Agendas
- Conversations

Recruitment Specialist Job Description Notes

1. Must have a knowledge of functions and division responsibilities.

2. Must develop a good working relationship with the management teams and workgroups.

3. Must be able to benchmark.

4. Should have experience interviewing.

5. Must have some experience in giving performance reviews.

6. Should be able to set goals and objectives with managers and new employees.

7. Must be able to read and interpret government hiring rules, rulings, court decisions, and regulations regarding personnel issues.

8. Must be able to answer questions, speak responsibly for the company, and think for themselves.

9. Experience: A bachelor's degree in HR related field or equivalent experience or higher.

10. Must be flexible and able to manage a number of projects simultaneously.

Daily Record of Events

Suggestions from Managers and Others

Excellent communications skills. Ability to work unsupervised and to solve problems without bugging others unnecessarily. John P.

Two languages would be very helpful. Maria

Manage the day-to-day recruitment and selection process. Work with all levels of management and employees across the corporation. Interviewing skills are important. J.W.

Writing skills. They must be able to write clearly and spell-check stuff! Kelly

Must be able to work with staffing agencies (like Manpower), Webmasters, and IT managers to ensure that new jobs are posted and advertised quickly. Don't leave me hanging all week with an important job that needs to be filled. Be a "get it done" type person. John S.

Interview candidates for a variety of positions at different levels and in different important functions in the company. Responsible for head-count monitoring. Terrie

Understand and experience the process of managing. A background in MBO or some similar background. Sachi

Be able to keep employee information confidential. Be a confident interviewer. Lexi

Be an effective communicator. Someone who can listen and hear what we are really saying about what our needs are. Ability to create Web pages is a plus. For example, they should know how to publish jobs on the Intranet. Marion

Degrees and Certifications

Most jobs require some sort of post-high school degree or certification. Companies often provide certifications for employees having demonstrated proficiencies with a particular software product or a technical skill. For example, many network engineers can receive certification from Microsoft for its networking Windows NT product. You will often see this kind of skill listed in a job description. Programmers may have to take tests to prove their abilities with programming languages such as Java, C++, or Visual BASIC.

Colleges and universities award degrees, including the following:

- Associate or technical degrees. These are usually two-year degrees.
- Bachelor's degrees, including Bachelor of Science (B.S.) or Bachelor of Arts (B.A.). These are usually four-year degrees.
- Master's degrees, including Master of Science (M.S.) or Master of Arts (M.A.). Usually two years of additional education are needed here. An MBA is a master's degree for business people. MBA stands for Master of Business Administration.
- Doctoral degrees include Doctor of Philosophy (Ph.D.). This usually requires four years of additional education.

Debriefing

Writing a great job description is challenging and requires dedicated effort. A recruitment specialist (RS) will need to write many job descriptions. This person will have to learn quickly how TeleView functions and what the needs of the various mission-critical functions are. The RS must be a good interviewer and be able to talk with prospective employees and interest them in working at TeleView. This requires a special kind of self-confidence. The RS must travel to college campuses and sometimes wake up in a new time zone excited to talk about jobs at TeleView.

Think and write about the following:

1. How would you evaluate a candidate's ability to perform this type of job?
2. How do you think you would perform in this position?
3. Does this sound like a job you would be interested in? Explain.

Save As:

Act4-2b

TeleView receives applications and resumes—by mail and in electronic form—every day from intelligent, capable individuals. TeleView appreciates talent and experience in applicants. When the time comes to make job offers, however, TeleView is looking for people who can function and thrive in a cooperative, team environment.

The following are the "super seven" skills TeleView looks for in its new recruits.

1. Problem-solving skills

2. Technical communications skills

3. Flexibility

4. Drive

5. Interpersonal skills

6. Project management skills

7. Teamwork skills

One way to learn whether a candidate has these skills is to develop interview questions that will reveal the presence or absence of the skills. Consider *flexibility*, for example. What is meant by flexibility? Here is a list of definitions a recruitment specialist summarized after a meeting with a workgroup in Corporate Communications.

Definitions of Flexibility

A person who is flexible
- Adjusts positively to change.
- Can do things in new ways.
- Responds to problems with viable solutions.
- Copes with unforseen circumstances without becoming anxious or upset.
- Is able to consider alternative courses of action.
- Is able to leap tall buildings in a single bound (or at least is willing to give it a try).

Figure 4-4
The AT&T Web site

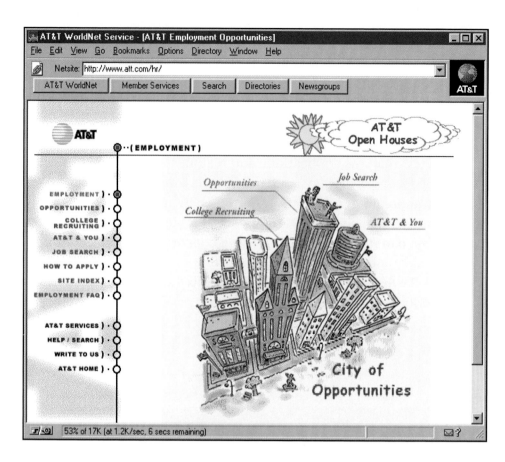

The **Least** You
Should Know
About...

Benefits

Benefits include anything a business provides an employee beyond the **base salary**. AT&T divides its benefits into the following general categories:

- **Performance and merit awards**, "to recognize, and reward, outstanding team or individual contributions to AT&T."

- **Health benefits**, which include "a flexible medical plan" with a "number of levels of coverage," allowing the employee to "tailor his or her benefits" to match personal lifestyle and needs. In addition, AT&T offers

"comprehensive dental and vision care plans, life insurance, long-term care and disability coverage."

- **Financial planning**, which includes "a broad array of investment options to assist employees in developing a personal investment strategy."

- **Work and family benefits**, which allow employees to "balance personal commitments and job responsibilities." This includes child care, leave of absence for the care of newborn or newly adopted children, family care leave, and elder care assistance.*

*AT&T. *AT&T Employment Benefits*. Online. Available: **www.att.com/hr/you/benefits.html**. August 21, 1998.

Everyone on a team must understand what is meant by certain words. Once a term or job skill has been defined, questions can be created that will help an interviewer learn whether a candidate has the skills being sought. Prior to an interview, the recruitment specialist, with the help of the workgroup concerned, will develop interview questions that test the candidate's strengths for working in the department.

Each job or situation will be different, so the questions will be different for each job interview. For example, these are the questions that the recruitment specialist, the Corporate Communications manager, and the workgroup team wrote for *flexibility* before they interviewed candidates for a new position in their group.

Possible Interview Questions Regarding Flexibility
- Describe a change that happened on a job you held. How did you adjust to the change?
- Have you ever had anyone angry at you? Describe the situation. How did you handle the situation?
- Describe a new situation you had to adjust to.
- Describe a situation in which you had to change your mind about something. What was the issue? Why did your opinion change?
- If we call the references listed on your resume, what will they say about your flexibility?

Just-in-Time Training

Writing Good Interview Questions

1. You have just seen how definitions were prepared, and interview questions written, about flexibility on the job. Choose three of the other TeleView super seven qualifications for employment (besides flexibility).

2. In a word processing file, list the three skills. Under each of the skills, key the department you are representing, such as Corporate Communications. Create four definitions and four questions for that skill. Look at this from the perspective of someone working in HR or one of the other mission-critical functions at TeleView. Here is the list of skills again to refresh your memory.

   - Problem-solving skills
   - Technical communications skills
   - Flexibility
   - Drive
   - Interpersonal skills
   - Project management skills
   - Teamwork skills

Save As:

Skills

Figure 4-5
Microsoft's Web site displays information about jobs at Microsoft.

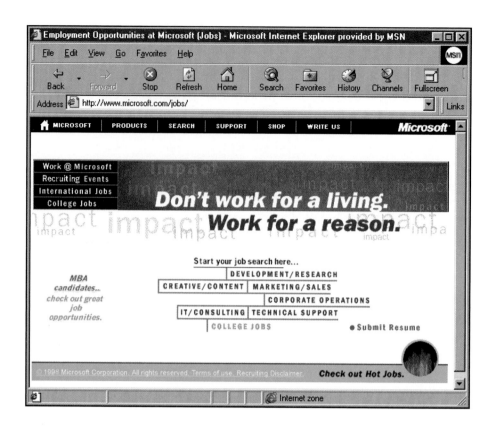

Business
Milestones

Interviews with a Twist

Before interviewing for a job, you should prepare for everything because you might be in for a few surprises! Some corporations ask bizarre questions, sometimes deliberately putting new candidates into humorous situations. This helps them see whether job candidates will be able to cope with the day-to-day stresses of the corporate world. For example, you may be asked about your hobbies and things you like to do after work. You could be asked to tell your favorite jokes. (Hope everyone laughs.) You could be asked to role-play some situations, perhaps one as bizarre as "You are lost in the Amazon rain forest and your battery on your portable computer has just died. Convince the natives to help you recharge your battery. Oh, and the natives don't speak your language. You have to explain everything without words."

What are these companies looking for with these kinds of creative interview questions? Would you feel comfortable in this kind of situation? Would this kind of interview help you relax or make you more nervous?

Debriefing

HR specialists try to match the skills of the candidate with the job. Because every job in every department in every corporation is different and requires a different kind of person, being an HR employee can get a bit complicated. Some people describe the job setting and the working conditions as the *job environment*. The job environment may be described in a job description.

Another important issue in interviewing is fairness. Questions must be consistent and fair for each applicant. Each person interviewing must have the same chance to get the job. Good questions can help HR personnel give every candidate the same opportunity to get the job.

Think and write about the following:

One question everyone needs to ask is, "Why am I working?" For a time, Microsoft boldly stated on its jobs Web site (see Figure 4-5), "Don't work for a living, work for a reason."* This is good advice.

1. What reasons do you have for looking for a job?

   _____

   _____

2. Why do you want or need to go to work?

   _____

3. Ask around. Why do your friends work? What do they want out of their jobs?

   _____

   _____

4. What do you think "Don't work for a living, work for a reason" means?

   _____

   _____

* Microsoft Corporation. *Employment Opportunities at Microsoft.* Online. Available: **www.microsoft.com/jobs/**. February 25, 1998.

Activity 4-4 *Evaluating Performance*

What a manager is and how a manager supports the company have changed significantly over the last 10 years. Management has traditionally been thought of as the top of the organization, with the manager distributing information, giving directives, and evaluating performance. A manager was someone whose job was handing out instructions or orders.

Today the role of management is quite different. The new bottom-up approach to management empowers everyone. Everyone takes part, and everyone gives input. Every idea matters, and the contribution of each individual is important to the mission-critical functions. The growth and competitive well-being of TeleView depends on it.

So here is our corporate view of management: The role of management is to facilitate and support a dynamic team environment at every level. Saturn built its reputation on this philosophy. So did Microsoft, Intel, HP, AT&T, and MCI. So has Corporate View and its TeleView business unit. At TeleView, management training teaches this philosophy and encourages the adoption of management skills that promote a cooperative work environment. As an intern, you are now in the middle of that training.

Role of Managers in Evaluation

Part of the role of management is to evaluate new candidates for job positions on their team. A manager must find not only qualified people, but also the kinds of people who can encourage and build the workgroup team they are responsible for.

After a candidate is hired, the responsibilities of his or her manager or team leader do not end. A manager must find ways to improve each team member's performance; recommend additional training to help employees grow in their jobs; review individual and team performance; and recommend bonuses, merit awards, and performance awards for personal and group achievement. Salary increases are also tied to performance evaluations.

Starting with the first job interview, a rapport must be developed between the team leader/manager and the candidate. After being hired, each employee is interviewed, and his or her performance is evaluated by the workgroup manager or supervisor every six months during the formal performance review process.

SCANS: The Secretary's Commission on Achieving Necessary Skills

In the early 1990s, the U.S. Department of Labor sponsored a study by SCANS (The Secretary's Commission on Achieving Necessary Skills) to determine what knowledge and skills are needed in modern business. Below is a summary of the workplace competencies and foundation skills the report, *Workforce 2000*, indicated businesses are looking for in employees. If you look at TeleView's super seven skills for new employees, you can see a strong parallel between them and those noted in the SCANS report guidelines.

Workplace Competencies

Effective workers can productively use resources, interpersonal skills, information, systems, and technology as described below:

- **Resources** They know how to allocate time, money, materials, space, and staff.

- **Interpersonal skills** They can work on teams, teach others, serve customers, lead, negotiate, and work well with people from culturally diverse backgrounds.

- **Information** They can acquire and evaluate data, organize and maintain files, interpret and communicate, and use computers to process information.

- **Systems** They understand social, organizational, and technological systems; they can monitor and correct performance; and they can design or improve systems.

- **Technology** They can select equipment and tools, apply technology to specific tasks, and maintain and troubleshoot equipment.

Foundation Skills

Competent workers in the high-performance workplace need:

- **Basic skills** Reading, writing, arithmetic and mathematics, speaking, and listening.

- **Thinking skills** The ability to learn, to reason, to think creatively, to make decisions, and to solve problems.

- **Personal qualities** Individual responsibility, self-esteem and self-management, sociability, and integrity.

Search for copies of the SCANS documents and summaries at ***http://infinia.wpmc.jhu.edu/***. At this address, you can find the *SCANS America 2000* publications and review this important body of work. Pay attention to everything written by Dr. Arnold Packer, former Assistant Secretary of Labor and coauthor of *Workforce 2000*. You can also visit the U.S. Department of Labor Internet site at ***http://dol.gov***.

Performance Review Process

The first part of the performance review, often called simply an evaluation, covers "outward" elements like absenteeism, meeting deadlines, and production goals. Goals and objectives are set with each employee and each team, usually during a *biannual* performance review. (Review The Least You Should Know About... Management by Objectives.) The starting point for this part of the evaluation is the individual's job description. If a person's job grows or changes, the job description can be updated. An updated job description can lead to a higher salary if the job's responsibilities increase.

The second part of the evaluation concerns personal improvement in summarizing any corporate training the employee has completed, educational achievements for those still attending college or working on a graduate degree, and improvements in productivity. For example, employees who attend seminars or pass in-house tests can get performance review credits that can increase their salaries or make them eligible for performance awards.

The third and final part of the evaluation highlights significant individual contributions to TeleView. This might be receiving a patent by someone in R&D or landing a big account by someone in Sales. Last year, TeleView gave a merit award bonus to a new employee in the Warehouse Department who proposed a change in physical layout that increased warehouse efficiency by 15 percent. (See The Least You Should Know About... Benefits.)

Teams are often evaluated biannually for their productivity and other contributions. Team bonuses or performance awards are divided evenly among team members and can be paid semiannually—once in time for summer vacation and once in time for the year-end holiday season.

Earning a good salary is important to everyone who works. The HR Department works closely with the Finance and Accounting Department to ensure that salary and benefits packages remain competitive. If our employees aren't paid as much as those of the competition, TeleView won't be able to keep the best people. There's more to a successful career than a paycheck, however. Enjoying a good working relationship with other employees and making a positive contribution toward corporate goals are also important to most employees.

Just-in-Time Training

Job Descriptions, Interviews, and Evaluations

Many corporations use a numbered scale to rank candidates for a new job or to evaluate performance after a job has been awarded. Often, more than one person will be involved in conducting an interview. It is a common practice to have the team leader or manager and an HR representative participate in a job interview. It's also common to have part or all of the team present during an interview. Team members may be asked to score the candidate on the interview questions to create *peer evaluations*. These scores can be added or averaged to determine a *composite score*.

Here is a sample ranking scale used by TeleView in conducting interviews.

Interview Rating Scale

5 *Excellent*

All major criteria and elements in the job description were addressed and the candidate's qualifications greatly exceed job requirements.

4 *Very Good*

Most major criteria in the job description were addressed with no major deficiencies in the candidate's qualifications.

3 *Good*

Some of the major and minor criteria in the job description were addressed. Some deficiencies exist in the candidate's qualifications, but none is a major concern.

2 *Weak*

Few of the criteria in the job description were addressed. Some major deficiencies exist and are of some concern.

1 *Poor*

Few criteria in the job description were addressed. Many deficiencies exist in the candidate's qualifications that could lead to major problems if the candidate were hired.

Managers and interviewers will often use a five-point scale like this one to help them evaluate candidates for a job or to help evaluate the ongoing performance of team members. The following exercise will give you a chance to become comfortable with this kind of evaluation scale.

1. Open the job-description document you wrote for Melissa Kim's HR recruitment specialist position in Activity 4-2 Writing Job Descriptions. Rank yourself for the recruitment specialist job using the 1-5 scale. What is your score for this position?

_____

2. How would you summarize your qualifications, skills, abilities, flexibility, and drive to get this job and do it well?

_____
_____
_____
_____

3. Write a 25-word summary of the additional skills you would need to compete successfully for this job.

_____
_____
_____
_____
_____

Debriefing

Managers, teams, and employees work closely with HR's Corporate Training group because virtually every person who joins a corporation requires some additional training. School can prepare candidates with general knowledge and skills, but in the corporate environment, many specific procedures and skills need to be learned to complete the mission-critical functions of a business. For example, new employees in

- Finance and Accounting need to learn how to use the company's financial software.

- Marketing and Sales need to learn about the products and services sold by their employer. They must also know the telecommunications marketplace (as in the simulation in Chapter 2, Activity 2-1).

- Customer Support representatives need to learn the proper protocols when working with customers and how to use the customer database.

Management training is important. Many businesses pay special attention to individuals involved in management training because they often fill management positions internally, or from inside the corporation.

Think and write about the following:

1. Have you ever worked with a manager you really liked? Name three strengths of this person's management style; then list two weaknesses.

    Strengths: _____, _____, and

    _____

    Weaknesses: _____ and _____

2. What kinds of training do you think this manager has received?

    _____

3. What kinds of additional training do you think this manager should participate in?

    _____

Chapter Review

Executive Summary

The Human Resources Department manages the services and benefits that attract, motivate, and retain a highly talented, committed, and diverse workforce. HR helps managers promote the fair and equitable treatment of all employees. It also provides ongoing training opportunities.

One key responsibility of a Human Resources Department is to prepare job descriptions and determine salary ranges for jobs. A job description lists the duties and responsibilities an employee is hired to fulfill. Job descriptions help in the evaluation of new candidates for job openings and are used in evaluating the performance of employees after they are hired.

Job descriptions can attract qualified candidates to a job. They should be short, clear, and to the point. Job descriptions are generally prepared only after researching the needs of the business and conducting interviews with the key people who will work with the new employee.

Salary ranges for jobs should be reviewed by Finance so that budgets are not exceeded. Also, many corporations limit the number of employees in each department as a cost-control measure. This number is called the "head count."

Helping interview people for new positions or jobs is also a key responsibility of the Human Resources Department. In preparation for a job interview, HR recruitment specialists will list the skills, traits, training, and experience they are looking for in candidates. These definitions guide them in preparing the questions they will ask in interviewing job candidates.

Many companies employ a numeric scale to help in ranking job candidates. For example, the highest score for excellent candidates may be 5 and the lowest score for poor candidates may be 1. If two or more people are interviewing a candidate, their rankings can be combined to form a composite score. A similar process can be used in employee performance reviews.

Technical Communications

Job descriptions are made up of several parts: job title, date posted and closed, department or group name, description of the job environment, job location, main responsibilities, and required education, skills, and experience. An informative job description will include each of these elements.

Corporations get lots of questions from phone calls, FAXes, and email. Even a letter or two will come in loaded with questions. Questions come from customers, employees, and other interested people. Sometimes the questions are sent to employees to answer. Here are some messages that need to be answered by someone in Human Resources. Answer these messages with the help of the Intranet and your own best judgment. If you need help preparing these documents, access the **_Style Guide_** under the **_Corporate Communications_** link.

CORPORATE VIEW

From the Desk of Robin Mills...

Dear Intern

A phone call came in today from Corey Thomas. Corey left a message asking where we post jobs, salary ranges, and salary schedules. Please send an email to cthomas@corpview.com with this information.

Thanks
Robin

TO: Intern
FROM: *mjones@corpview.com*
SUBJECT: MBO
MESSAGE:

Several questions have come to me recently about MBO (management by objectives). It might be a good idea to add some information about it to our Intranet FAQs. Please prepare an answer to this question that can be posted to cover the topic.

What is MBO and do Corporate View and TeleView use it?

Just email the information to me, please.

Thanks for your help.

Mariette Jones
Corporate Communications

Voice Mail

Hi, this is Melissa Kim. I need your help, please. We often get questions from new employees and interns about the performance review process at TeleView. Would you please create an email message that I can keep on file to send in response to these questions? Please describe our performance review process in detail. Thanks. Just send the email to me, and I'll forward it to others as needed.
Bye.

Save As:

Inbox4C

CORPORATE VIEW

From the Desk of Hilary Francis...

HR, help please.

How do we rank candidates for jobs when more than four of us are interviewing?

Hilary

Please send Hilary an email with this information at hfrancis@corpview.com.

Thanks,
Robin

Access the Corporate View Web site. (A live Web connection is needed to check stock quotes. If you do not have access to a live Web connection, move on to the second part of this exercise under When a Few Words Will Do.) Click the **_Stock Watcher Links_** on the **_Regular Features_** page and follow the instructions. Identify the following ticker symbols and learn how each of these companies did in the stock market today.

Current Date _____

Ticker	Exchange	Company Name	Current Price
MAN	NYSE	_____	_____
HWP	NYSE	_____	_____
MSFT	NASDAQ	_____	_____
INTC	NASDAQ	_____	_____
T	NYSE	_____	_____

When a Few Words Will Do

Answer the following questions using what you have learned reading the Business Milestones and The Least You Should Know About... reports. Use 25 to 50 words to write your answers in a word processing document.

1. What is MBO? Why is this a popular management system? What are its strengths and weaknesses?

2. Why would large companies use a company like Manpower to provide job candidates?

3. Evaluate Hewlett-Packard's attitude toward its new employees. What are the strengths and weaknesses of HP's approach?

4. Many jobs require some sort of educational degree. What do you consider the minimum degree to obtain the job of your dreams and why?

5. What is your opinion of AT&T's benefits program? List the strengths and note any possible weaknesses.

Save As:

Online4

Portfolio-Building Project

Working in an Online World

Everyone would like to write his or her own "perfect" dream job description. What would your dream job be? Demonstrate your technical communications skills by writing a job description for your dream job for your portfolio.

1. Write a job description for your dream job. Include the job title; a description of the job environment; the desired location; the main responsibilities of the job; and the education, skills, and experience needed for the job.

2. Review Technical Communications Online Job Descriptions with a Style All Their Own in this chapter before you begin.

3. Spell-check your report before you print or share it, and remember to proofread.

Save As:

Pfolio4

High-Performance Workgroup Project

Team up with three or four others and share the dream job descriptions you just completed in the Portfolio-Building Project for this chapter. Evaluate each job description and discuss how much a company should pay a person for doing the job.

Include answers to the following questions in your job evaluation:

1. Why do some jobs pay more than others do?

2. What do other businesses pay for this kind of work?

3. What would be a competitive starting salary?

4. What would a proper salary range be for this kind of work?

5. What kinds of bonuses and benefits should accompany this position?

Save As:

HP4

Thinking and Writing About Your Business

Corporate View and its strategic business units all look for certain skills in an employee. (See the list on page 121.) The SCANS report lists many additional skills. Review the Business Milestones SCANS: The Secretary's Commission on Achieving Necessary Skills.

Which skills do you think TeleView should add to the super seven list? Choose at least three additional skills and explain why each of these skills is fundamental to a high-performance workplace. Why should it be added to TeleView's super seven list?

Key your answers of 25 to 50 words in a word processing document.

Save As:

Think4

Overtime

Comparing Corporate Job Descriptions

1. Select five fortune 500 corporations and visit their job or employment Web sites. Links to several companies can be found on the Corporate View Web site. Click on the ***Human Resources & Management*** link on the Corporate View Intranet Home page. Choose the ***Competitive Job Employment Listings*** link.

2. Find the description of one job from each of the five corporations that you would find interesting to do.

3. Write a summary of each job description. Include the job title; date posted and closed (if shown); department or group name (if shown); a brief description of the job environment; the location of the job; the main duties of the job; and the education, skills, and experience required for the job.

4. Copy and paste one or two key phrases or sentences from each of the five job descriptions from the Web into your word processing document to use as direct quotes. If you need help with this process, click the ***Intranet FAQs*** link on the ***Regular Features*** page. Read ***Copying and Pasting Information from the Web and the Intranet*** .

Save As:

Otime4

5. Place each job description on a separate page. Cite the source of information for each job description as a note at the bottom of the page. If you need help creating reference notes for electronic sources, access the ***Style Guide*** link on the ***Corporate Communications*** page. Choose the ***Citing Electronic Sources*** link.

Applications to Small Business

Outsourcing

There are many jobs that a business unit like TeleView might "outsource," or have another company or consultant do for them. This could save the company a lot of money, particularly if the job were only needed for a short period of time. Explore some of these jobs.

1. Access the local Intranet or the Corporate View Web site. Click on the **_Human Resources & Management_** link, and choose **_Current Job Openings @ TeleView_**.

2. Access some job openings and find three you think could be done by an outside consultant working at a location outside the company.

3. Write a memo to Melissa Kim about these three jobs and recommend that it would be a win-win situation to outsource this work instead of hiring full-time employees and adding to the departments' head counts unnecessarily. Record notes about the job descriptions as you read them to help you in writing the memo.

Save As:

ASB4

Online Evaluation

Access the Corporate View Web site and take the Online Evaluation for this chapter.

1. Click on the **_Employee Training and Evaluations_** link on the **_Regular Features_** page.

2. Select the **_Online Tests_** link. (You must be a registered user to access the online tests. If you are not a registered user, click the **_Register_** link and follow the instructions on the screen. Then click the **_Online Tests_** link to return to the Online Tests page.)

3. Choose the **_Chapter 4 A View from Human Resources and Management_** link on the Online Tests page.

4. Enter the username and password you selected when you registered.

5. Take the test. Click the **First**, **Back**, **Next**, and **Last** buttons to navigate through the questions. Click the **Finish** button to submit your test for grading. If you wish to close the test without submitting it for grading, click the **Cancel** button. Any answers you have entered will be lost if you cancel the test.

Chapter 5

A View from Corporate Communications

The Voice of the Corporation

"Hi. My name is Maria Bravo. I'm one of several coordinators in the Corporate Communications Department. Think of our department as the voice of Corporate View.

"Corporate Communications is the heart of the company, if you think about it. Corporations like Corporate View depend on information to survive and remain competitive.

"When you came in, I was putting some finishing touches on our new *active server* Web site. Our team worked together on the design, artwork, and content of our Web site; then we handed it off to the Information Technology (IT) team for the HTML work. The IT Department takes care of running the site, but we control the content.

"I guess you've already seen the corporate Intranet; that's ours, too. The Intranet is the way we keep all our employees informed on all the happenings at Corporate View. It's how employees interact and share information. It is *the* way employees stay informed at Corporate View.

"Our Web site is one way Corporate View communicates with the outside world. There are many other ways, too, and our department handles all of them. We work closely with our ad agency in Chicago and with Marketing, Sales, and Customer Support to develop promotional campaigns that include television, radio, print, and Web advertisements. For instance, we recently started a magazine advertising campaign outlining five good reasons to buy Corporate View's video conferencing products. As a direct result of the campaign, sales went up 11 percent.

"We work with our *trade show* team and sales personnel to develop some really exciting multimedia sales presentations. We blew everybody away at *COMDEX*, our biggest trade show, last year!

"Our department is responsible for developing product and service brochures, reference manuals, installation guides, service contracts, and other kinds of product literature. We also write *press releases* and sensitive letters for our colleagues in other departments. We send out press releases whenever there's a market shift, an acquisition, or a change in upper-level personnel. Every time we release a new product, we send a *press kit* to a long list of consumer magazines, trade journals, and other periodicals. We send hardware to authors who write about our products or conduct comparison tests. We basically handle any kind of communications that will promote Corporate View."

Assisting Other Mission-Critical Functions

"Once people buy our products, they need to know how to use them. When R&D is developing a new product, we work with them to write installation or user instructions. (Sometimes these very smart inventors have a hard time writing simple instructions.) These instructions are tested along with the product. This way, we are sure we get clear instructions to customers.

"Another important aspect of what we do is writing service copy, or service information, and distributing it to our Customer Support representatives. If a problem arises with a product, we make sure all our support personnel have clearly written answers to customer concerns. We may also post this information as FAQs on the Web site for our customers.

"We market in more than 40 countries, so we need to *localize* our products, documentation, press releases, Web FAQs, installation instructions, and so on. That is, we need to translate our product literature into a variety of languages and adjust our promotional materials to interest people of different cultures and in different countries. This process is called *localization*. We often outsource our localization work to consultants who are experts in different languages, countries, and cultures. Our Corporate Communications managers make sure the outsourced work meets Corporate View's high standards.

"We work with other departments, such as Finance and Accounting, to help prepare an easy-to-read *annual report* for stockholders. We also collaborate with Human Resources to write and edit policy manuals, training materials, job descriptions, and any other literature used by the staff.

"Legal Services often issues official statements, like copyright or liability information. Sometimes the corporate lawyers need our help translating what they mean from 'legalese' into plain English that our customers will understand."

Summarizing the Role of Corporate Communications

"The role of Corporate Communications is to convey information inside and outside the company. When you get right down to it, everything we do fits into four broad categories: (a) we promote our image, (b) we promote our products and services, (c) we keep our employees informed, and (d) we assist our SBUs and our mission-critical departments with their communications needs."

The **Least** You **Should** Know About...

Outsourcing

Twenty years ago, the corporate trend was to do everything in-house. Departments like Corporate Communications grew and grew as the workload increased. As more individuals were hired, more people were needed to handle accounting and payroll. More office space meant more facilities with more associated maintenance costs. More Information Technology people were needed to keep the technology systems growing and working. More training had to be done. More managers had to be in place. Some companies got so bloated with new personnel that they couldn't survive!

In the 1990s, the downsizing trend began. Companies started cutting their workforces and hiring outside contractors to do work that used to be done in-house.

Outsourcing is the practice of hiring independent contractors to provide specific services. Here's a good example. Suppose Corporate View has a huge stack of materials that need to be photocopied, organized, and bound for an upcoming conference. Contracting with an independent copy center to do this work might cost a little more per page. However, when you figure in the savings of not having to buy and maintain expensive copy machines—not to mention hiring a staff to operate them—outsourcing saves money in the long run.

A large corporation may outsource many tasks in every mission-critical department:

- Corporate Communications may outsource technical writing, proofing, media production, artwork, and printing.

- Human Resources could outsource a new-employee training program. Localization experts could be hired to ensure that the training will be effective in branch offices located in foreign countries.

- Security, building maintenance services, and food services are often outsourced to subcontractors.

- Marketing and advertising campaigns may be outsourced to professional advertising agencies.

- Information Technology may outsource the maintenance of computers, FAX machines, copy machines, and printers.

- Research and development tasks can be outsourced to specialized independent research labs and manufacturing facilities.

- Legal services can be outsourced by retaining a law firm and consulting its attorneys only as needed.

- Finance and accounting needs, like tax preparation and payroll services, can be contracted to an outside financial firm.

- Telemarketing firms can be hired to help with sales and customer support tasks.

Outsourcing is one way business gets done. And if anything, the trend is growing. Many people leave large corporations and establish a business to do the work that is being outsourced by their former employers.

Activity Overviews

Corporate Communications is one of the most visible teams in any corporation. The job of Corporate Communications is *informing*. In doing this job, Corporate Communications takes on a lot of responsibilities, including

- Informing employees of important decisions made by the corporation that affect their jobs.

- Informing investors and customers of the strength of the corporation and its products.

- Helping other mission-critical departments prepare a variety of documents, including job descriptions and listings, installation instructions, press releases, letters, memos, operations manuals, technical specifications, and instructional materials.

- Proofreading, editing, and correcting work done by others.

- Answering correspondence from customers.

- Helping direct the work of outsourcers, localizers, and other consultants.

- Assisting in the upkeep and maintenance of the Intranet and Web site content for the company.

Corporate Communications employees work with people in nearly every department of a corporation. They usually know about everything that is going on, and they use their skills to help other employees do a better job communicating important information.

Activity 5-1 What Is a Press Release? will introduce the press release, an important tool that Corporate Communications uses to get the word out about new products and newsworthy events.

Activity 5-2 Rules for Writing Press Releases will take you to a **style guide** on the Intranet to investigate the guidelines Corporate Communications has developed for press releases coming from Corporate View.

Activity 5-3 Analyzing the Audience and Purpose will introduce you to three kinds of press releases: general, detailed, and specific. Learning about these three types of releases will help you determine your audience and fine-tune the purpose, personality, and length of your press releases.

Activity 5-4 Writing Press Releases will take you step-by-step through writing three press releases.

Corporate ShopTalk

Understanding the meanings of these terms will help you learn the concepts and develop the skills related to Corporate Communications covered in the chapter. In preparation for completing the chapter activities, access the Intranet and find the definition for each of these terms by clicking the ***ShopTalk*** link on the ***Regular Features*** page.

- Active Server
- Annual Report
- COMDEX
- Listservs

- Localize
- Press Kit
- Press Release

- Style Guide
- Trade Show
- Webzine

It's up to the company to spread the news about a product, a merger, or a shift in corporate direction. One way the company does this is with the press release (sometimes called a *news release*). A press release is a short document usually prepared by Corporate Communications about some newsworthy subject relevant to the company or the company's customers. It might be about a new product, the formation of a new strategic business unit (SBU), a problem with a current product, or a breakthrough in technology.

The purpose of a press release is simple: Get your company's message out quickly and accurately to the right people—customers, reviewers, stockholders, and employees.

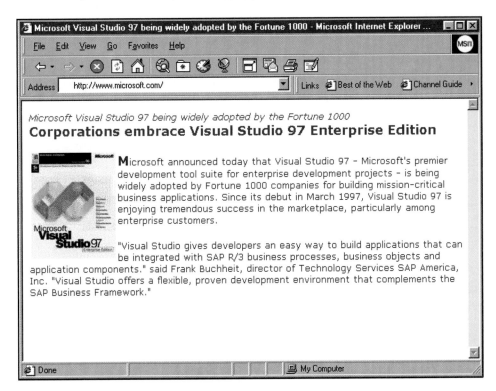

Figure 5-1
Major corporations like Microsoft issue press releases nearly every working day.

A press release is usually rather short—about one page. It was traditionally sent to "the media"—newspapers, television and radio stations, and trade journals—as well as to vendors and other interested parties. Now, a press release, besides going to traditional sources, is also posted on the company's Web site, the Intranet, and other relevant Web sites like online magazines or *Webzines*.

A document can't be all things to all readers. Different documents have different functions. You wouldn't run a marathon in expensive

Italian dress shoes, nor would you wear logging boots to a formal dinner. The shoes and the boots have different functions. Similarly, different types of press releases meet the needs of different types of readers.

Figure 5-2
Media organizations like Time Warner post press releases from other corporations.

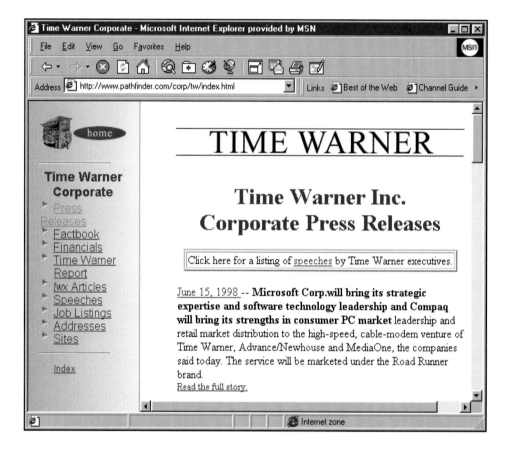

The **Least** You **Should** Know About...

Posting Press Releases

Press releases are sent to newspapers, television stations, radio stations, magazines, trade journals, vendors, and other interested parties. They can also be posted on the company's Web site and on other relevant sites on the Internet like online magazines or Webzines. Press releases can be emailed to online customers, stockholders, and industry analysts. They are often published by trade magazines or magazines that focus on a specific industry, like *PCWeek Online* for computer users and *LAN Times Parts*, a Webzine for Internet technologies. Financial press releases can be quoted in *The Wall Street Journal* or other investor-oriented publications.

Many corporations use *push* technology to transmit press releases to employees and Web site visitors. Push automatically updates Web pages on personal computers (PCs) or network computers (NCs) without the employee or Web site visitor requesting the information. Push is pretty amazing, but it may be considered too pushy unless the information that is pushed is worth reading or seeing.

Copies of press releases can also be sent via email, using *listservs*, to customers who have registered product purchases online. Email is a very inexpensive way to communicate with hundreds of thousands of customers at one time. For customers who don't have email, companies can send information through the U.S. Postal Service to addresses obtained from registration cards mailed in by customers.

General Information Press Release

Most press releases fall into the general category. The audience needs to know about the product, event, or promotion, but only in general terms. For example, suppose a company has developed a new word processing program. The company would send out a press release discussing the program's features, comparing them with those of similar products, and mentioning availability and price.

Detailed Information Press Release

Some readers need more detailed or technical information about the product. For example, a reader in charge of purchasing new office software for a corporation would need facts to justify purchasing the product. Details listing the software's requirements would be needed. The press release should discuss the kind of computer required to run the software, the amount of memory needed, and the amount of hard disk space the software occupies.

Specific Information Press Release

The reader of a specific information press release is an expert who needs specific data or answers to specific questions. Perhaps a structural engineer needs a sophisticated software package to test the tensile strength of steel in suspension bridges and needs to know whether the company's software has the mathematical formulas required to make that sort of calculation.

A press release is a carefully written document and an important business tool. You will learn more information about press releases in this chapter and in the style guide on the Intranet.

Just-in-Time Training

Evaluating Press Releases

1. Access your local Intranet or the Corporate View Web site.

2. Select the **_Corporate Communications_** link from the Corporate View Intranet Home page and read **_About Corporate Communications_**.

3. In a word processing file, write a brief description in your own words of what Corporate Communications is all about.

4. On the **_Corporate Communications_** page, access the **_Style Guide_**. Click the **_Press Releases_** link and choose **_Sample Press Releases_**. Access and read the three sample press releases.

Save As:

Act5-1

5. Which press release most closely matches the description of a general information press release?

_____

6. Which one most closely matches the description of a detailed information press release?

_____

7. Which most closely matches the description of a specific information press release?

_____

8. Which press release did you find the most informative?

_____

9. In your view, which press release was the least valuable or helpful?

_____

10. Which titles or headlines worked the best? List the three titles from the most effective to the least effective.

_____

_____

_____

Business
Milestones

Time Warner

This quote from the *Time Warner Factbook* says it all:

The merger of Time Warner and Turner Broadcasting has created the world's foremost media and entertainment company with the strongest and best-known brands in our industry.*

You would naturally expect the foremost media company in the world to have a formidable internal communications system. Time Warner (NYSE:TWX) takes its corporate communications function one step beyond that of the average corporation by producing an online magazine just for employees. Take a peek at what the employees see at *www.pathfinder.com/corp/ie/*.

Time Warner has many strategic business units, each of which is a household name and a significant business in its own right:

- Time Warner Inc. Corporate
- Time Inc.
- Warner Bros.
- Warner Music Group
- HBO
- CNN
- Turner Entertainment Networks
- Time Warner Cable

By focusing on strategic mergers and acquisitions, Time Warner has become the premier entertainment and news organization in the world. Learn more about these strategic business units by visiting *www. pathfinder.com/corp/*.

*Time Warner. Time Warner Factbook. Online. Available: www.pathfinder.com/corp/fbook/fbframe.html. February 1, 1998.

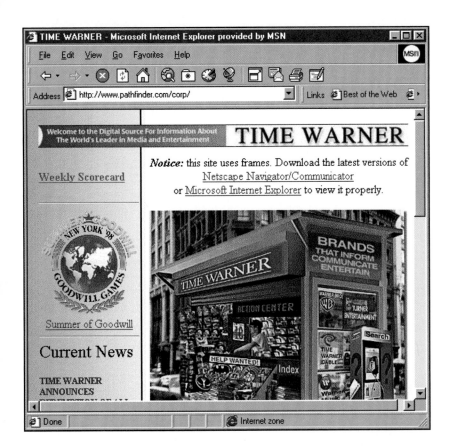

Debriefing

In this activity, you have identified three kinds of press releases. Now that you have had a chance to read several press releases, summarize what you have learned.

Think and write about the following:

1. What are three similarities among the press releases you have read?

_____

_____

_____

2. What do you think is the primary motivation for a business to issue press releases?

_____

_____

_____

3. How can press releases help a corporation like Corporate View?

_____

_____

_____

Activity 5-2   *Rules for Writing Press Releases*

A press release is an issue-driven document that has a specific

- Audience
- Purpose
- Personality (including style, mood, and objective tone)
- Length (of sentences, paragraphs, and the entire document)

In a press release, the issue or purpose is to inform the reader. A press release sometimes fails because the author didn't really understand the audience, the purpose of the release, or the style of writing (personality) required. A press release can also fail simply because it is too long to keep the reader interested.

Technical Communications

The topics of audience and purpose are investigated in more detail in Activity 5-3. This activity focuses on sentence and paragraph length and personality (including mood and use of verbs and adjectives).

Press Releases

A press release or news release, as the name implies, is a short document (generally a page or less) about some newsworthy subject prepared by organizations for the media and other audiences. Press releases, like newspaper articles, tend to be factual and informative. Like newspaper articles, press releases begin with the most important information. The first sentence or two of a press release should discuss the *who, what, when, where,* and *why* of the story. Information that is less important is included in subsequent paragraphs.

Press releases are written in this way for the same reason that newspaper articles are—so that, if the audience is too busy to read the entire release or if the publication does not have space for all of it, the most important information is still likely to be included and read.

Press releases tend to be simple and straightforward and have an objective or neutral tone. Like newspaper articles, they report the news without commenting on it, although writers of press releases, unlike journalists, try to present their news in a way that is advantageous to the company.

Just-in-Time Training

Press Release Guidelines and Format

1. Access your local Intranet or the Corporate View Web site.
2. Select the ***Corporate Communications*** link from the Corporate View Intranet Home page and click the ***Style Guide*** link. Select ***Press Releases***.

Style Guides

Many businesses and professional organizations have their own style guides. A style guide (sometimes called a *style sheet*) gives the organization's preferred standards for formatting documents such as letters, memos, and reports. It may include information on grammar, punctuation, and usage. For example, a style guide might suggest that one way to avoid sexist language in documents is by using *he or she* instead of just *he* or *she* alone.

Style guides help corporations maintain consistency in the many documents issued by their different departments and present a consistent image to the public.

Guidelines for formatting and organizing press releases vary from corporation to corporation. Corporate View's guidelines for writing and formatting press releases were created by Corporate Communications and appear on the Intranet.

3. The style guide discusses the language to be used in a press release. In a word processing file, list the key points and summarize the concepts in your own words.

Save As:

PRStyle

4. The style guide also examines how press releases at Corporate View should be formatted and organized. In your *PRStyle* document, list and describe the parts of a press release. Save your file again using the same name.

5. Access the ***Sample Press Releases*** under the ***Press Releases*** link on the ***Style Guide***. Select the first press release and look over it quickly. How many of the parts of a press release described in the style guide does this press release use?

_____

6. Read the press release and analyze it in terms of length and personality. How well does it meet the style guide criteria for the following?

Sentence length: _____

Paragraph length: _____

Use of verbs: _____

Mood: _____

Debriefing

Before a press release is sent out, it usually has to be reviewed and approved by one or more people in a corporation. A public relations director, an editor, a team of editors, or a program director might perform this function.

Your goal is to have your release taken seriously and approved for distribution. Writing the press release according to the guidelines in the style guide will improve your chances of having the release approved. If you don't take the style guide seriously, an editor or other decision maker probably won't take your work seriously either.

Put yourself in the place of a Corporate Communications editor. You might review 20 or 30 press releases every day. Of that 20 or 30, only one may be printed or posted on the Web. A very important consideration in whether to approve a press release is how timely and newsworthy the topic is. If you have 30 press releases to choose from, however, you will probably consider the ones that follow the style guide first and send the others back to be reworked.

Think and write about the following:

Corporate Communications is responsible for maintaining the corporate image. Put yourself in the role of a Corporate Communications editor. Suppose a press release comes to your desk from a workgroup team member. The press release is scheduled to go to trade magazines, newspapers, and Webzines around the world. How would you explain the following to a team member without offending him or her?

1. The press release contains information that is inaccurate.

   _____

   _____

   _____

2. The press release contains grammatical and spelling errors.

   _____

   _____

   _____

3. The press release is hard to read, and the important information is at the bottom of the release.

   _____

   _____

   _____

When you write a press release—or any issue-oriented document—you must keep in mind your audience and the exact purpose of the document. If a document fails, the failure can almost always be traced to a lack of understanding of one of these two important elements.

Ask yourself, "Exactly who is going to view this document?" Then ask yourself, "Why do they need (or want) to view it?" In other words, what is their purpose for reading this document?

After you have identified your audience and purpose, consider what information would be helpful, necessary, or interesting. What information would be distracting to this particular audience?

A useful technique is to picture an actual person or make up a person for whom you can write your release. Remember, you're writing it because someone will be reading it—someone who will have an interest in the information.

In the next activity, you will write three press releases introducing a new and improved CF4000/SE phone to the college market. But first, you will take some time in this activity to analyze the audience and purpose for each press release. This will make the writing go faster.

Business Milestones

America Online

America Online (NYSE:AOL) is the world's largest Internet service provider, or ISP. It is a global leader in a highly competitive interactive Internet services industry. In just two years, America Online (AOL) surpassed its two main rivals—CompuServe and Prodigy—to capture the number-one spot in the ISP world. During fiscal year 1997, AOL's revenue exceeded $1.6 billion. The company had the largest subscriber base of any ISP, with more than 8.5 million members as of June 1997. This number increased to more than 11 million six months later. Pushing to increase its subscriber base keeps America Online ahead of its competitors.

America Online has not limited itself to the North American market. It has expanded its services to more than 100 countries, localizing its online service for Austria, France, Germany, Japan, Sweden, Switzerland, the United Kingdom, and other countries.

America Online has three primary business units:

- AOL Networks
- AOL Studios
- ANS Communications

America Online helps people stay informed, conduct business, learn, shop, and have fun online. Many small start-up businesses have used AOL to provide Intranet services for their employees. Businesses can advertise on AOL and sell products in its online stores.

Figure 5-4
AOL outperformed its competition and became the number-one ISP.

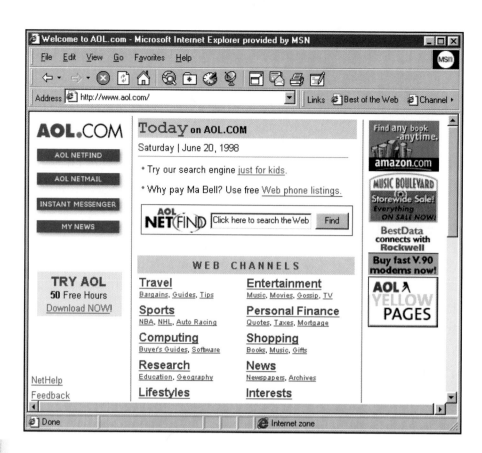

Just-in-Time Training

Identifying Audience and Purpose

1. Access your local Intranet or the Corporate View Web site.

2. In Chapter 2, you completed the CF4000/SE training scenario. You learned all about the product. You analyzed its strengths and weaknesses. With a team, you identified a problem with the phone, which has now been fixed. In this activity and the following one, your goal will be to acquaint the public with the newly improved product. Spend some time on the Intranet, reacquainting yourself with the phone product. Take a few notes.

Purpose

Record your answers to questions 3-11 in a word processing file.

3. Suppose you were writing a press release for a readership needing general information about the phone (for instance, a college student buying the CF4000/SE for personal use). What type of information would be useful to this reader?

4. Write a profile or description of this type of reader.

5. What would be the exact purpose for the press release as it relates to this group of readers?

6. Suppose you were writing a press release for a readership needing detailed information (for example, the manager of a pizza place near a college campus who thinks that giving digital phones to his drivers would make their jobs safer and help them stay in touch). What type of information would be useful to this reader?

7. Write a profile or description of this type of reader.

8. What would be the exact purpose for the press release as it relates to this type of reader?

9. Suppose you were writing a press release for a readership needing specific information (like an expert reviewer who would be comparing several similar phones in a magazine "round-up" article on digital phones. This could even be the reviewer from *Technophobia* magazine who reported problems with the phone in an earlier article). What type of information would be useful to this reader?

10. Write a profile or description of this type of reader.

11. What would be the exact purpose for the press release as it relates to this group of readers?

Technical Communications

Split Audiences

Writers of press releases frequently encounter split-audience problems. Although the public is often the main audience, the same press release may have several distinct audiences. For example, a CEO or an office supervisor might have to approve the release before it is issued. The editor of a newspaper or magazine also reviews a release before deciding whether to print it. Sometimes one part of the audience that reads the release is looking for general information, and another part of the audience is seeking more detailed information.

A split audience can present problems for a document writer. Which audience do you write your press release for? As a rule, you'll want to target your release to the audience that needs the information the most or the audience you are told to write for.

One often-used technique is to place the general information at the beginning of the press release and the details near the end. If you let your readers know that the details appear later in the document, people who need the more detailed information can read to the end to find it.

Debriefing

When writing a press release, always assume that your audience is capable and intelligent—but not versed in this subject. Assume that your reader will be interested in the information you are going to impart. Your job is to inform, not entertain—to help the audience understand your message as easily and as quickly as possible. Be careful not to "talk down" to your reader, making the reader feel you think he or she doesn't know anything about this or related topics.

Suppose you are asked to write a general information press release for the average customer, but you learn that some people with highly technical backgrounds are also going to read the release. Read Technical Communications Split Audiences to learn more about split-audience problems.

Think and write about the following:

1. Think about times you may have been talked down to. How did you react in such situations?

   _____

   _____

2. How can you write a press release that will satisfy both a general and a detail-oriented audience at the same time?

   _____

   _____

   _____

When drafting a press release, use an objective tone. This can be tricky because you're trying to present your product in the best light possible, but it can be done if you write your release carefully. A press release is a carefully written, informative document, not a place to praise your product with superlatives or unnecessary adjectives. Save that writing style for advertising copy. Never lose sight of the fact that the purpose of a press release is to inform, not to impress. One of your major targets is the press—a press that is objective or impartial in its writing. Objectivity is something editors will be looking for in your writing.

Unlike claims in advertising copy, in a press release, the writer has to be able to prove everything he or she says. It's best not to overstate or exaggerate, which is why we suggest you use an objective, journalistic style. Exaggerations can seriously damage your company's professional reputation. Your press release must remain credible—honest and down to earth.

Getting It Right

Look at several examples of exaggerated writing. Examine this sentence:

The XJK is the world's smallest and best personal computer.

This is a very difficult statement to prove. The sentence would be more effectively written like this:

The XJK is a high-tech computer the size of a matchbox.

Consider this example:

This is the clearest cell phone on the market.

Unless an impartial research laboratory presents documented proof that this is the clearest cell phone on the market, this sounds like advertising copy and is very difficult to prove. This sentence would be more effectively written like this:

This cell phone is six times clearer than the popular Tencon 387 model.

Here is another example:

The Navigator 12 is the most user-friendly ATM on the market today.

Keep your wording objective. This doesn't read like journalistic copy. This sentence would be more effectively written like this:

User-friendly features of the Navigator 12 ATM include... (list the features).

Writing Efficiently

Corporate Communications writers often work on several related press releases at once. For example, a writer might need to prepare several press releases on a given product for different audiences. A technique professionals use to save time in these situations is to use text from their earlier written works, altering it appropriately for a new audience, and using it again in another press release. You will practice this technique in this activity, using some of the text you write in the first press release to help you write the next two press releases.

Just-in-Time Training

Writing Related Press Releases

Press1

Press2

Press3

1. Write a general information press release about the CF4000/SE. Consider audience, purpose, personality, and length. Keep the press release between 90 and 150 words. Review your notes from Activities 5-1, 5-2, and 5-3 to help you complete your release. As you write, follow the guidelines in the Corporate View Style Guide.

2. Adapt the general press release you just wrote *(Press1)* into a detailed information press release. Don't start from scratch. Adapt your previous work and build upon it. Make this press release a little longer, between 100 and 180 words.

3. Adapt your detailed information press release *(Press2)* by modifying the purpose, personality, and length to communicate with an audience looking for specific information. You might be able to pick an issue from your detailed press release and expand on it. It could be how the phone was improved or one or two of its key features. Your release should be 100 words or more in length.

Debriefing

A press release is a short but important business document—one that corporations take seriously. On the surface, writing a press release doesn't seem that difficult. For your press release to be effective, however, you have to fine-tune your message, making sure you have the audience targeted and the exact purpose clearly identified. Perhaps the most difficult aspect of writing a press release is making the document clear and concise. The proper tone is absolutely essential.

Think and write about the following:

1. Consider yourself for a minute or two. How good are you at writing press releases? In answering this question, describe some writing strengths that helped you finish this activity successfully. Don't say anything negative about yourself. Think and write only about the positive!

_____

_____

_____

_____

_____

2. Explain some strategies you can use to get the media to take your press releases seriously.

_____

_____

_____

_____

_____

Chapter Review

Executive Summary

Corporate Communications is one of the most visible departments in any corporation. Corporations depend on information. The team responsible for distributing the appropriate information to all the important constituencies in a business is Corporate Communications.

Corporations often outsource much of their work. Tasks that can be outsourced include writing, translating, advertising, artwork, legal support, janitorial functions, and security services. Outsourcing can save the corporation money and still get the work done effectively.

Corporate Communications helps other mission-critical functions and departments prepare their communications. For example, a Corporate Communications coordinator or editor might edit a job description for Human Resources before it is posted on the World Wide Web. Corporate Communications can help the Marketing Department with an advertising campaign or complete the annual stockholders report for the Finance and Accounting Department.

One important communications task for which Corporate Communications is directly responsible is the preparation of press releases. A press release is a short document about some newsworthy subject prepared for the media. Press releases can be designed to provide general information, detailed information, or specific information.

Technical Communications

When preparing a press release, the writer must consider four elements: audience, purpose, personality, and length of the release. The audience can include people looking for general, detailed, and specific information. The purpose is to share information in a positive way. Most press releases are written in a factual, objective manner that portrays the company in a positive light. Short sentences and short paragraphs are the norm for press releases.

Generally, Corporate Communications prepares a style guide that provides guidelines for press releases and other company documents, such as memos, letters, and reports. These guidelines may be posted on the corporate Intranet.

Here are some messages that need to be answered by someone in Corporate Communications—perhaps an intern like you. Answer these messages with the help of the Intranet using your own best judgment. If you need help preparing these documents, access the **_Style Guide_** from the **_Corporate Communications_** page.

Save As:

Inbox5A

Outsource Services International

23 Prospect Avenue
Princeton, NJ 08542-9123
609-555-0102/FAX 609-555-0104

Current Date

Ms. Maria Bravo
Communications Coordinator
Corporate View
One Corporate View Drive
Boulder, CO 80303-0103

Dear Ms. Bravo:

Do you need expert help with writing corporate communications? For ten years, Outsource Services International has been providing writing and documentation services, including translation services, for companies with international markets such as Corporate View. Our translators are business professionals proficient in Spanish, German, and other languages. Our writing staff is expert at producing press releases, job descriptions, and other business documents.

Outsource Services International specializes in product documentation. Our technical writers work with your staff to produce clear, well-written, and accurate documentation in many languages.

Please contact me if we can be of assistance to you in meeting your corporate communications outsourcing needs.

Sincerely,

Ms. Astrid Frankle

Ms. Astrid Frankle

Intern,

Please prepare a letter in reply for my review and signature, giving Ms. Frankle some information about Corporate View. She seems to have the kind of credentials we are looking for to expand our European operations. Address outsourcing opportunities in the areas I've highlighted.

Thanks,
Maria

CORPORATE VIEW

From the Desk of Maria Bravo...

Dear Intern:

We've received an email from Steppen Abitbol, a strategic marketing manager for a large retail store chain. He wants information about the CT4000/ST student bundle that he can share with prospective customers. Please write a press release we can FAX to him. I think something general would be in order. Dust off some previous work, make any necessary adjustments, and get it to me. Don't spend all day on this one.

Thanks,
Maria

Voice Mail

Hi, this is Maria. We have had a request for a press release from Technophobia *magazine providing general information about Corporate View and specifically about the TeleView division. I don't like any of the press releases we have in our archive. You know how picky* Technophobia *editors can be. If they see any weakness, however small, they will report it. Can you put a new press release together for us? The first part needs to give general information about Corporate View. I think it should include information about the Research Park here as well. The second part should provide more specific details about the TeleView division. Get me your draft ASAP, and I will give it to Stephanie for editing.*
Thanks for your help. Bye.

> **TO:** Intern
> **FROM:** *rmills@corpview.com*
> **SUBJECT:** Job Description
> **MESSAGE:**
> _____
>
> Our department has created a position for a
> press release writer. Maria suggested that I
> ask you to put together a job description for
> this position. Please email the job description
> to me within 24 hours. I need to fill this
> position quickly. Are you interested in
> applying?
>
>
> Thanks,
> Robin

Online Business Trends

Access the Corporate View Web site. Use the **Stock Watcher Links** on the **Regular Features** page to identify the following ticker symbols and learn how each of these companies did in the stock market today.

Current Date _____

Ticker	Exchange	Company Name	Current Price
TWX	NYSE	_____	_____
AOL	NYSE	_____	_____

When a Few Words Will Do

Answer the following questions using what you have learned reading the Business Milestones, Technical Communications, and The Least You Should Know About... reports. Use 25 to 50 words to write your answers in a word processing document.

1. Name five Time Warner strategic business units.

2. American Online is the world's largest ISP. What is an ISP? Can you name some ISPs that compete with AOL? How does AOL stay on top?

3. What are some problems associated with a split audience, and how can you overcome them?

4. What are some pros and cons of using push technology to send information to customers?

5. Why has outsourcing become so popular? Describe outsourcing and list some reasons why corporations use outsourcing.

Save As:

Online5

Portfolio-Building Project

Press Releases for an Online World

Select a product that interests you that could be sold by one of the strategic business units of Corporate View. For example, RetailView might want to introduce a new brand of jeans. MediView could come up with a new and more competitive brand of headache medicine. TravelView might launch a new package tour to the Mexican coast.

Write a press release announcing the product you've selected as if it were being released to the market for the first time. Write a general press release for the average consumer. Follow the guidelines for writing and formatting press releases given in the Corporate View Intranet Style Guide. Spell-check and save your press release before you print or share it, and remember to proofread.

Save As:

Pfolio5

High-Performance Workgroup Project

You have now completed six press releases—three in Activity 5-4, another two in The Corporate Inbox, and one in the Portfolio-Building Project. You've gotten pretty good at this kind of writing. But what do your team members think of your work?

At Corporate View, every press release goes through the Corporate Communications editorial loop. Usually, an editorial team is assigned to review each press release. Because nearly everyone in CC is a trained writer, employees there often pass their work around the department for editing and feedback.

1. Form a team with three or four coworkers. Together, review the press release you prepared in the Portfolio-Building Project. Be ready for some constructive criticism of your work. Evaluate and take notes on the following:

   • **Audience:** Is the press release appropriate for the audience?

- **Purpose:** Is the purpose of the press release clear to the reader?

- **Personality:** Does the press release have a factual style and objective tone while conveying a positive image of the corporation?

- **Length:** Are the sentences and paragraphs generally short, as recommended in the Corporate View Style Guide?

2. Review your notes. Make the changes suggested by your team that you think will improve your work.

3. Proofread your press release and save it, using a new name.

HP5

Thinking and Writing About Your Business

The role of a Corporate Communications Department is flexible. The department can grow or shrink, depending on the requirements placed on it by Management. Below is a list of other mission-critical functions. Brainstorm specific jobs that Corporate Communications personnel can do for each of these departments. Record your answers of 25 to 50 words in a word processing document.

1. Human Resources

2. Research and Development

3. Marketing, Sales, and Customer Support

4. Finance and Accounting

5. Legal Services

6. Information Technology

Think5

Overtime

Sizing Up the Competition

In this activity, you will search for and critique press releases from large corporations. To save time, work with several other employees as a team.

1. Search for press releases from several corporations. Using your search engine, enter the search words *press releases* followed by the name of a major corporation. Links to some large corporations can be found on

the Corporate View Web site. Click on the **_Human Resources & Management_** link on the Corporate View Intranet Home page and choose **_Competitive Job Employment Listings_**. Once you reach the company's Web site, look for press releases.

2. Critique several press releases. Do they follow a pattern? Are they effectively written? What kinds of releases are they—general, detailed, or specific?

3. Of all the press releases you find, select the one you consider the most effective. Write 50 words or so on why you think it is so effective.

Otime5

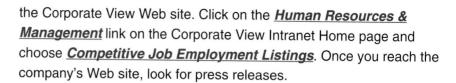

Applications to Small Business

Company Communications

A large business often has an entire Corporate Communications Department devoted to promoting the company image, products, and services; keeping employees informed about company issues; and assisting other departments with their communications needs. A small company, however, might not be able to support an entire department, or even one employee, devoted exclusively to these tasks.

Think and write about the following:

1. In a small company without a Corporate Communications Department, who is likely to be in charge of final approval for press releases?

2. If you work in a small company and must prepare a press release, whom can you ask for help in critiquing or proofreading your work?

3. How might the tone or personality of a press release from a small company differ from that of one released by a large corporation?

ASB5

4. What might be some advantages to oursourcing the writing of press releases, advertising copy, or Web pages for a small company? What might be some disadvantages?

Access the Corporate View Web site and take the Online Evaluation for this chapter.

1. Click on the ***Employee Training and Evaluations*** link on the ***Regular Features*** page.

2. Select the ***Online Tests*** link. (You must be a registered user to access the online tests. If you are not a registered user, click the ***Register*** link and follow the instructions on the screen. Then click the ***Online Tests*** link to return to the Online Tests page.)

3. Choose the ***Chapter 5 A View from Corporate Communications*** link on the Online Tests page.

4. Enter the username and password you selected when you registered.

5. Take the test. Click the **First**, **Back**, **Next**, and **Last** buttons to navigate through the questions. Click the **Finish** button to submit your test for grading. If you wish to close the test without submitting it for grading, click the **Cancel** button. Any answers you have entered will be lost if you cancel the test.

Chapter 6

A View from Research and Development

It's Not a Bug; It's a Feature

"How are you doing? My name is David Wu. Please call me Dave. I head up R&D for Corporate View's TeleView division.

"Welcome to the Corporate View **Research Park** facility. We're pretty informal around here. Every day is dress-down Friday. We don't have a lot of face-to-face contact with individuals outside the Research Park—and the people we do keep in contact with aren't concerned about outward appearance—so we dress informally.

"Research and Development is primarily concerned with new products and with enhancements or innovations for existing products. Occasionally, a product is uniquely ours, but often it's technology available in other forms that we've improved upon or modified in some way.

"Let's use the example of TeleView's series CF4000/SE digital phones, which went to market last year. We didn't invent the idea of digital wireless communication—it's actually a combination of several distinct technologies—but we developed the capacity to boost the signal reception area while lowering the cost to consumers.

"Our job is to stay ahead of the competition in terms of innovation and new products. Our goal is to be the company with the most advanced products in the consumer market.

"As soon as we introduce a product, some other company will buy it, *reverse-engineer* it (figure out how we created it), and manufacture a cheaper version of it in about six to ten months. Even if that's illegal, the courts are often too slow to be an effective deterrent. The best thing to do is stay ahead of the pack technologically.

"This means we have to look ahead and try to predict what the consumer will need in one year, in three years, in ten years. We have to look at where technology is taking us and couple that insight with customer needs and demands.

"In one sense, Research and Development is the heart of Corporate View. Without exciting, innovative products continually being introduced to the market, Corporate View would soon wither and die.

"Research and development can be very expensive. Therefore, we have to use our research dollars effectively. One way to do this is to share ideas among research teams. For instance, the research we do for TeleView may have applications for other products in other business units of Corporate View. To avoid duplication of effort, Corporate View keeps its research teams together at the Corporate View Research Park.

"While Corporate View concentrates its R&D teams in one location, some companies follow a different strategy, placing research facilities around the world.

"There is a lot of research to be done. Here at the Research Park, we are free to find out what customers want and to build customer-driven, marketable products."

Market-Driven, Cooperative Research

"It's one thing to think of neat products; it's another thing to think of neat products people will buy. We work closely with Marketing and Sales to help determine how well our proposed products will be received by consumers. If it's not a marketable idea, we put it on the shelf.

"Here's an example. Last year, one of our TeleView research product teams was working on design specs for a pair of glasses that could interface with a personal computer. Sensors embedded in the eyewear could read and respond to various eye movements.

"The thinking was that quadriplegics or people without the use of their hands could operate a computer with this kind of interface instead of a mouse and keyboard.

"Marketing pulled the plug on the idea—and rightly so. Their surveys and research indicated that *speech-recognition software* might make the eyeglass interface unmarketable for several more years by reducing the total number of potential customers. Everything we develop has to be marketable, or we're just spinning our wheels. This is what we mean when we say we are *market-driven*.

"We were in the break room, lamenting about having to kill this particular research project, just as one of the **Virtual Reality (VR)** games research team members was grabbing a jelly donut. She heard what we were saying and asked to see our **prototypes**. A few days later, we gave our research and prototypes to the VR games team. They continued to work on the technology and created some great VR game products. Later, when it was proven that voice and VR technology can work together, we borrowed the improvements from the games workgroup and modified the concept further. They learned from us; we learned from them. This is called *synergy*. This kind of exchange would not have happened if we weren't together at the Research Park."

The **Least** You **Should** Know About...

Strategic Market Research

Strategic markets can be described as integrated systems that share common market characteristics. For example, the medical profession has one set of needs; the telecommunications industry has a very different set of needs. Although there is some overlap in what products both markets may buy, like computers, for the most part corporations must adopt very different strategies to sell to each of these markets.

For example, making a telephony system compliant with **FCC (Federal Communications Commission)** regulations is important for the telecommunications market. The medical market is more concerned about getting **FDA (Food and Drug Administration)** approval for certain prescription drugs than it ever will be about wireless communications. Each market requires a different strategy, a different way of thinking, and unique products and services. Just as foreign markets require localization, these strategic markets require the customization of products to fit their specific needs.

Corporate View's strategic business units (SBUs) were created to meet the demands of key strategic markets.

- TeleView: Telephony, Electronics, and Computers Business Unit

- RetailView: Retail Consumer Products Business Unit specializing in sports equipment and sports apparel

- MoneyView: Banking, Insurance, and Financial Business Unit

- MediView: Medical and Pharmaceutical Business Unit

- PublishView: Online Publishing Business Unit

- TravelView: Travel and Vacation Business Unit

Business units can be wholly owned subsidiaries or divisions that are relatively separate and independent from each other. One advantage of a large corporation like Corporate View is that research from one business unit, designed to meet the needs of a strategic market, may also have applications in a different strategic business unit.

For example, computer technology developed at the Research Park for the TeleView business unit may have applications in the games division of the RetailView consumer products business unit. A laser process developed at TeleView could find its way into the manufacturing process for the next line of sports clothing or sporting goods sold in retail stores across North America, Asia, South America, and Europe through RetailView.

Three Phases of Research

"At the Corporate View Research Park, R&D is divided into three phases. Some of our people work in all three phases; some work in one or two. It depends on the individual.

"The first phase involves thinking and dreaming. The people on a 'phase-one team' tend to be the technicians, computer programmers, and engineers. They work in a ***think-tank*** atmosphere where new things are discussed—where they try to come up with things nobody has ever thought of before. Working on this team can be a lot of fun. Out of a hundred wild ideas, maybe five will be technologically feasible. A lot of talk, a lot of consulting, and a lot of research go into weeding out those five ideas.

"The second phase involves prototyping. The folks on a 'phase-two team' are a little more down to earth. They have a great deal of technical knowledge, and they know how to turn good ideas into workable designs and functioning prototypes.

"In the second phase, researchers spend a good part of their day keeping up-to-date on the latest technology trends, techniques, innovations, and research being conducted. Some information comes from private institutions, but a lot of it comes from universities in different parts of the world. We use the Internet to communicate with partners and contacts around the globe. That's what the Internet was built for, after all.

"Phase three involves product testing. Members of a 'phase-three team' enjoy interacting with other people as a part of testing the new product. Once we have a good working prototype, called a *beta model*, we can subject it to various kinds of tests to find bugs in the programming, flaws in the design, structural weaknesses, or other problems. Often members on this team are communicating directly with *beta testers* on the outside who are trying out the new product."

Types of Testing

"There are many ways to test a product. Four common testing methods used in corporate research and development are

- ***Usability testing***
- Product safety testing
- Consumer quality or comparative value testing
- ***Beta testing***

"Corporate View relies heavily on usability testing. We have an entire lab dedicated to it. In that lab, cameras, computers, and sensors track every movement a person makes as she or he uses one of our prototypes. Usability testing is fun to watch. It's where you first get a chance to see whether your products are really as good as you hope they are.

"We also do product safety testing. You've heard of the **UL (Underwriters Laboratories Inc.)** label? UL tests our products and helps us determine their safety and quality. UL acts as an outside consultant and gives us an independent view of our products' safety features.

"Consumer quality or comparative value testing is often conducted by other organizations like the Consumers Union, which publishes **Consumer Reports**. Its consumer tests compare products for quality, price, and customer satisfaction. Independent, outside opinions, like those found in *Consumer Reports*, are very helpful as we research improvements to our products. Other industry magazines, like *Technophobia,* also give us reviews.

"Not all reviews are favorable. We read industry reviews carefully and try not to make the same mistakes twice. You may have heard about the problems we had with the CF4000/SE that *Technophobia* hit on. We fixed the problems in the next version. So, even negative reviews can help improve products.

"Beta testing is also important. Testing begins as soon as we have a workable beta product. As problems with the beta model are corrected or as the product is modified or improved, beta testing continues. Before we send a product to market, we test it with customers. They give us feedback. Hardware and software products can soak up a lot of person hours, so R&D outsources some of the work to labs that specialize in beta testing.

"I hope all of this didn't go *zip*...over your heads! We are often accused of being too technical when we talk to others. Enjoy your stint here. And remember, no matter what part of the corporation you end up working in, we all have a stake in the quality and testing of products coming out of R&D."

Activity Overviews

Many people think R&D is all about invention, high-tech computers, and chemistry experiments. And they are correct. Invention is at the heart of every R&D facility. But R&D today is much broader than that.

Did you know that:

- Tommy Hilfiger (NYSE:TOM), The Gap (NYSE:GPS), Mossimo (NYSE:MGX), Nautica (NASDAQ:NAUT), Nike (NYSE:NKE), and Reebok (NYSE:RBK) all have R&D Departments testing new products, materials, fabrics, colors, designs, and competitive trends?

- Banks, major stockbrokers, and insurance companies have research departments or hire research consulting firms to help them improve and expand their services to customers?

- Medical research laboratories and pharmaceutical companies are constantly researching new techniques, tools, and prescription drugs?

- Because of corporate research, computer processing speeds have doubled every 1.5 years for the last four decades?

The day a high-tech company—or any company for that matter—stops R&D is the day it decides to put itself out of business. In this training session, you will work in all three phases of research and development at Corporate View.

Activity 6-1 Strategic Market Research will allow you to explore R&D research efforts across a variety of strategic markets and strategic business units.

Activity 6-2 Reviewing Usability Reports will show you how usability studies are conducted and what a ***usability report*** contains. Later in this chapter, you will write your own usability report.

Activity 6-3 Conducting Usability Tests will put you in the role of the R&D researcher, learning how products can be made better through careful observation.

Activity 6-4 Writing Usability Reports will allow you to analyze how consumers use a product so that you can suggest improvements and capture a larger market share. You will put your observations in the form of a usability report.

Understanding the meanings of these terms will help you learn the concepts and develop the skills related to Research and Development covered in the chapter. In preparation for completing the chapter activities, access the Intranet and find the definition for each of these terms by clicking the ***ShopTalk*** link on the ***Regular Features*** page.

" *Corporate* **ShopTalk** "

- Affiliate
- Beta Testing
- *Consumer Reports*
- FCC (Federal Communications Commission)
- FDA (Food and Drug Administration)
- Fieldwork
- Market-Driven
- Prototype
- Research Park
- Reverse-Engineer
- Speech-Recognition Software
- Strategic Markets
- Think-Tank
- UL (Underwriters Laboratories Inc.)
- Usability Report
- Usability Testing
- Virtual Reality (VR)

Activity 6-1 — Strategic Market Research

TeleView spends most of its R&D dollars on telephony-based electronics equipment. Other Corporate View SBUs have R&D efforts aimed at a variety of strategic industries or strategic markets:

- **TeleView:** Telephony products, electronics, and computers
- **RetailView:** Sporting goods and sports apparel
- **MoneyView:** Banking, insurance, and financial services
- **MediView:** Medical supplies and pharmaceuticals
- **PublishView:** Online publishing materials
- **TravelView:** Travel and tourism packages

Each of these industries is considered a strategic market. That is, the banking industry is different from the medical industry. Clothing products are very different from computers. Banking services are very different from medical devices. If you were designing products for these unique markets, they would be very different.

Business Milestones

AT&T's Bell Labs

In addition to improving the basic telephone invented by Alexander Graham Bell in 1887, AT&T is responsible for such technological break-throughs as the first FAX machine in 1924 and the first electrical digital computer in 1937. In 1947, three AT&T Labs researchers shared a Nobel Prize for inventing the transistor, a small electronic component that made the current information age possible and was the forerunner of today's silicon chip.

In 1951, AT&T Labs devised the technologies that allow you to make a long-distance call by dialing direct. The company also made low-cost transoceanic calls possible. In the 1950s, AT&T discovered how to convert sunlight into usable energy. Every time you use your solar calculator, you can thank AT&T.

In the 1960s, AT&T pioneered the Touch-Tone phone and the UNIX operating system and created the core technologies and telecommunications systems supporting the Internet, then in its infancy.

In the 1970s, things didn't slow down. AT&T improved "picturephone" computer technology and fiber optics. In the 1980s, the company pioneered cell phones and the C++ programming language. C++ popularized object-oriented programming and forms the basis of Java, the programming language of the Internet. At the end of the decade, AT&T was experimenting with HDTV (high-definition television).

With the reorganization of AT&T Labs and the emergence of Lucent Technologies, the corporation seems ready for yet another period of outstanding R&D. See for yourself by visiting **www.att.com*** and looking for the **AT&T Labs** link, or visit Lucent Technologies at **www.lucent.com**.

*AT&T Welcome Page. *AT&T*. Online. Available: **www.att.com**. February 13, 1998.

174   *Chapter 6*   *A View from Research and Development*

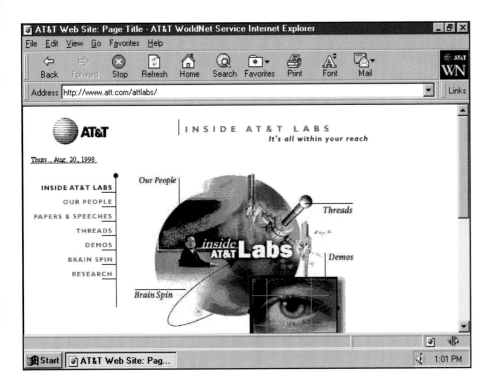

Each strategic market requires its own special kind of research and product development. Regardless of the strategic market, however, research at Corporate View is divided into three phases:

Phase 1: Envisioning (thinking of products that people will want to buy)

Phase 2: Designing and prototyping (designing and building quality products)

Phase 3: Product testing (testing products for safety, durability, and other qualities before they go to market)

In this session, you will be a part of a think-tank, where the invention or envisioning process begins.

Just-in-Time Training

Strategic Market Think-Tanks

1. Access the local Intranet or the Corporate View Web site.
2. Select the ***Research & Development*** link from the Corporate View Intranet Home page. Read ***About Research and Development***.

3. Write a 25-word description in your own words of what R&D is all about.

   _____
   _____
   _____
   _____
   _____

4. Choose three Corporate View SBUs from the list in the Activity Overviews. In a word processing file, list each of the three SBUs. Under each SBU, create a list of five new products that could be researched and developed by Corporate View's R&D workgroup responsible for the SBU's strategic market. (Assume that any products not generally available in the real world are also not marketed by the SBU.) Briefly describe what makes each product new or different.

Save As:

Prodlis

Debriefing

The main goal of R&D in corporations is to create marketable products. Therefore, all research is guided, at least in part, by the need to make a profit. Return to the lists of new product ideas you just created. Choose the five products you think most clearly meet the following subjective criteria:

- The product can be researched and made marketable for under $100,000.

- The product can be sold at a list price of $30 to $50.

- More than 50,000 units of this product can be sold every year.

Rank the five products below, with the product most likely to meet these criteria in the number-one position.

1. _____
2. _____
3. _____
4. _____
5. _____

To paraphrase a famous quote, R&D is 1 percent inspiration and 99 percent perspiration. After products have been envisioned, it still takes a lot of research and testing to develop them. One aspect of R&D that requires lots of work is product testing. Product testing is essential if customers are to be satisfied. Four common kinds of testing are

- Usability testing
- Product safety testing
- Consumer quality or comparative value testing
- Beta testing

The following story from Dave Wu illustrates the value of one of these kinds of testing—usability testing:

The average consumer has no idea of the extensive research that led to the development of viable speech-recognition software. It was expensive research conducted by many corporations and smaller businesses. To keep the cost down so consumers could afford this new technology, inexpensive headsets with three- to four-foot-long cables were packaged with the software.

We ran these headsets through usability testing. We set up desks, very similar to what you would find in a home office or in a typical cubicle in an average corporation.

We quickly learned that the microphone cord became entangled with the mouse cord and other cords attached to the computer. On the desktop in a busy office, objects like staplers, reports, or reference books wound up stacked on the cord. On one desk, the phone cord became so entangled in the headset cable that it took more than ten minutes to unravel them.

Additionally, users wanted to move around their offices as they dictated, but the cord was usually too short. In some instances, the cord was stretched to its limit and the headset fell off the user's head. The cord would get caught underneath people's elbows and often was knocked off the desktop and fell on the floor. In short, the headset was annoying.

As a result of this rather simple usability study, we began re-searching some of the first wireless dictation headsets in the industry. This type of headset was more expensive, but usability tests told us it was a much better product to use. We thought that consumers would pay extra for this added convenience.

Usability testing helped us discover the need to reduce microphone noise and increase the dictation range from 20 to 30 feet. This way, people could dictate while they were watering their plants or looking up facts in reference books on the other side of their offices. One home office usability test had a user cooking dinner while dictating letters into a speech-recognition program running on a computer located in another room.

Business Milestones

This story helps demonstrate how even the simplest usability test can lead to new products and innovations.

Underwriters Laboratories Inc.—Over a Century of Public Safety

Underwriters Laboratories Inc. (UL) is an independent, nonprofit organization devoted to product safety testing. A goal of UL, which was founded in 1894, is to increase public safety. UL has developed a unique system of voluntary testing for possible defects and safety risks, which now extends across the world.

UL is an impartial organization that evaluates products from more than 40,000 manufacturers around the world. Its laboratories, strategically located worldwide, conduct well over 75,000 product investigations and safety tests for more than 16,500 products every year. UL subsidiaries and *affiliates* are located in Mexico, Japan, Hong Kong, Korea, Singapore, Taiwan, Denmark, England, and Canada.

The UL mark is important. For example, a corporation like Corporate View will seek the UL seal of approval for many of its products. Consumers and retail stores depend on UL safety tests. In the interest of consumer safety, many retail stores will not carry certain products unless they have the Underwriters Laboratories seal or a similar independent assurance of safety. Therefore, if Corporate View wants to sell such products, it should submit them to UL for review against UL's published safety standards.

To learn more, visit UL at ***www.ul.com***.

Figure 6-2
UL provides safety testing for consumer products.

Just-in-Time Training

Inside Usability Reports

1. Access your local Intranet or the Corporate View Web site.
2. Select the ***Research & Development*** link from the Corporate View Intranet Home page.

3. Click the **_Teleview_** link and read the **_Voice Dictation Headset (Model CF85/Voice) Usability Report_**.

4. Identify the six parts of the usability report.

_____

_____

_____

_____

_____

_____

Save As:

Usesum

5. In a word processing file, summarize the usability report in 50 to 100 words.

6. Who do you think might be the audience for this report?

_____

_____

_____

7. How would you define or describe the personality or style of writing of this usability report?

_____

_____

_____

_____

_____

Figure 6-3
The UL seal assures customers that a product has passed UL safety tests.

The **Least** You **Should** Know **About...**

Underwriters Laboratories and Product Safety Testing

Underwriters Laboratories Inc. specializes in testing the safety of products. UL has top engineers testing products in a variety of settings, labs, and onsite evaluations. When a product passes UL's rigorous examination, the product can carry the UL seal. This mark is seen on all sorts of products, including:

- Household appliances
- Computer equipment
- Furnaces and heaters
- Electrical equipment
- Fire detectors and fire extinguishers
- Life vests and buoyant immersion suits
- Children's toys
- Smoke detectors
- Water additives and treatment chemicals
- Food preparation equipment for fast-food restaurants
- Building materials

Safety testing adds value to products. The UL mark inspires confidence in consumers and demonstrates the willingness of a corporation to stand by its products.*

*Underwriters Laboratories Inc. Home Page. _Underwriters Laboratories Inc._ Online. Avaliable: **_www.ul.com_**. February 4, 1998.

Usability reports fall into the category of in-house or private documents. They aren't meant for outside consumption. Thus, the audience for a usability study is not the same as the audience for a press release. A press release is meant for an audience outside the corporation; it is an outside or public document.

Think and write about the following:

Consider the similarities and differences between press releases and usability reports. Compare the personalities or styles of the press releases you wrote in Chapter 5 with the usability report you just read.

1. How are they different?

_____

_____

_____

_____

2. How are they similar?

_____

_____

_____

_____

In this exercise, you will conduct your own usability research. Usability testing can be carried out in labs or in situations where the product is to be used. Observing how products are used in true-to-life situations is often called *fieldwork.*

You may associate fieldwork with watching birds in the Amazon jungle for a *National Geographic* special, but fieldwork is conducted extensively in business, as well as in science. Fieldwork is performed on the job, in homes, at schools—wherever the product being tested is going to be used.

In this activity, you will choose a product and observe at least one person using it. Find out what people do with the product and discover what problems they have. Choose any product you wish. For instance:

- *Software or video game:* Observe participants using an applications program or playing a video game for the first time. Take notes on how they learn. Which parts are easy to learn? Which are difficult to learn?

- *Exercise or sports equipment*: Observe participants using a new piece of exercise or sports equipment. How do they learn to use the equipment? If it has a high-tech, computerized monitoring system, how comfortable are participants with the system? How long does it take them to become proficient with the equipment?

- *Clothing accessory*: Investigate the ease of use and functionality of a purse, bag, jewelry clasp, barrette, scrunchy, watch, scarf, crimp, pair of gloves, hat, ribbon, bandy, or headband. How user-friendly is this accessory?

- *Fast-food restaurant equipment:* View participants as they use a piece of equipment at a fast-food restaurant. Can you think of any ways to improve the equipment or increase efficiency?

The **Least** You **Should** Know **About...**

Keeping Your Notes

Some organizations require employees to keep their notes for several years after a report has been completed. Being able to refer to the original notes on a project helps in the analysis of results and allows others to reproduce your methods if they wish. You might also need to return to your data to defend the company in a legal challenge. So don't throw those notes away!

Because some notes are so important, many business people keep a legal-style ledger or notebook planner in which they write their day-to-day observations. They include the dates of observations and the time of day. They include the names of those present at the time of the observations. These notes become an ongoing record of how the conclusions were drawn. They become, in a sense, a legal document if someone should ever wish to question the results in court.

When you are dealing with products worth millions and millions of dollars, it is important to keep good notes.

- *Car or sport utility vehicle (SUV):* Watch participants learn to use the controls of a car or SUV for the first time. How ergonomically efficient are all the controls? How easy is it to use all the controls and still maintain control of the vehicle?

- *Home electronics product:* Watch participants as they read the installation instructions and attempt to use a DVD player, CD player, VCR, or boom box. Are any procedures unclear?

- *Digital phone:* Watch as participants try to program their digital phones. Have them read the instructions and see whether they can follow them. Are the instructions clearly written? Can users follow the instructions?

- *Speech-recognition software:* Observe people trying to use speech-recognition software to dictate a letter for the first time. What, if any, problems do they encounter?

- *The Corporate View Intranet:* Watch carefully as participants use the Corporate View Intranet for the first time. Do they have any difficulties? If so, what are they?

Technical
Communications

Note Taking

There are two schools of thought about observational note taking. The first school would have you record every detail, everything that happens, no matter how insignificant it might seem at the time. With this kind of note taking, you will then need to go back to your computer and organize the observations you made into important categories. After you have reviewed your notes, specific patterns will emerge. These patterns will become the basis for the conclusions you draw in your usability report.

Another school of thought takes a slightly different angle. Michael Agar, a professor of anthropology at the University of Maryland, very astutely points out the need for focus in taking notes:

Field notes, then, are a problem. In their worst form, they are an attempt to vacuum up everything possible, either interrupting your observation to do so or distorting the results when retrieving them from the long-term memory. Not that you shouldn't keep notes, but they should be more focused in topic... (Agar, p. 113)*

Using this method, you would only take notes on the particular areas you are interested in. You would focus your note taking on specific observations, not on trying to document every event you observe.

It is difficult to decide which approach to take. Do you write down everything you see, however insignificant, or do you focus on just those things that seem to make a difference in what you are trying to learn? You might find it advantageous to try both methods and find your own balance between the two methods. What cannot be disputed, however, is the need for accurate and descriptive notes.

*Agar, M. H. (1980). *The Professional Stranger*. New York: Academic Press.

Figure 6-4
Taking good field notes is an essential part of the usability research process.

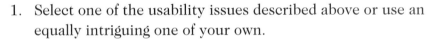

Just-in-Time Training

Performing a Field Study

1. Select one of the usability issues described above or use an equally intriguing one of your own.

2. Observe carefully as someone uses the product.

3. Take many detailed notes. (See Technical Communications Note Taking.)

4. Try to get other participants to try the product as well. Watch them while you continue to take notes. The more observations you can make and the more participants you use, the more representative and reliable your notes will be.

5. Go to your computer and organize your notes. Create three to five main categories. For example, if you were observing the use of a new piece of software, you could have categories such as

   - Launching the software
   - Opening files
   - Saving files
   - Using the mouse
   - Exiting the software

If you are observing how firefighters use a fire hydrant, you might have these categories:

- Location of the fire hydrant for firefighter access
- Connecting to the fire hydrant
- Reliability of the fire hydrant
- Disconnecting from the fire hydrant

Save As:

Rptnts

6. Organize your notes under your categories. Write key observations or summary points. Reference your notes by page number to indicate where more details can be found.

Debriefing

During the fieldwork part of usability testing, you make observations while taking notes. Fieldwork is fun. In the field, you learn all sorts of things you can't really learn in books, in the lab, or from any other source. The next stage, forming conclusions, requires a little more nose-to-the-grindstone effort. But first, one additional step can't be forgotten: validation of your results by questioning your participants.

You may need to ask very specific questions. In this case, you want to learn your participants' thoughts about the product. Remember that they see the experience from a different perspective. Their perspective may be more accurate than your own. For example, compare the view a football player on the field has with the view a sportscaster has from high atop the stadium in the press box.

After observations are complete, a researcher will ask the subjects testing the products a set of prepared questions in the form of an exit interview to gain a user's perspective. The exact questions researchers ask vary. Here are a few sample questions:

- What did you like or dislike about the product?
- What did you learn about the product?
- What did you not understand about the product?
- How would you describe your experience?
- What would you change about the product you are testing?

Think and write about the following:

1. Write three to five questions you should ask your participants.

   _____

   _____

   _____

   _____

   _____

2. Ask your questions. Record your participants' responses on a separate sheet of paper. What new information did you gain by formulating and asking good questions?

   _____

   _____

Business Milestones

Consumer Reports

Probably the most influential consumer product magazine ever published is *Consumer Reports*. *Consumer Reports* provides independent reviews and comparisons of a wide variety of products as diverse as cars, computers, CD players, and kitchen sinks. *Consumer Reports* examines the quality of these products and provides comparative value analysis.

Consumer Reports has gone online with a Webzine called *Consumer Reports Online*. The online service requires the payment of a subscription fee. This makes sense because *Consumer Reports* does not accept advertising. The editors of *Consumer Reports* think that advertising might bias their product evaluations. *Consumer Reports* works hard to be as fair and as unbiased as it can be.

Consumer Reports can make or break a product. An unfavorable review in *Consumer Reports* can cripple sales. A favorable review can greatly increase sales. Other magazines also review products, but few enjoy the consumer loyalty of *Consumer Reports*.

Learn more about *Consumer Reports* at **www.consumerreports.org**.*

*Welcome to Consumer Reports. *Consumer Reports*. Online. Available: **www.consumerreports.org**. February 4, 1998.

Activity 6-4   *Writing Usability Reports*

Field and lab work can lead to a pile of interesting notes and pieces of information. But it requires a little more work to take the research data and turn them into something useful to the corporation.

The end result of a usability study is the usability report. In this activity, you will write a usability report based on the data you collected in Activity 6-3.

A usability report has six parts:

1. *Overview and Scope:* A brief statement explaining why the usability study was conducted.

2. *Product Description:* A brief description of the product being reviewed.

3. *Testing Environment:* A description of the testing situation or environment, along with a brief description of the subjects who tested the product.

4. *Observations Summary:* A summary in the form of a step-by-step description of all the observations that were made.

5. *Exit Interview Summary:* The questions asked and a summary of the comments given by the subjects in an exit interview after the testing has been completed.

6. *Conclusions and Recommendations:* Conclusions from the researchers about the product and how it can be improved.

Figure 6-5
Thomas Edison

Business
Milestones

The Menlo Park Experience

Thomas Alva Edison was born in 1847 in Ohio. At the time of his death in 1931, he held 1,093 patents, the most by any individual.

One of Edison's research facilities was in Menlo Park, New Jersey. There, Edison pioneered the modern industrial research lab and earned the title of the Wizard of Menlo Park.

Edison often worked up to 20 hours a day. He once said, "Genius is 1 percent inspiration and 99 percent perspiration." A team of talented assistants from around the world helped Edison translate his ideas into working devices.

Edison believed in inventing things that people wanted. To meet popular demand, these products had to be produced rapidly and cheaply. Some of his patents were for the phonograph, batteries, motion picture, typewriter, and telephone. He also invented or made improvements to electric meters, motors, and lights.

The final usability report is an important decision-oriented document. It will be used by executives in the corporation in deciding how to improve the product or even whether to continue offering it. Decisions made on the basis of a usability report can make or cost corporations millions of dollars. A usability report has to be clear, accurate, and well documented. It has to be reader-friendly and provide direction and suggestions for those in the corporation who must make decisions about the product.

Just-in-Time Training

Usability Reports with Style

1. Access the local Intranet or the Corporate View Web site.

2. Review the ***Voice Dictation Headset (Model CF85/Voice) Usability Report*** under the ***Research & Development***, ***TeleView*** links.

3. Close the report and access the ***Corporate Communications*** link.

4. Go to the ***Style Guide*** and click the ***Usability Reports*** link.

5. Read ***Writing Usability Reports*** and summarize the four elements presented there.

   Audience: _____

   _____

   _____

   Purpose: _____

   _____

   _____

   Personality: _____

   _____

   _____

   Length: _____

   _____

   _____

6. Return to the beginning of the ***Usability Reports*** page, select ***The Six Parts of a Usability Report***, and review each part.

7. In a word processing file, write your usability report based on the data you collected in Activity 6-3.

8. After you finish writing a first draft of your report, access the ***Style Guide*** and format your document according to the instructions found there.

Save As:

UR1

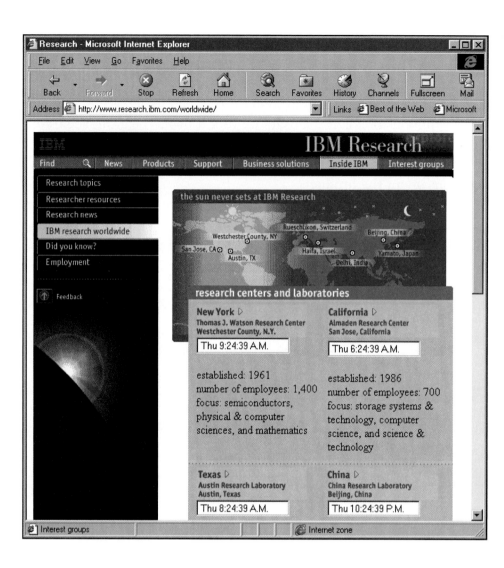

Business
Milestones

IBM's Research Facilities

IBM has many top research facilities around the world, including these:

- Thomas J. Watson Research Center, Westchester County, New York
- Almaden Research Center, San Jose, California
- Austin Research Laboratory, Austin, Texas
- China Research Laboratory, Beijing, China
- Haifa Research Laboratory, Haifa, Israel
- Tokyo Research Laboratory, Yamato, Japan
- Zurich Research Laboratory, Rueschlikon, Switzerland

These labs work on computers, semiconductors, databases, storage systems, design techniques, high-performance microprocessors, language and speech recognition, mathematics, multimedia, image technology, and manufacturing research.

Learn more about these R&D facilities on the IBM Web site. Search for IBM Research at ***www.ibm.com***.*

*IBM Research Home Page. *International Business Machines.* Online. Available: ***www.research.ibm.com/worldwide***. February 2, 1998.

After product testing is complete, another process takes over: the manufacturing process required to make products on a massive scale. For example, TeleView can make the best phone on the market, but if it costs over $1,000, no one will buy it. TeleView must find ways to reduce the cost of the phone and make it affordable to consumers. Many companies offer phones at very low prices with their calling plans. These corporations must count on selling lots of phones and calling packages to make a substantial profit.

The techniques you have learned for studying how a product is used and for determining how it can be improved can be applied to the manufacturing process as well. Making products efficiently requires specialized tools, specialized training, and streamlined techniques. Turning a $100,000 prototype into an inexpensive consumer product takes excellent planning, thinking, creativity, invention, and constantly improving manufacturing techniques.

Visit a manufacturing facility and observe the process used to create a product. (If you are not able to tour a facility, choose a product you have used and write to the product manufacturer.) Ask the manufacturer these questions and summarize the answers.

1. What type of research was done to aid in creating the manufacturing process for the product?

   _____

   _____

   _____

   _____

2. What improvements to the manufacturing process have you considered now that the process has been in place for a period of time?

   _____

   _____

   _____

   _____

3. Could any part or tool used in the manufacturing process benefit from a usability study?

   _____

   _____

Executive Summary

New products and services keep a corporation competitive. A corporation greatly values its R&D researchers because without them the company could fall behind in the race to stay competitive. R&D employees are responsible for creating new products and improving existing ones.

Three phases of research were presented in this chapter: envisioning, designing and prototyping, and product testing. Research is conducted for every strategic market a corporation has defined. Products vary a great deal among the various markets: Medical industry needs are very different from the needs of a bank or other financial institution. Retail consumer products, like clothing and accessories, are very different from high-tech telephony and computer products. Every market requires specialized research.

Many research organizations in corporations are market-driven. This means they try to focus their R&D on products that can eventually make profits for the corporations.

One important part of research is testing. There are many kinds of testing. Four testing methods commonly used in corporate R&D are usability testing, product safety testing, consumer quality or comparative value testing, and beta testing.

Many laboratories and organizations can help a corporation with its testing needs. One of the most important testing needs is product safety testing. Outside, third-party laboratories, like Underwriters Laboratories Inc., test products against published safety standards.

Many federal agencies are also important in the product testing process—for example, the Federal Communications Commission for telecommunications systems and the Food and Drug Administration for foods, cosmetics, medicines, medical devices, and radiation-emitting products.

Technical Communications

Usability research involves learning how a product is actually used by participants. Researchers test products, looking for ways to make them easier to use. A usability report consists of the purpose of the study; descriptions of the product, testing environment, and subjects; and summaries of the observations, exit interviews, and conclusions reached.

Here are some messages that need to be answered by someone in Research and Development. Answer them with the help of the Intranet and your own best judgment. If you need help preparing documents, access the **_Style Guide_**, under the **_Corporate Communications_** link.

TO: Intern
FROM: **_dwu@corpview.com_**
SUBJECT: Press Release
MESSAGE:

Maria Bravo in Corporate Communications just sent me an interesting email. Apparently, *Technophobia* magazine and several national prime-time news programs have launched a series of reports critical of product safety in the telephony industry. She wants us to make a statement in a press release about how we work with Underwriters Laboratories to guarantee the safety of our products. Please prepare a press release that explains UL's role in our product safety testing. She thinks this will help ensure that we don't lose any customers as a result of uninformed publicity. Please give the release to me to look over before we send it to Maria.

Thanks,
Dave

Voice Mail

Hi, this is Dave Wu. I need your help in responding to an inquiry I received regarding how government agencies affect research and development at TeleView. Basically, the researcher asked two questions: "With what government agencies, if any, does TeleView interact in product development? How do these agencies help or hinder your work?"
Of course, TeleView works with the FCC; and it is very helpful to us.
Please prepare a reply to the two questions and email it to me for review. Stress safety concerns. I know these questions are tough to answer.
Please keep our reply very formal.
Thanks. Bye.

Hi. This is Dave Wu. A new vice president, Mariette Taylor, just came to RetailView from Levi Strauss & Co. last week. She has heard a lot about our usability testing here at the Research Park. Please prepare a memo for Ms. Taylor, describing the process we go through, how we observe, how we take notes, the kinds of notes we take, and how we categorize our data. Also, let her know how we report our results. Explain the parts of a usability report and how it should be organized. Give me a draft of the memo before you send it, please.

Thanks,

Bye

Save As:

Inbox6C

CORPORATE VIEW

From the Desk of Melissa Kim...

Dear Intern:

We are going to create a new position in TeleView R&D. We need a full-time technical writer to write and edit usability studies. Can you prepare a job description for this job? Because you went through the usability process recently, I thought you might have the most insight as to what this job will require.

Please email the job description to me sometime today.

Thanks,
Melissa

Save As:

Inbox6D

Access the Corporate View Web site. Use the **Stock Watcher Links** on the **Regular Features** page to identify the following ticker symbols and learn how each of these companies did in the stock market today.

Current Date _____

Ticker	Exchange	Company Name	Current Price
IBM	NYSE	_____	_____
T	NYSE	_____	_____
TOM	NYSE	_____	_____
GPS	NYSE	_____	_____
MGX	NYSE	_____	_____
NAUT	NASDAQ	_____	_____
NKE	NYSE	_____	_____
RBK	NYSE	_____	_____

When a Few Words Will Do

According to what you have read in the Business Milestones, Technical Communications, and The Least You Should Know About... reports, answer the following questions in a word processing document.

1. Describe two different philosophies on note taking.

2. List five possible strategic markets.

3. Explain strategic marketing and how a corporation can adjust its R&D efforts to maximize profits in certain strategic industries.

4. What do you think are the advantages or disadvantages of a corporation having a central research facility, as opposed to spreading its research facilities around the world?

5. Why is it important for business researchers to keep good notes on the products they are working on?

6. Why are organizations like UL and Consumers Union (publisher of Consumer Reports) important to R&D divisions of major corporations?

7. Who was Thomas A. Edison, and why is he considered so important in the development of the modern corporate research facility?

Save As:

Online6

Portfolio-Building Project

Usability Reports for an Online World

Learning to write great usability reports takes practice. A good way to improve your report-writing skills is to read and consider successful usability reports written by others.

1. Borrow five or six usability reports from your workgroup team members and read them.

2. Discuss the reports with the authors for ideas.

3. Armed with this new information, edit the usability report you created in Activity 6-4. Improve how it reads. Try to say more in fewer words. Make your report as reader-friendly as you can. Review the information in the **_Usability Reports_** section of the Corporate View Style Guide about audience, purpose, personality, and length.

4. Spell-check your report before you print or share it, and remember to proofread.

Save As:

Pfolio6

High-Performance Workgroup Project

Working effectively in a group requires cooperation and mutual respect among all members of the workgroup. Does the way a person is dressed affect the respect or cooperation that person receives from others? You will explore this issue with your team members in this workgroup project.

David Wu made some very interesting comments in his opening remarks:

> *We're pretty informal around here. Every day is dress-down Friday. We don't have a lot of face-to-face contact with individuals outside the Research Park—and the people we do keep in contact with aren't concerned about outward appearance—so we dress informally.*

What should the corporate dress code be for employees? Dave has an obvious opinion about what the rules should be for people in R&D, but does his attitude apply to all company departments and positions? Do the clothes you wear really affect your performance on the job? Is there a need to dress for success?

1. Form a discussion group with three or four coworkers. Search the Internet or business magazines for articles on current trends in business dress. Summarize and share the articles with the workgroup.

2. Together, consider the dress standards that corporations should impose and discuss appropriate business dress options for people in the following positions:

- A Marketing manager for a new line of products

- A Corporate Communications senior coordinator

- A Human Resources benefits manager

- An accounts receivable associate in the Finance and Accounting Department

- A patent lawyer in Legal Services

- A team leader in the Manufacturing Department

- An administrative assistant in the R&D Department

3. Record the conclusions of the group in the form of a dress code for Corporate View. Submit your policy statement document as a team assignment.

Save As:

HP6

Thinking and Writing About Your Business

Based on what you have learned in this chapter, answer the following questions in your own words. Key your answers in a word processing document.

1. If you decide on a career in R&D, what kinds of research would you like to do?

2. Would your research interest be available in a corporate research lab, in a university, or in a public research environment?

3. What kinds of products would your research interest lead to?

Save As:

Think6

4. Name three corporations that might benefit from your research.

Overtime

SBU Competitors

An important part of any research effort is keeping up on the latest trends, new inventions, and progress of others around the world. The World Wide Web will help you stay informed, no matter what your job description might be. It is particularly valuable for researchers.

1. Access the Corporate View Web site.

2. Review the information provided for each SBU by clicking the appropriate link on the Corporate View Intranet Home page.

3. Choose three of the Corporate View SBUs and list them in a word processing file.

4. For each SBU you have selected, find two natural competitors or corporations on the Web that make similar products. List each of them under the appropriate SBU.

5. Examine the products of the competitors you have found. List several products under each competitor that Corporate View should be considering for research and development. List these products in bold in your notes.

6. Do you see any trends? Where are these other corporations spending their research dollars? For each competitor, summarize in your notes the areas in which you think they are spending most of their research money and energy.

7. Reference each competitor in your notes by recording the URL for each competitor's Web site you have included in this exercise. (Read ***Citing Electronic Sources*** on the Corporate View Style Guide for help with this step.)

8. Based on your research in steps 1 through 7, think of new products, enhancements to existing products, or research paths the R&D team in each SBU you selected should pursue to be competitive.

Save As:

Otime6

9. Write a memo to David Wu, summarizing your recommendations. Attach your notes in a separate document that Dave can refer to.

Applications to Small Business

Research and Development

How can small or home-based businesses compete with the well-financed R&D efforts of the Fortune 500? Well, they do every day. Smaller companies can compete if they focus on products or services they can afford to research, develop, manufacture/provide, and market.

Think and write about the following:

1. Choose a product or service you think a small business or a consultant who telecommutes from a home-based business can successfully develop. (Perhaps one of products you listed in the Debriefing in Activity 6-1.)

2. How much do you think it would cost to develop and bring this product or service to market?

3. How long do you think it would take to develop the product or service from R&D to the point of sale—that is, to the time customers actually buy it?

4. How would a small business be able to test its products like the big companies? List the four types of testing discussed in this chapter and give your ideas on how a small company could accomplish these tests.

Save As:

ASB6

Online Evaluation

Access the Corporate View Web site and take the Online Evaluation for this chapter.

1. Click on the ***Employee Training and Evaluations*** link on the ***Regular Features*** page.

2. Select the ***Online Tests*** link. (You must be a registered user to access the online tests. If you are not a registered user, click the ***Register*** link and follow the instructions on the screen. Then click the ***Online Tests*** link to return to the Online Tests page.)

3. Choose the ***Chapter 6 A View from Research and Development*** link on the Online Tests page.

4. Enter the username and password you selected when you registered.

5. Take the test. Click the **First**, **Back**, **Next**, and **Last** buttons to navigate through the questions. Click the **Finish** button to submit your test for grading. If you wish to close the test without submitting it for grading, click the **Cancel** button. Any answers you have entered will be lost if you cancel the test.

Chapter 7

A View from Marketing, Sales, and Customer Support

Show It! Pitch It! Make the Sale!

"Nice to meet you. My name is Casey Jones—I know, like the railroad engineer. People make that connection all the time, so I'm used to it. I'm here to help you learn a little bit about Marketing and Sales.

"The product line expansion is keeping us pretty busy these days. Thank you for giving me a legitimate excuse to take a breather. I don't know how Dave and his R&D teams do it. He's not an easy person to keep up with.

"Let me tell you about Marketing and Sales from my point of view, starting with the big picture of how business works.

"Corporate View and its various business units like TeleView exist because consumers are willing to give up some of their resources—we're talking about money here—in exchange for the products Corporate View produces and the services we provide. And why are they willing to spend that money? Because a salesperson convinced them to do it.

"The goal of Marketing and Sales is to increase the **market share** of our products. For instance, of all the digital phones and services sold in the world, we want to increase TeleView's share from 11 percent to 15 percent this year. Just this small increase in the percentage of the market share could mean tens or hundreds of millions of dollars more in total revenue because the total **market** for digital phones is in the billions of dollars. To increase our share, our salespeople must convince people to join the TeleView family of digital phone customers.

"It would be difficult to name many items you've paid money for that somebody didn't convince you to buy. For example, look at one main product of TeleView: wireless phones. Not long ago, they didn't exist. Frankly, people got along fine without them. Then, when wireless phones were invented, the marketers and salespeople went to work. They talked with consumers about the advantages of having mobile communications. They talked about things like being more productive, getting more work done, security in the event of an emergency, and staying in touch with family.

"People were convinced, and a new industry called wireless communications was born. Now it seems as if we can't live without these things. I'm lost without my digital phone. But the point is, it happened because of Marketing and Sales. All businesses exist because of Marketing and Sales.

"Marketing, Sales, and Customer Support teams are the very heart of Corporate View and all its business units. None of this would be here if it weren't for us—neither the buildings nor the Corporate View Research Park—and all the people would be working somewhere else.

"Many corporations have Marketing, Sales, and Customer Support as separate functions. But here at Corporate View, we try to connect them as much as possible to each other to create better working relationships and to generate synergy. This arrangement works well for us; these departments are closely related, but there are some differences. Let me explain."

What Marketing Does

"Marketing focuses on reaching large numbers of people and informing them about what Corporate View is, what its business units do, and why they should take notice. Marketing concerns advertising and brand-name recognition. Putting the Corporate View and TeleView *logos* on the side of a blimp and flying it around a football

F i g u r e 7 - 1
Trade shows showcase new products.

stadium is marketing. No money changes hands and no products are delivered, but the Corporate View name is put in front of people and gets noticed.

"Marketing handles exhibitions at the big trade shows like COMDEX. It seems like the more buzz we make at the shows, the more products we end up selling that year. We want to get people excited; we want to get everyone in the industry talking about us.

"Marketing works closely with our Manufacturing Department, advertising agencies, and artists to come up with the best possible packaging for our products. Sadly, many people never look at what is inside the box. They buy the image or the impression we give them from the packaging. I would never buy a product that way, but many people do; so it's important to get it right. Packaging is an essential part of marketing a product.

"Marketing works hand-in-hand with Corporate Communications to develop product-related Web site information, product press releases, and promotional campaigns. The goal is to find the best possible approach for presenting products and services to consumers. We're always looking for ways to get people's attention, to show them the possibilities, to help them feel secure with the quality and technical innovation that define TeleView's products and services.

"Marketing also works closely with R&D to determine ways to present new products to consumers so that they will be interested. Sometimes Marketing has to give a new project the ax because the product isn't marketable. Perhaps an idea is a good one, but the market isn't ready yet, so we have to put it on the back burner. Sometimes we give R&D ideas for products that could be marketable, and they go to work on them.

Figure 7-2
Our survey teams discover what customers want in products.

"A big part of marketing involves consumer *surveys*. We have an insatiable appetite for people's opinions. We want to know what they will buy and what they won't buy and the reasons behind their decisions. Our survey teams go to work in malls, at sporting events, at county fairs, at monster truck rallies—anywhere people are. And in exchange for their opinions, we give people T-shirts, hats, pens, free calling cards—you name it.

"Of course, all the stuff we give away has the TeleView and Corporate View logos stamped all over it; that's marketing, too. It is called *branding*. We want our brand names associated with every great product and every great product idea. We want people to know who we are and what we make, market, and sell.

"*Focus groups* are another way marketing people learn what their audience is thinking. Focus groups are usually conducted away from our corporate offices, out where the consumers are. A focus group can involve 25 people or more. Questions are asked and responses are recorded in a group or person-to-person session with a marketing research team."

The **Least** You **Should** Know **About...**

Marketing

Consider the following tips on timing and marketing:

- *Don't market your product before all the bugs have been worked out—no matter how tempting it is to do so or how ready you think the market is.* Make sure your product can do what you say it will. Otherwise, you will ultimately lose sales and the consumer's goodwill.

- *Don't rush your marketing or ad campaign.* Do it right the first time. Plan carefully and act accordingly. Marketing and advertising are expensive, so make sure your efforts will produce the desired results.

- *Plan to have written materials arrive in the mail on Tuesday or Wednesday.* Mondays and Fridays are bad days to get mail. Monday is catch-up day from the weekend—or a planning day for the week. On Friday, thoughts are moving ahead to the weekend, and your materials may get put aside or lost.

- *Try to get free media coverage of your new product.* Send press releases liberally. It

goes without saying that you should be very obliging to media personnel.

- *Don't send your press releases out too early.* Media attention will create public interest, and that interest means the public will want to purchase your product. With the exception of insider or industry journals, don't court media attention until your product is nearly ready for distribution. A rule of thumb is that customers should be able to buy it at the time they read about it.

- *Be creative with your competition.* For instance, suppose you sell equipment for fly fishing. Like your competitors, you send out a catalog in the spring—the traditional season for casters to purchase gear for the coming summer. Can you make an extra marketing push when your competitors are relaxing? How about an early-bird Christmas sale catalog in September?

- *Plan to have your distribution system (often called the **channel**) firmly in place when the product is released.* It will do little good to have a blue-ribbon ad campaign and no product for the consumer to purchase.

What Sales and Customer Support Do

"Sales goes right to the point of getting people's money. After all the marketing is done, after all the ads and free T-shirts and blimps flying around stadiums, at some point someone who knows the product and knows how to talk to customers has to close the deal. That salesperson has to tell consumers why they should spend their money on Corporate View products; then he or she needs to take the money. It happens a billion times each day, and each time it happens somebody walks out of a store happy to have a new TV, or a new wireless phone, or a bar of soap.

"Our Customer Support team is one of our most important groups. While Customer Support representatives are helping customers solve problems, they can often suggest solutions in the form of additional new products the customer might want or need. This helpful, low-pressure sales strategy is a good one. It results in what we call *after market sales*. And because the customers are on the phone and are communicating directly with the Customer Support team, it is easy to close a sale with a credit card.

"Another great opportunity for low-pressure advertising and after market sales is when customers visit our product support Web sites. When customers visit us on the Web, looking for information, they might find a product they are interested in and decide to buy it. On the Web, customers can order, make a payment, and track the progress of their purchase as it finds its way to them through a delivery service like UPS or FedEx. Like many corporate Web sites, ours allows two-way video conferencing between customers and sales representatives and/or customer support people. It is an amazing way to talk face-to-face with customers.

"We are constantly working to expand our team and help our salespeople learn everything they can about our products. To this end, we have a Sales Training and Development team that travels around and works with our people in the field. The team visits retail outlets that carry our products and trains the salespeople on how to sell our brand. We also have teams of account managers who service large- and medium-sized corporate accounts. They work long, hard hours, and they get paid very well.

"The bottom line with Marketing, Sales, and Customer Support is that this is where the business makes a profit. This is where we either stay in business or close our doors. The way Corporate View is growing, I'd say you should plan on seeing that blimp floating around the stadium for a long time."

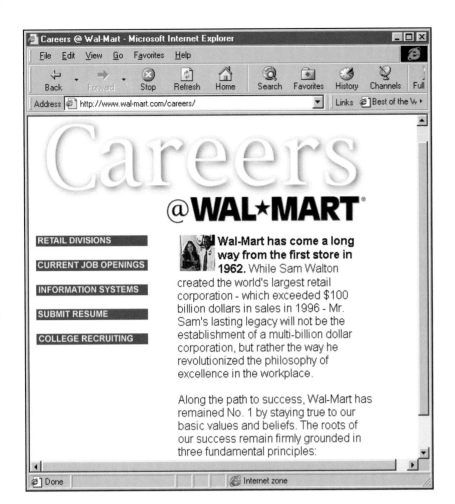

Careers @ Wal-Mart - Microsoft Internet Explorer

File   Edit   View   Go   Favorites   Help

Back   Forward   Stop   Refresh   Home   Search   Favorites   History   Channels   Full

Address   http://www.wal-mart.com/careers/   Links   Best of the W ▸

Careers
@WAL★MART®

RETAIL DIVISIONS

CURRENT JOB OPENINGS

INFORMATION SYSTEMS

SUBMIT RESUME

COLLEGE RECRUITING

Wal-Mart has come a long way from the first store in 1962. While Sam Walton created the world's largest retail corporation - which exceeded $100 billion dollars in sales in 1996 - Mr. Sam's lasting legacy will not be the establishment of a multi-billion dollar corporation, but rather the way he revolutionized the philosophy of excellence in the workplace.

Along the path to success, Wal-Mart has remained No. 1 by staying true to our basic values and beliefs. The roots of our success remain firmly grounded in three fundamental principles:

Done   Internet zone

Business
Milestones

Wal-Mart's Successful Product Line

Looking at Wal-Mart's (NYSE:WMT) history, you must think that the retail giant will soon become the largest company in the world. Its rise up the ranks of the Fortune 500 is legendary. It is now competing with General Motors (NYSE:GM), Ford (NYSE:F), and Exxon (NYSE:XOM) to become the world's largest company, with annual revenues well over $100 billion. Here is a list of the categories in which Wal-Mart stocks and sells products:

- Appliances and Home Accents
- Baby Shop
- Books
- Clearance
- Gourmet Food and Floral
- Health and Medical Supplies
- Jewelry and Gifts
- Music and Videos
- Computers
- Electronics and Office
- Sporting Goods
- Toys and Hobby

When Sam Walton began Wal-Mart in 1962, no one could have predicted that his little Arkansas company would soon surpass such retail giants and Fortune 500 corporations as Kmart (NYSE:KM), J.C. Penney (NYSE:JCP), and Sears (NYSE:S). Walton built his company on this belief:

*We're all working together; that's the secret. And we'll lower the cost of living for everyone, not just in America, but we'll give the world an opportunity to see what it's like to save and have a better lifestyle, a better life for all. We're proud of what we've accomplished; we've just begun.**

*Wal-Mart. *Wal-Mart Corporation.* Online. Available: **www.wal-mart.com**. February 24, 1998 and July 16, 1998.

Paying with Plastic

More and more companies are issuing credit and debit cards rather than giving cash to their employees to use in paying for business expenses. There are thousands of different cards to choose from. VISA cards are the most widely used and are issued by banks. The Discover Card is associated with Sears, Roebuck & and Co. department stores (NYSE:S), but the cards are actually issued by Dean Witter, a financial services company. The Discover Card was launched nationally in 1986. It soon became the largest and most successful bank card issued by a single source. It achieved record profits three years later and became a separate business unit of Dean Witter Financial Services, which is now affiliated with Morgan Stanley.

One of the most influential business cards is issued by the American Express Company. (NYSE:AXP). American Express has its corporate headquarters in New York City's financial district.

Like other leading business cards, American Express provides lending services through its credit card operations and travel support services.

The American Express card is attractive to businesses because it is a charge card, not a credit card. Businesses obtain these cards for their employees so they can charge business-related expenses each month. All charges on the card must be paid in full each month. Therefore, no interest charges are incurred. An annual fee is charged for each card.

As the saying goes, if you're in business, don't leave home without some plastic in your pocket. Suppose you are at a trade show and the computer used in your key presentation goes down. If you have a credit card, you can rent another computer for the rest of the trade show. This might seem expensive, but it's probably more cost-effective than losing all those prospective customers. Because few employees carry enough cash to cover these kinds of expenses, a credit card is a good idea.

Activity Overviews

The goal of Marketing and Sales is to make a profit. Marketing managers lead this effort. They manage the products companies sell and coordinate every aspect of product success. Marketing managers make lots of product decisions. For example:

- What products go to market?

- When is the best time to launch the product?

- What should the packaging look like?

- How should the product be described to others?

- What is the **price point** for the product?

- How is the product best distributed to prospective buyers?

- How should advertising campaigns be structured to build product interest and loyalty?

To be successful, managers must understand their audience. Among marketing people, the phrases "the **market segment**" or "the **market niche**" are often substituted for the word *audience*. Analyzing the market to understand your market niche is crucial.

For example, you wouldn't want to try to sell a hamburger-making machine to Victor's Vegetarian Restaurant or a soybean beef substitute to Sam's Sirloin Steakhouse. These two restaurants represent very different market segments, or market niches.

In this chapter, you will work through some of the same problems faced by Marketing managers the world over. You will explore various methods of customer research and discover how people share ideas, stay informed on new marketing trends, and get customers' opinions of their products.

Activity 7-1 Focusing on Your Market Niche will present questions you need to think about to identify your market segment. You will learn to apply strategies for targeting an audience or a market niche.

Activity 7-2 Inside White Papers will have you examine **white papers** that discuss market trends and decide how products and marketing efforts must change so that Corporate View can profit from these trends.

Activity 7-3 Writing a White Paper will put you into the role of a Corporate View marketer, analyzing trends and markets and discussing your findings and ideas with your peers in a white paper.

Activity 7-4 Customer Surveys will introduce ten tips for effective Web surveys you will use in assessing a survey planned by Corporate View.

Corporate ShopTalk

Understanding the meanings of these terms will help you learn the concepts and develop the skills related to Marketing, Sales, and Customer Support covered in the chapter. In preparation for completing the chapter activities, access the Intranet and find the definition for each of these terms by clicking the **_ShopTalk_** link on the **_Regular Features_** page.

- Addressable Advertising
- After Market Sales
- Branding
- Channel

- Demographics
- Focus Group
- Logo
- Market
- Market Niche

- Market Segment
- Market Share
- Price Point
- Survey
- White Paper

There's an old saying among ad agency veterans: "You can jump the ditch once, or you can keep trying to jump it again and again." That is, you can take the time and effort to construct your marketing campaign right the first time, or you can do it sloppily, make mistakes—and end up redoing your campaign again and again.

Each time you try to jump the marketing ditch, it costs you a great deal of money. Advertising and marketing aren't cheap. Doing a sloppy job the first time not only costs you the price of advertising and lost revenues, but also it allows the competition to leap ahead in the marketplace.

So what is the best way to create effective ad and marketing campaigns? In simple terms, the best way is to do your homework and find your audience. As we discussed earlier, you have to know your audience, or your potential customers, and you have to know your audience's needs. To put this in advertising terms, you have to identify your segment, or niche. Then you have to focus or target your product to the segment you've selected.

When a member of the Marketing team spots an important trend that opens a new market niche for company products, he or she will often prepare a white paper. A white paper, or position paper, explains the trend to others. It describes how existing company products can be targeted to the new market niche or suggests products that could be developed for it.

White papers are informative and are meant to generate interest and discussion. Often a white paper will influence corporate decisions, product development, and marketing efforts.

Casey Jones saw many of the Marketing managers "jumping the ditch two and three times." So Casey held a meeting and gave them some advice. The discussion was recorded, written up as a white paper, and placed on the Intranet for others at Corporate View to read. In this activity you will analyze the comments.

Technical Communications

White Papers and ROIs

A white paper is a document that explains a position or suggests change. It might identify new market niches and new products or propose improved methods. A white paper is usually intended to help others look at something in a new way or think about doing things more efficiently.

A white paper is a comparatively easy document to write. White papers are generally short and concise, with a personality that is interesting, informational, and often informal.

ROI (pronounced *roy*), which stands for return on investment, is a term you will frequently encounter in business circles. In the plainest terms, a ROI report is a document showing the amount you are likely to gain from a business venture compared to how much you will have to invest. In other words, after you've spent your money, how much net profit will you receive?

A ROI report gives managers and executives all the figures so that they can determine whether a project is worth doing. In contrast with a white paper, a ROI report is much more detailed and specific. It requires a lot of research. For such a report, a Marketing manager will need to test different possible financial outcomes and use several mathematical formulas to project whether a proposed expenditure is worth the investment.

1. From what you have learned in the chapter introduction, explain in your own words what Marketing is all about.

_____

_____

_____

2. From what you have learned in the chapter introduction, explain in your own words what Sales is all about.

_____

_____

_____

3. From what you have learned in the chapter introduction, explain in your own words how Customer Support can help a corporation's marketing and sales efforts.

_____

_____

_____

4. Access the local Intranet or the Corporate View Web site.

5. Select the ***Marketing, Sales, & Support*** link from the Corporate View Intranet Home page. Read ***About Marketing, Sales, and Customer Support***.

6. Why does Corporate View encourage a close working relationship among the Marketing, Sales, and Customer Support functions? Explain some of the beneficial effects working together can have.

_____

_____

_____

_____

7. On the ***Marketing, Sales, & Support*** page, click on the ***White Papers*** link and read ***Understanding Your Market Niche***.

8. In a word processing file, list seven important questions you believe someone should ask to identify accurately a market segment for a restaurant or fast-food establishment.

9. How does the white paper define *market segmentation*?

_____

_____

Save As:

Market1

In this activity, you learned about the kinds of questions marketers ask to identify the market segment for a product. How well do such marketing strategies work?

1. Review the seven questions you identified in step 8 of the Just-in-Time Training.

2. Visit three restaurants with different geographic locations, prices, and cuisine. Sit in each restaurant for 25 to 30 minutes. Observe the customers. Are they in a hurry? Are they looking for a quick bite to eat or a romantic dinner? Take notes that will help you answer the seven questions you identified and write a description of the market niche each of these restaurants is serving.

3. Open the word processing file *Market1*, created earlier. Answer each of the seven questions for each restaurant. Use your answers to help you identify each restaurant's market segment or niche.

Save As:

Market2

Activity 7-2   *Inside White Papers*

A white paper is written to prove a point, express a new idea, or generate interest in a new product or a new product idea. One very important function of a white paper is to give people a means of expressing ideas clearly.

Have you ever tried to explain an idea to someone, only to find that you couldn't make the person understand? Later, after your conversation, did you think of a better way to explain your idea? If you have ever had this experience, you are ready to write your first white paper. A white paper gives you a chance to think about your idea, explore it in more detail, and think clearly about how your audience will receive your idea.

As you have seen from the previous activity, white papers are not difficult to write. They are not as tightly written as other business documents, such as press releases, usability studies, ROI reports, and annual reports. White papers instead allow for a greater degree of personal interpretation, opinion, and style. Just remember to make your key points.

In the next activity, you will write a white paper. But first, in this activity, you will examine several examples of white papers on the Corporate View Intranet. You will look at content, implications for marketing, value to the audience, purpose, personality and tone, and length.

Just-in-Time Training

Reviewing White Papers

1. Access your local Intranet or the Corporate View Web site.
2. Select the ***Marketing, Sales, & Support*** link from the Corporate View Intranet Home page.
3. Click the ***White Papers*** link and read ***Demographics and Market Trends***.
4. Define the word ***demographics***.

   _____

   _____

Key the answers to questions 5 through 14 in a word processing file.

5. Summarize the main points and positions outlined in this paper.

6. What implications might this white paper have for Marketing managers in the RetailView division (Corporate View's retail consumer products SBU specializing in sports equipment and sports apparel)? What kinds of new products or new advertising campaigns should RetailView be considering?

7. What implications might this white paper have for Marketing managers in the MoneyView division (Corporate View's banking, insurance, and financial SBU)? What kinds of new products or new advertising campaigns should MoneyView be considering?

8. What implications could this white paper have for Marketing managers in the PublishView division (Corporate View's online publishing SBU)? What kinds of new products or new advertising campaigns should PublishView be considering?

9. Return to the **_White Papers_** list on the **_Marketing, Sales, & Support_** page. Read **_The Outdoor Market_**. What are the main findings and positions presented in this white paper?

10. Which division of Corporate View might be able to capitalize on the trends the white paper indicates?

11. Who do you think is the audience for this white paper? Is the content appropriate for this audience?

12. Briefly describe the purpose and value of the white paper.

13. How would you describe the style of writing or personality used in the white paper? What is the tone? For example, is it scientific? Objective? Opinionated? Informative?

14. How appropriate is the length of this white paper? Is it too short, too long, or just right?

Save As:

WPReview

Debriefing

You just read several white papers defining growing audiences or markets for Corporate View products. What other trends do you foresee?

Think and write about the following:

1. What expensive high-tech items will become inexpensive high-tech items in a few years (such as cell phones, pagers, and laser printers are today)?

   _____

   _____

2. What new sports will be popular in the future, and what kinds of equipment will they require?

   _____

   _____

   _____

3. What fashion trends will become popular in the next three years?

   _____

   _____

4. How can Corporate View benefit from these trends?

   _____

   _____

   _____

In this activity, you will write a white paper on a consumer trend, product, or business situation that needs improvement. You can use one of the following sample topics from the strategic business units at Corporate View, or you can choose your own concept or position. Even if you have already thought of a topic, read the following suggestions before you start. You might find a few ideas that will be useful to you.

- *Interactive Web games*: More and more games are being played over the Internet with participants who live half a world away. The trend is for faster, more realistic games. Write a white paper that explains this trend and how Corporate View can make a profit in this industry.

- *Exercise and sports equipment:* People now are more interested in health and recreation equipment than at any other time in history. The market is in the billions of dollars. New kinds of equipment and techniques have reinvigorated the industry in the last few years. Write a white paper that traces this trend and suggests how Corporate View can make a profit in this industry.

- *Digital wireless phones, wireless Internet connections, and wireless television:* The Federal Communications Commission recently auctioned off an entirely new segment of the electro-magnetic spectrum to entrepreneurs who think they can bring consumers higher-quality phone, computer, and television services at a lower cost without using wires. These new communications industries will lead to hundreds of new inventions, products, and services. Write a white paper that traces this trend and explains how Corporate View can make a profit in this industry.

- *New speech-recognition technologies*: When most people think of speech-recognition technology, they think of talking to a computer, which types their document. But speech recognition has given birth to a wide range of new products—for example, a handheld, pager-sized device that can record 25 to 50 pages of digital information you can upload to your word processor later; a car that knows your voice and allows you to start it and turn on the lights, the radio, and the air conditioning by speaking; a house that, at the sound of your voice, heats or cools itself, starts dinner, and plays your favorite CD. Write a white paper that traces this trend and describes how Corporate View can make a profit in this industry.

F i g u r e 7 - 4
The growing market for sports or exercise equipment represents an opportunity for Corporate View.

- *New Internet banking services*: Available since 1996, online Internet banks are growing. Many major banks allow customers to make deposits, transfer funds, pay bills, and withdraw money over the Internet. SmartCards can carry electronic cash from your personal computer's Internet bank. Online banking is becoming increasingly popular, and today includes loans and even investment services. Write a white paper that traces this trend and explains how Corporate View can make a profit in this industry.

- *Medical services for elderly people*: The U.S. population is living longer, getting older, and requiring more cost-effective health care solutions. One of the fastest-growing health care markets is geriatric care (care of the aging). Any medical division should pay attention to this growth pattern. Write a white paper that traces this trend and explains how Corporate View can make a profit in this industry.

- *Medical services for active people*: Another major trend in the health care field is the growing number of sports-related industries. As people have been getting off their couches and starting to bike, snowboard, surf, and play soccer or golf, the number of sports-related injuries has increased significantly. Physical therapy and other medical services and devices are needed to deal with the injuries. Write a white paper that traces this trend and describes how Corporate View can make a profit in this industry.

- *The corporate Intranet*: Intranets and their technologies have proliferated faster than any other aspect of business and computer technology. Web pages for the internal use of company employees have proven to be a very effective way to keep employees informed. Still, improvements can be made. Write a white paper that traces this trend and explains how Corporate View can make a profit in this industry.

Just-in-Time Training

White Papers with Style

1. Select one of the issues described above or use an equally intriguing one of your own.

2. Before you begin writing your white paper, take some time to consider:

   - Your *audience,* their knowledge of and interest in the subject.

   - The *purpose* and value of your white paper to your audience.

- The *personality* of the paper. Ask yourself, "Should it be fun and exciting, or serious and thoughtful?"
- The overall *length*— not so long as to bore the reader, but not so short as to leave out important details.

3. Research your white paper, if necessary, by using library resources or the Internet.

4. Write your white paper. Keep your paragraphs short and the total length between 150 and 200 words. Format your paper so that the design adds to the readability of the document.

Save As:

WhiteP1

Debriefing

Like usability reports, white papers are usually in-house documents, not meant for outside consumption. Some well-written white papers, however, will find their way to customers or interested shareholders outside the corporation. There the similarities between usability reports and white papers cease.

Think and write about the following:

Compare the white paper you wrote in this activity with the usability report you wrote in Chapter 6.

1. Which document has a more formal, structured style?

   _____

2. How might the research or testing done in preparation for the two documents differ?

   _____

   _____

3. Which document deals with current or in-development product(s), and which deals with ideas for products?

   _____

   _____

4. Which document discusses broad trends or issues, and which discusses specifics about a particular product?

   _____

Activity 7-4   *Customer Surveys*

Research is a key factor in determining how to identify, focus on, and capture your target market. It is crucial that you stay on the cutting edge by looking for trends and for new consumer bases. In this activity, you'll examine a marketing base that is sometimes overlooked in the effort to find new markets and identify new trends—your current customers.

The customers who have bought your products already have informed opinions about what you have to offer. Their opinions are very valuable. Working with them and identifying trends within your current customer base is essential for several reasons.

- *All feedback is useful.* It is important to listen to negative comments, as well as to positive ones. Learn from your research. Never make the same mistake twice. It is common to make adjustments in response to new information.

- *Learn what your customer base likes and does not like.* As an old cliché says, "monitor and adjust." Learn how to focus more narrowly on the segment you are dealing with so that you can spend your advertising dollars more effectively.

- *Your current customers are your best source of future sales.* Make a customer a customer for life. If customers are happy with your product and service, there's a good chance they will buy from you again.

- *Your current customers are your best sounding board for what worked and what did not.* Knowing that you are interested in what they have to say will make your customers feel important and build brand loyalty.

Speak with your customers to determine their perceptions. This is important because the perception, or previously formed ideas, consumers have about your product might not be the perception you think they have. In advertising, perceptions are important.

How can you gather information from your customers or a target group you hope to make your customers? Surveys are a major part of the information-gathering process. Survey data can be collected in many ways. Some of the most commonly used methods are

- Surveys sent to customers through the mail, by email, or by FAX.

- Phone surveys conducted by telemarketers. Customer Support operators usually make great interviewers because they know how to approach customers.

- Person-to-person surveys in focus groups or at malls, sporting events, or other locations where the demographic segment of potential customers can be found.

- Surveys on the World Wide Web.

- Some organizations, such as InetSurvey.com, even specialize in helping you create surveys for use on the World Wide Web. They provide you the URL to create the link from your Web page. What's more, they provide you the tool to analyze the data online.

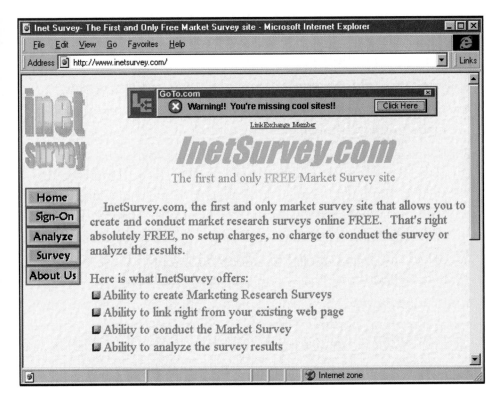

Figure 7-5
InetSurvey.com offers you the ability to create market surveys online.

Surveys are perhaps the easiest way to get feedback. A survey can be as simple as a form with a few boxes to check or as complicated as a six-page, single-spaced questionnaire. Surveys can range from quite formal to extremely informal. You must structure the survey, however, to attract your target demographic group or else the results will not be accurate.

The object of any survey is to receive feedback. The length of the survey depends on what you need to know and your purpose for conducting the survey. Unless you are paying survey respondents for their time, long surveys should be avoided.

Because your audience has a limited amount of time to take a survey and a limited amount of patience, a survey should be thought through very carefully. The concepts of *audience, purpose, personality*, and *length* play a big role in survey preparation, just as they do in other forms of technical communications.

The key to any survey, especially a Web-based survey, is to ask clear questions. Poorly worded questions will not yield any useful information. Worse, they can confuse customers so much that they do not finish the survey. In this activity, you will analyze several survey questions.

Just-in-Time Training

Evaluating Surveys

Save As:

Surveys

1. Access the local Intranet or the Corporate View Web site.

2. Select the **_Marketing, Sales, & Support_** link from the Corporate View Intranet Home page.

3. Click the **_White Papers_** link and read **_Writing Web Surveys_**.

4. In a word processing file, summarize each of the ten points made in this white paper.

5. Before a survey goes out to the public, employees are usually asked to try it and to make suggestions on how to improve the survey. You have been asked to complete and make suggestions for a pre-release survey on the VoiceCom III software. Return to the **_Marketing, Sales, & Support_** page and click the **_Surveys_** link.

6. Select the **_VoiceCom III Pre-release Survey_** link. Read the information about the survey and the survey questions.

7. In your *Surveys* word processing document, comment on how well each of the survey questions meets the ten points outlined in the **_Writing Web Surveys_** white paper. In several areas, the survey is weak and needs improvement. You might want to create a table or chart to help you organize your analysis of the survey.

Debriefing

It is important that you have a precise purpose or focus when you write a survey. You then write survey questions to accomplish this purpose. A poorly worded survey is a waste of time and money. Before you begin, decide what the exact objectives of the survey are. In other words, what do you want to learn from the survey?

Think and write about the following:

1. Have you ever taken a marketing survey at a mall or over the phone? Was it a positive or a negative experience for you?

   _____

2. What was the purpose of the survey? Were you told the purpose right away in easy-to-understand terms?

   _____

3. How long did it take to complete the survey? Did you think the time was too long, too short, or about right?

   _____

4. What rewards, if any, were you offered for completing the survey?

   _____

The **Least** You
Should Know
About...

Telephone Surveys

Let's look at the telephone survey in a little more detail because it is one of the least expensive ways to reach the most people.

Telephone surveys are an economical way to get information, but the size of your survey group is limited. Such surveys are geared toward shorter answers and answers that aren't personal. It is a phone call, after all, with an interviewer the audience doesn't know and may not trust. Few people will be candid about private or personal feelings over a phone line.

Telephone surveys can be conducted in-house or outsourced to other companies. Some companies have a staff specifically trained for this work. These people have pleasant voices and know the ins and outs of telephone surveys. Outsourcing is a desirable way to conduct a phone survey when, as is frequently the case, the surveying will take a short time to complete and the sponsoring company doesn't want to use its own staff.

Even if you outsource your phone survey, you will still be responsible for writing your own survey questions. This task is too important to leave to someone outside the company. Remember to keep your questions short. They should be clearly worded so that they are easy to understand. Ask the most important questions first and avoid the temptation to ask too many questions. Many people don't want to be bothered by a marketing call at all—let alone answer a dozen questions over the phone from a complete stranger. Keep it short.

A general phone survey will average a 9 through 14 percent return. To ensure the maximum results, test your questions with a small group before you start making calls. This way you can salvage any questions that might be ambiguous or misleading.

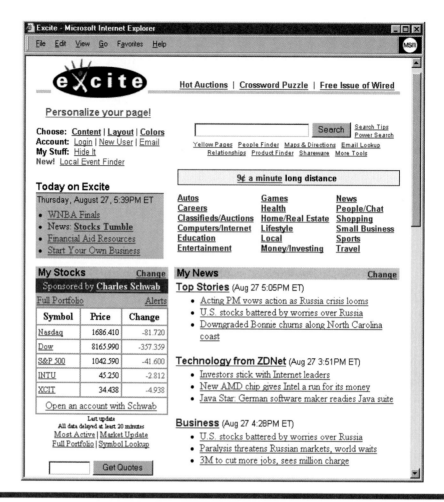

Figure 7-6
*Internet portals like Excite are experts in addressable advertising. Visit **www.excite.com** and look for banners or ads. You can also check stock quotes.*

Business
Milestones

Addressable Advertising

Most advertising is not focused on the specific market segment it is intended to reach. It is estimated that 80 percent of television advertising money is wasted on people who are uninterested in the products being advertised. ***Addressable advertising*** means that commercials can to be focused on demographic groups likely to be interested in the products.

For example, Internet advertising is much more focused than television advertising. Through the use of special user data files transmitted by Web browsers, companies gather information from Web users about their Web surfing habits and interests. This information is rendered into a demographic profile that allows advertisers to target a well-defined market segment or niche.

This concept has been successfully used by state-of-the-art cable television systems where set-top boxes monitor your viewing habits, report the results, and adjust the advertising to fit your specific demographic profile. This breakthrough in market research was successfully tested in the Bell South regional cable system in the late 1990s.

New digital set-top boxes have been installed in millions of living rooms during the last few years. As television and the Internet become more closely integrated, every Web site you visit and every television show you view will help paint a picture of who you are, your interests, and what you are likely to buy, thus creating opportunity for addressable advertising.

Addressable advertising commercials can be focused on different demographic groups—even if the groups are watching the same television programs or clicking the same Web pages. For example, a group of consumers watching the same football game will be segmented. Some consumers will receive advertisements for corn chips, while other viewers at the same time can receive advertisements for digital telephones, laptop computers, or new long-distance services.

Executive Summary

Corporations don't make it to the top of the Fortune 500 without selling products and lots of them. Wal-Mart made it by selling hundreds of thousands of products in a wide variety of product categories, whereas Ford, General Motors, and Exxon maintain a large market share in just a few product categories. Despite their different strategies, each corporation has a formula for marketing and selling that works.

A corporation exists because customers are willing to spend their money in exchange for products the corporation produces. Convincing someone to buy the company's products is the role of Marketing and Sales. Keeping customers is the job of Sales and Customer Support.

No one will buy the company's products if they aren't aware of who the company is and what it sells. Brand-name recognition, a marketing responsibility, is an important factor in generating consumer confidence.

To accomplish their sales goals, Marketing managers participate in trade shows, hire advertising agencies, and improve the packaging design for products. Together with the sales team, they create a channel, or a means of distribution to the customer. They write press releases with Corporate Communications and manage other information campaigns.

Marketing also has a say in what kinds of products are developed and when products are released to the marketplace. To avoid making costly mistakes, Marketing managers conduct surveys or create focus groups to find out whether a product idea is a winner before the company invests money in the product.

Marketing managers often prepare white papers to discuss product ideas, marketing issues, trends, and changing market forces. White papers can help Marketing managers clarify their positions on various issues, get the ball rolling on a new idea, or highlight new consumer demographics.

Finding the correct market segment or niche is often difficult. Marketing managers can spend months identifying market trends and the precise market segment that is interested in buying a particular product. Time spent in this endeavor, however, will pay off because advertising efforts will be more focused and more successful. Two tools used to ferret out this information are surveys and focus groups.

Technical Communications

The white paper is one of the easiest documents that Corporate View personnel are asked to prepare. Yet it can have significant and far-reaching effects. A simple idea shared in a well-presented white paper can eventually turn into a major new product line or marketing campaign. White papers need to be clear, concise, and interesting. Key points must be easy to identify. A little personal style will help sell others on the ideas you are presenting.

Surveys are a great way to identify the needs of a market segment or market niche. They must be very carefully constructed. Before sending out a survey, always have people you know and trust take the survey and give you feedback on the questions you have asked.

The Corporate Inbox

Save As:

Inbox7A

Here are some messages that need to be answered by someone in Marketing, Sales, or Customer Support. Answer them with the help of the Intranet and your own best judgment. If you need help preparing documents, access the **_Style Guide_** under the **_Corporate Communications_** link.

TO: Intern
FROM: _cjones@corpview.com_
SUBJECT: White Papers
MESSAGE:

This is a switch, writing a white paper about white papers! Please answer Maria's request and create a white paper that explains white papers and how we use them. Let me see a draft as soon as it's ready. Thanks.

<<From Maria Bravo, Forwarded by Casey Jones>>

Marketing's white papers have scored major points with people in different parts of the corporation. There has been a lot of interest in how you use them to generate ideas, discuss trends, and figure out better ways to do things.

Can you prepare a white paper for me on how white papers are written and used? The paper should discuss what others should know about writing white papers so that they can be as successful with them as you have been. I will post your white paper on the Intranet for other departments to access.

Thanks,
Maria

Hi, this is Casey Jones. I received a call from Momoko Kochi, a RetailView Marketing manager. He would like help coming up with seven questions he can use to help identify a market segment that would be interested in a new line of snowboards.

Can you tackle this one for me? You are good at identifying customers and market segments. Please email your questions to me for review.

Thanks,

Bye.

Save As:

Inbox7B

VoiceCom III Survey

1. Was the software easy to load on your computer?
   ☐ Yes   *940*   ☐ No   *60*

2. Did the software live up to the manufacturer's expectations?
   ☐ Yes   *845*   ☐ No   *155*

3. Did the software save me time?
   ☐ Yes   *820*   ☐ No   *180*

4. I was happy with the product.
   ☐ Yes   *841*   ☐ No   *159*

5. This is a good product.
   ☐ Yes   *867*   ☐ No   *133*

6. Did you need customer support?
   ☐ Yes   *288*   ☐ No   *712*

7. If you did use customer support, was it helpful?
   ☐ Yes   *243*   ☐ No   *45*

10. Would you recommend this software to a friend?
   ☐ Yes   *919*   ☐ No   *81*

Dear Intern:

We need a press release, fast! We are about to launch the VoiceCom III. Our survey results are just coming in. We have all but questions 8 and 9 tabulated. It will take another week to tabulate those questions, and we can't wait. With the product release set for Monday, we are under a lot of pressure to report something to the media.

Here are the early results. Please make some sense out of them and put them into a press release that will interest the media and new customers.

Thanks,
Casey

Save As:

Inbox7C

TO: Intern
FROM: *cjones@corpview.com*
SUBJECT: Job Description
MESSAGE:

The problem we faced with the VoiceCom III survey has caused us to rethink our survey procedures. As you know, only part of the survey information was ready before the product was released. We must find ways to streamline the survey process so that the data we gather is useful and timely.

We've decided to create a new full-time position. One half of the new employee's time will be spent as a survey writer preparing better surveys, and the other half will be spent making sure our surveys are being conducted and tabulated in a timely manner. We will call this half of the job survey coordinator.

Can you prepare a job description that we can give to Robin Mills in Human Resources? Please list as many skills and qualities as you can identify that will be important in this job. We will post the opening immediately and close in two weeks. We need to get this person on the team!

Thanks,
Casey

Save As:

Inbox7D

Online Business Trends

Access the Corporate View Web site. Use the **Stock Watcher Links** on the **Regular Features** page to identify the following ticker symbols and learn how each of these companies did in the stock market today.

Current Date _____

Ticker	Exchange	Company Name	Current Price
AXP	NYSE	_____	_____
S	NYSE	_____	_____
WMT	NYSE	_____	_____
GM	NYSE	_____	_____
F	NYSE	_____	_____
XOM	NYSE	_____	_____
KM	NYSE	_____	_____
JCP	NYSE	_____	_____

When a Few Words Will Do

According to what you have read in this chapter or on the Corporate View Intranet, answer the following questions in a word processing document.

1. What do you think are the keys to Wal-Mart's success?

2. What do you think is the most efficient way to deliver a survey: over the phone, over the Web, or through the mail? Why?

3. Of all the white papers you have read, which was the most valuable? Why?

4. Why would a company issue credit cards to its employees?

5. List the top five Wal-Mart product categories that Corporate View would be most interested in.

Save As:

Online7

Portfolio-Building Project

Writing a Survey

After receiving the surveys on the VoiceCom III, TeleView has decided to launch two advertising campaigns. One will be geared directly to people suffering from, or at risk for, carpal tunnel syndrome.

You have been asked to conduct a phone survey to help Marketing and Sales target the VoiceCom III to carpal tunnel and potential carpal tunnel sufferers. You don't have time to do another direct mail survey, so you will get the help of several Customer Support operators to administer the survey over the phone to 2,000 individuals. Your audience will be those people who were sent beta copies of the VoiceCom III software who suffer from carpal tunnel syndrome.

The goals of the survey are to learn

- What kinds of features your audience is looking for in a speech-recognition product.

- What participants liked and disliked about the beta version of the product.

- What kinds of advertisements and packaging would attract this audience the most. For instance, should the packaging be formal and sophisticated, or fun and lively? Would a radio or television campaign be best? Should the Web be part of the campaign? Should the advertising be placed in magazines?

1. In preparation for writing your survey questions, review The Least You Should Know About... Telephone Surveys (page 219) and the **VoiceCom III Pre-release Survey** on the corporate Intranet.

2. Write 10 to 15 survey questions.

3. Write a brief opening statement for the survey call. Remember to thank your audience for participating.

Save As:

Pfolio7

4. Format your survey so that it will be easy for Customer Support operators to read and for you to tabulate.

5. Spell-check your survey before you print or share it, and remember to proofread.

High-Performance Workgroup Project

Save As:

HP7

Form a team with three or four other employees. Share the surveys you created in the Portfolio-Building Project with each other. Get feedback on how your survey can be improved. Then combine your best efforts into one survey of 10 to 15 questions.

Spell-check and proofread carefully before printing your survey.

Thinking and Writing About Your Business

Based on what you have learned in this chapter, answer seven of the following questions in your own words. Key your answers in a word processing document.

1. If you decided on a career in Marketing, Sales, or Customer Support, what specific product would you most like to work with?

2. What do you think would be the ideal price point for the product you selected in number 1?

3. Who would be interested in your product choice? Describe the market segment.

4. What kinds of stores or retail outlets would carry your product?

5. Could your product be successfully marketed online over the Web? If so, what would be some advantages of online marketing?

6. Why is market share important? Can market share grow and profits still drop?

7. What does it mean to brand a product?

8. Why is it important for corporations to attend trade shows?

9. How can Customer Support help acquire information from customers?

Save As:

Think7

Overtime

Identifying Markets

How do you get information about a new market? The first place to look might be the Intranet. If the market has been identified, a white paper in the archive might address the market segment. If you fail to find anything on the Intranet, you can always turn to the World Wide Web for answers.

The Web gives marketers many resources for facts and figures that can help them identify new markets and trends. Suppose, for example, you needed demographic information on

- Areas where the population has grown
- Households with two people with college degrees
- Towns and cities with colleges nearby

You can find all these answers and a wealth of other useful demographic information at the U.S. Government's Census Web site.

1. Access the Corporate View Web site and select the ***Marketing, Sales, & Support*** link.

2. Click on the ***U. S. Census Statistical Abstract*** link.

3. Scroll down the page to see a variety of links broken out into categories.

4. Access each link and prepare a summary of the kinds of data you find on the site.

Save As:

Otime7

Applications to Small Business

Product Packaging

When a large corporation is about to launch a new product, it will test-market the packaging in a variety of segments to see whether it is effective. Surprisingly, sometimes the best-looking packages are not the most effective at attracting customer interest. Plain or colorful packaging can attract people faster than some fancier-looking packaging. The goal in packaging is to attract attention and inspire confidence at the same time.

Small businesses frequently lack the funds needed to test-market their packaging. Entrepreneurs often must use their personal impressions and experience to help them determine the best possible way to package their products. Explore some strategies small businesses use for packaging.

Key your answers to the following questions in a word processing file.

Visit a small business or store. Take note of the packaging used for the products.

1. What type of business or store are you visiting? What products are made or sold here?

2. Which boxes and packages are people attracted to? Which ones do they pick up and look at? Which ones do they pass by?

3. Why do you think some packaging seems to work and other packaging doesn't help sell a product?

4. Interview the business or store owner/manager. How does he or she make decisions about how to package or display the product?

Save As:

ASB7

Access the Corporate View Web site and take the Online Evaluation for this chapter.

1. Click on the ***Employee Training and Evaluations*** link on the ***Regular Features*** page.

2. Select the ***Online Tests*** link. (You must be a registered user to access the online tests. If you are not a registered user, click the ***Register*** link and follow the instructions on the screen. Then click the ***Online Tests*** link to return to the Online Tests page.)

3. Choose the ***Chapter 7 A View from Marketing, Sales, & Customer Support*** link on the Online Tests page.

4. Enter the username and password you selected when you registered.

5. Take the test. Click the **First**, **Back**, **Next**, and **Last** buttons to navigate through the questions. Click the **Finish** button to submit your test for grading. If you wish to close the test without submitting it for grading, click the **Cancel** button. Any answers you have entered will be lost if you cancel the test.

Chapter 8

A View from Finance and Accounting

The Long and Short Term of It

"Hi, my name is Spencer Malone. I work in TeleView's Finance and Accounting Department in a team called *Liquid Assets*. I'll explain what my team does in more detail later on, but basically we're in charge of managing a big chunk of TeleView's money. Our goal is to make even more money and keep the executives at our parent company, Corporate View, ecstatically happy with our unit's performance."

The Money Game

"As a former college football player, I like to compare finance to football because they both involve a lot of strategy. Like football, finance is about reading the field (the market) and following trends and patterns to take advantage of opportunities. Some plays are kind of risky, but they can pay off big when they work. Some plays are conservative, but being safe means you only move the money ball a little at a time.

"One strategy is to play it safe until the opportunities come along for big gains. Sometimes you get pushed back and you lose some ground, but if you play the game right, you can always end up with more gains than losses.

"Our team looks for ways to keep a constantly fluctuating amount of money earning interest but not tied up in any long-term commitments. Anytime TeleView needs a lot of money for something, and it needs it in a hurry, our team's job is to keep it where we can access it quickly. Give me a million for two years, and I can just about guarantee you a positive return. Give me a million for a few weeks, and that makes things a lot more interesting. How do you make the short-term gains? Well, it depends on what the market looks like during those few weeks.

"In any business, money is the most valuable employee; if it's managed properly, every corporate dollar will work very hard and earn its keep through returns and financial gains. TeleView is a big, successful business unit, and part of its success has to do with how we handle the money. If our finances are mishandled, all the Marketing and Sales people in the world wouldn't be able to save the company.

"Finance and Accounting is the heart of any business, and money is the blood. As long as we keep the blood circulating at the right pace, TeleView will continue to do well. If *we* do well, that helps all of Corporate View do well, Corporate View stock goes up, and more investment money will be available for new corporate ventures."

The Big Accounting Picture

"Actually, my team's role in the big picture of money management is relatively small. Let me tell you about some other financial functions.

"The various Accounting workgroups have the enormous responsibility of making sure all of TeleView's revenues are accounted for and distributed appropriately. We have to know where every dollar is earned, where every dollar is spent, and where our money is invested . . . every dollar. Without that information, the Corporate View Board of Directors can't plan and can't make the right decisions. Accounting means to 'account' for all the money so that those making decisions know where we stand.

"Within Accounting there are different departments. Around here, everyone's favorite department is *Payroll*, for obvious reasons. It keeps food on our tables and cars in our driveways. Then there's *Accounts Payable*, the people at TeleView responsible for paying all the bills, including payments to outside contractors. The counterpart of Accounts Payable is *Accounts Receivable*, the team that tracks and verifies that others pay what they owe to us.

"Another important team associated with Finance and Accounting is *Purchasing*. They're like TeleView's professional shoppers. Most departments handle their own budgets for small purchases such as office supplies, but Purchasing takes care of any big-ticket or large-scale purchases. Think of all the little parts that go into a phone, for example. All those parts are made by other companies, many of which are located in Asia or Central America. Purchasing finds the best prices for the highest-quality components and then buys them in huge quantities. The system is global, and within days the components show up via boat, train, plane, or truck, and Manufacturing takes it from there.

Figure 8-1
Purchasing finds the best prices for high-quality products.

"Others work in Finance and Accounting in positions such as ***controller***, ***analyst***, ***auditor***, ***bookkeeper***, ***clerk***, ***account manager***, ***adjuster***, and ***actuary***. We have managers to direct travel, medical, and dental reimbursements. We have teams of insurance and tax accountants.

"For any multinational ***corporation***, accounting is a huge task. You have to manage multiple currencies and navigate the tax and insurance laws of multiple countries. There is much work to do. All the work gets broken down, and each Finance and Accounting person has a piece of the pie to attend to.

"One major job of Accounting is to make sure every department has a realistic budget and that every department sticks closely to its budget. A budget is just a financial game plan detailing how much money the department plans to spend on particular products or services. For example, a travel budget is often prepared and approved before an employee takes a business trip. Upon completion of a trip, actual expenses are recorded on a travel reimbursement form so that the employee can be reimbursed, as needed, and so that the corporation can claim the costs as a business expense on its tax return.

"At TeleView, budgets don't come from the top down. Every team leader works with the team to propose quarterly and yearly budgets.

The team leaders know best how much money they need and what they need it for. Sometimes management has to bring them back down to earth a bit, or maybe it will say to a team, 'We want you to do this much more, so you'll need a bigger budget.' Everything is negotiable, but when the numbers are set, everyone sticks to them."

Corporate Investment

"Some corporate profits are put into short- or long-term investments. This is a significant profit center because we can make a lot of money with TeleView's money. A big chunk of the corporate profits go out to the investors in the form of **dividends**. The investors took a financial risk by investing in us—all investments are a financial risk, even the safe ones—so we want that risk to pay off for them.

"One of our Finance teams manages the accounts we have with major commercial banks and lending institutions. We have lines of credit like anyone else, and the strength of our credit is directly connected with the financial strength of the TeleView division and Corporate View. When the powers that be decide that the company should expand—for instance, build a new production plant in Phoenix—we make arrangements with our lenders for a new building loan. TeleView probably has enough funds available to pay cash for the building, which is where my team would come in. But sometimes it makes better financial sense to not tie up money in a long-term commitment like a new building. Sure, we pay interest on the building loan, but we can usually earn more than the interest we pay if we don't have to invest all those millions of dollars in a building.

"It's all about strategy; it's all about making small gains, and sometimes large gains, depending on the circumstances. It's about maintaining the flow of money, or **cash flow**, so that TeleView can function smoothly.

"Just like in football, we need scouting reports on the various financial options we have as we invest the corporation's money. Just like coaches and players create a game plan, we must do our financial research and prepare a strategy. We use several services to help us formulate our plan. These services give us the scouting reports we need.

"Are you familiar with Dun & Bradstreet (NYSE:DNB) or any of the marketing research firms? No? I'm surprised Casey didn't mention Dun & Bradstreet when you were working with that group. I know the group uses them all the time to help with marketing research.

"We use Dun & Bradstreet, Primark (NYSE:PMK), McGraw-Hill (NYSE:MHP), and several other financial research consulting firms to track companies that deliver financial and investment services. We also track new companies that want to work with us to see whether they are **solvent** and are good risks.

Figure 8-2
Dun & Bradstreet is a global research giant.

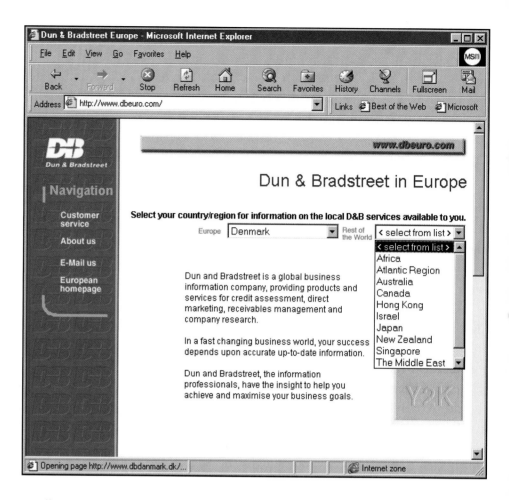

"We need to make credit decisions and prepare recommendations on different investment options. To do all of this successfully, we need reliable financial information. Most of this information is available over the Web. Some financial information is free; some requires an up-front fee. This information is easy to access through the Web. It doesn't take us much time to find out what we need to know, but it is important to do so. If we don't, we can make a bad play and cost the corporation.

"Now you have an overview of what Finance and Accounting is all about. Remember, finance is a game of strategy. Consider all your options carefully before you call a play."

Activity Overviews

The Finance and Accounting function is essential to the survival of every business, large and small. There are three major business types:

- **Single or sole proprietorships:** A business owned by an individual is called a *single* or *sole proprietorship*. Many consultants in business for themselves manage sole proprietorships.

- **Partnerships:** A business owned by two or more people is called a *partnership*. Many legal and accounting firms are organized into partnerships.

- **Corporations:** Businesses incorporated under state laws are called corporations. A corporation can be any size, from a small business of two or three people to a huge organization of 100,000 or more employees.

Ownership in a corporation is held by *shareholders* (also called *stockholders*), who buy shares of ownership. The shareholders of a corporation elect a board of directors to oversee the company. For the various divisions and business units of the corporation, the board may hire a CEO (chief executive officer), CFO (chief financial officer), CIO (chief information officer), COO (chief operations officer), plus the president and vice presidents who run the divisions.

Business Milestones

Dun & Bradstreet

In 1841, during the height of the U.S. Industrial Revolution, Lewis Tappan anticipated the information age. He created a mercantile agency and provided other businesses and traders with information about credit needs and market trends. This was at a time when westward migration and settlement were fueling business opportunities in North America. Eventually, his company created business information and financial research data as we know it today.

Tappan's dream evolved into Dun & Bradstreet (NYSE:DNB)*, a global provider of business-related information. With more than 16,000 employees, D&B serves business needs in 40 countries. The company researches and catalogs the performance of 45 million companies around the world.

In business, you might not have time to do extensive research yourself on financial markets, sales potential, or the performance of other companies. Time is money, and D&B and firms like it can save you a great deal of money by providing reliable information to help in decision making.

If you are a credit manager and need credit references on other companies and potential business partners, better check D&B's database. If you are a senior financial analyst and need to see whether the bank you are borrowing investment *capital* from is solvent and profitable, check D&B. If you are a product marketing manager and need market research to help define a market segment or niche, better check D&B. If you need to validate your position in a white paper for a new financial or marketing plan, better include data from D&B. If you create a new service you want other companies to know about, better let D&B know about it first. It can pass the information along to interested potential business partners.

Every decision in business requires some risk. Data from D&B and businesses like it can help you make informed decisions and minimize your risks.

A few other prominent business information services are Primark, McGraw-Hill, and J.D. Power and Associates.

*Dun & Bradstreet Europe. *Dun & Bradstreet*. Online. Available: **www.dbeuro.com/eu_abou.htm**. February 27, 1998.

Regardless of the kind of business or its size, all corporations need good accounting to

- Provide financial data on which decisions can be made.
- Assist in tax preparation.
- Report to stockholders.
- Organize and plan department and business-unit budgets.
- Pay bills and receive and account for payments made to the business.
- Maintain solvency and track profits.
- Audit medical, dental, and insurance plans.
- Supervise purchasing, travel, and miscellaneous spending.

Activity 8-1 Jobs in Accounting will have you visit various members of the Finance and Accounting team at TeleView on the Intranet. You will consider how you would enjoy a job in Finance and Accounting. You will get an idea of what accountants do, how much preparation they need, and where they fit in the overall company.

Activity 8-2 Forms, Forms, and More Forms will help you understand the financial needs behind many of the different forms and reports a corporation needs to have filled out, filed, and reported on.

Activity 8-3 Reviewing a Quarterly Report Summary will give you a look at the bottom-line health of Corporate View. You will need to make some decisions on the health of the company and whether it is a good investment risk.

Activity 8-4 The Major Accounting Firms Online will take you to the Web to visit some of the most recognized accounting and consulting firms. Each company you visit, along with countless smaller firms, can help a company organize and maintain an effective accounting system.

Understanding the meanings of these terms will help you learn the concepts and develop the skills related to Finance and Accounting covered in the chapter. In preparation for completing the chapter activities, access the Intranet and find the definition for each of these terms by clicking the **_ShopTalk_** link on the **_Regular Features_** page.

- Account Manager
- Accounts Payable
- Accounts Receivable
- Actuary
- Adjuster
- Analyst
- Assets
- Auditor
- Balance Sheet
- Bookkeeper
- Capital
- Cash Flow

- Clerk
- Controller
- Corporation
- Dividends
- Earnings Statement
- EPS (Earnings Per Share)
- Fiscal Year
- General Ledger
- IRS (Internal Revenue Service)
- Liabilities

- Liquid Assets
- Owner Equity
- Partnership
- Payroll
- Purchasing
- SEC (Securities and Exchange Commission)
- Single or Sole Proprietorship
- Solvent
- Stock Options

Accounting personnel have many different jobs to perform. Although accountants concern themselves with many issues, in broad terms, they consider three main areas:

- Solvency
- Profitability
- Cash flow

Solvency asks, "Can the corporation pay its bills?" Profitability asks, "Is the corporation making money?" And cash flow asks, "Is there enough money on hand today to meet today's needs?"

A business may be very profitable and still experience cash-flow problems. For example, if a business spends a great deal of money developing a new line of designer jeans in the first, second, and third quarters of the year but the jeans won't be ready to sell until the fourth quarter, it might develop a cash-flow problem. The business might need to borrow money from a lending institution or pull cash out of other liquid assets to remain solvent until the new product line starts to sell. The corporation may post a first-, second-, or even a third-quarter loss but post a huge fourth-quarter gain, allowing it to pay back investors and creditors alike, thus erasing the deficit and posting a year-end dividend.

In the final analysis, a business must have a good "bottom line." The bottom line refers to the last line of a **balance sheet**, which summarizes a corporation's financial performance. A balance sheet lists the company's **assets**, **liabilities**, and **owner equity**, providing a snapshot of the total worth of the corporation.

Many accounts are required to create a balance sheet. A company's **general ledger** includes all of these accounts.

Keeping these financial records complete and accurate requires a workgroup of highly

The **Least** You **Should** Know About...

CPAs

CPAs are the backbone of any Accounting Department. CPA is short for certified public accountant. To become a CPA, a candidate must pass an examination given by the American Institute of Certified Public Accountants (AICPA). To qualify for the CPA designation, a candidate must also have experience in the accounting field and a degree in accounting from a university or college.

Although a CPA is often at the top of an Accounting Department, many other people contribute to the financial well-being of the corporation, including bookkeepers, payroll clerks, accounts payable clerks, accounts receivable clerks, administrative assistants, and other office workers who help "prepare the books."

The CPA designation opens the doors to many complex accounting jobs besides those in Accounting Departments. For example, corporations hire outside auditors with CPA backgrounds to verify the accuracy of their records. This way, there can be no question about the accuracy of the corporation's books. Tax specialists are essential to the success of a corporation. Without good tax advice, a corporation's revenue can suffer. A CPA has the necessary background to move into corporate tax work.

Figure 8-3
The AICPA prepares CPAs
in the use of generally
accepted accounting
principles.

trained people. Teams of clerks, bookkeepers, administrative assistants, accountants, and CPAs contribute to the accounting in a business by maintaining everything from department budgets to investments and assets to federal and state tax records.

One of the best ways to learn about these "accountant types" is to visit them in their offices and cubicles. Barring that, view their online biographies on the Intranet to discover what they do, what they need to know to do it, and how they relate to each other.

Just-in-Time Training

The Players in the Money Game

1. Access the local Intranet or the Corporate View Web site.

2. Access the *Regular Features* page and choose the *Employee Contacts* link.

3. To view the online biographies of the key contacts in this department, choose the ***Contacts in Finance and Accounting*** link.

4. What is the reason given by the Finance and Accounting Department for listing these particular employees on the corporate Intranet?

_____

_____

5. Select five of the biographies and read them. In a word processing file, give this information about each biography you read.

   • Name

   • Title

   • What does this person do on the job?

   • From what you have read, what kind of education or on-the job experience did this person obtain prior to taking this job?

   • How interesting do you think this person's job would be for you?

Save As:

F&Abios

Debriefing

Sometimes, when you are new to an organization, you wonder, "What do all these people do?" Learning the names of others and what they do is beneficial in a number of ways—not the least of which is to gain an understanding of how career paths work. For example, by knowing what people do in the Finance and Accounting Department, you can learn what a logical career path might be should you choose a career in accounting. By knowing the team members in the Finance and Accounting Department, you would be better able to answer questions such as: Where does one start? What is considered an entry-level position? What does one have to do to move up to a job having increased pay and greater responsibility? Knowing who is who and what they do can help you understand career paths.

Think and write about the following:

In this Debriefing, you will play the Career Ladder in Accounting game. Fourteen job titles are listed below. Rank them in the order you think they would appear in the chain of command for accountants. For example, in the military, the highest position is a general, with colonel, major, captain, and lieutenant following in a descending order.

Rank these jobs, with a 1 being assigned to the highest position and a 2, 3, or 4 being assigned to less demanding or entry-level position(s). Some jobs are roughly equivalent to others, just as math and science teachers may be considered on the same level. In this exercise, you may have several positions with the same numeric ranking.

Use these questions to help guide your rankings and look at the **_Contacts in Finance and Accounting_** biographies for clues. Also, access the **_Human Resources & Management_**, **_Current Job Openings @ TeleView_**, **_Finance and Accounting_** links to find other clues to help you rank the jobs.

- Does this job involve supervising others?
- Does this job require greater experience?
- Does this job require a higher level of education?
- Does this job merit a higher rate of pay?

HMO Manager	_____	Internal Auditor	_____
Tax Accountant	_____	Travel Clerk	_____
CFO	_____	Credit Card Accounts Manager	_____
Payroll Manager	_____	Life Insurance Accounts Manager	_____
Alternative Medical/Dental		Financial Analyst	_____
Accounts Manager	_____	Director of Investment Operations	_____
Senior Financial Analyst	_____	AP Manager	_____
401(k) Investment Manager	_____		

Activity 8-2   *Forms, Forms, and More Forms*

A new employee in a corporation has lots of forms to fill out. Most people sign them after only glancing at them. Most of the forms are required by law. The forms will vary from business to business, but they frequently include

- W-4 Form
- Life Insurance Beneficiary Form
- Health Choice Provider Form
- Retirement or 401(k) Investment Form
- Direct-Deposit Form
- Accident Information Form
- Proof of Citizenship Status Form

- Additional or Supplemental Insurance Forms
- Dental Plan Selection Form
- Corporate Credit Card Form
- Travel and Other Reimbursement Forms
- Security Card Information Form

This is just a sample of the forms you might need to complete while on the job. Many of them are essential to the financial well-being of the employee and of the corporation. For convenience, most of these forms are distributed and collected by HR personnel; then the information is passed on to the appropriate departments and functions. Many of the forms end up in someone's inbox in Finance and Accounting. HR will work with others, and because most of the forms are required by law, Legal Services will often get involved to make sure the forms are accurate and meet specific legal standards.

Business Milestones

The American Institute of Certified Public Accountants

The 330,000-member American Institute of Certified Public Accountants, or AICPA, is the primary organization overseeing the accounting profession. The AICPA sets standards for auditing, tax, and other accounting practices. It is a primary source of technical and professional information for accountants.

The setting of professional accounting standards began back in 1887. The AICPA ensures the quality of its accountants by conferring a professional certification. To be certified, candidates must pass the CPA qualification exam administered by the AICPA. The exam is given twice each year. The AICPA provides training and seminars to help its members prepare for exams and to help current CPAs stay on top of their trade.

The AICPA also provides conferences and training sessions for accountants and publishes the respected *Journal of Accounting*. These training sessions and publications help CPAs learn to follow the GAAP (generally accepted accounting principles). The Financial Accounting Standards Board and the Governmental Accounting Standards Board develop GAAP principles. These committees are sponsored by the AICPA. They affirm the appropriate accounting principles for CPAs to follow.

AICPA Online. *American Institute of Certified Public Accountants*. Online. Available: ***www.aicpa.org***. March 4, 1998.

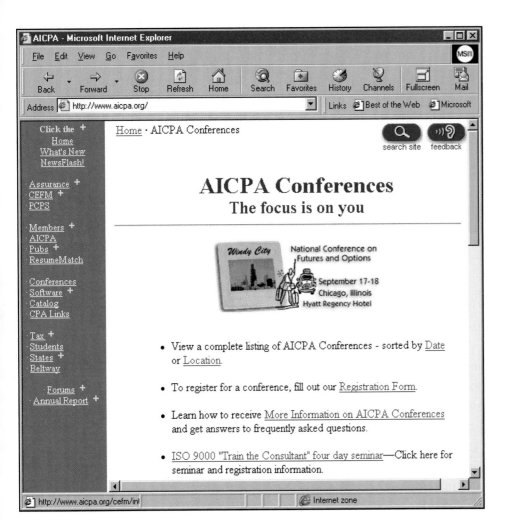

Figure 8-4
The AICPA provides seminars to help members improve accounting and management skills.

In this activity, you will use the Corporate View Intranet to learn what each of these forms is for and then determine whose inbox the forms may eventually be forwarded to.

Just-in-Time Training

The Purpose of Forms

1. Access the local Intranet or the Corporate View Web site.

2. Select the ***Human Resources & Management*** link from the Corporate View Intranet Home page.

3. Click the ***Forms, Forms, and More Forms*** link.

4. Select five of the forms found on the list that you believe will likely be passed from HR to a member of the Finance and Accounting team.

5. List your five forms in a word processing document.

6. In your own words, provide a short description (10 to 15 words) of each form.

Forms

7. Access the **_Contacts in Finance and Accounting_** under the **_Regular Features_**, **_Employee Contacts_** links.

8. From your knowledge of the employees in Finance and Accounting, determine where your five forms will eventually end up. Whose inbox will your five forms be delivered to? Add the name and job title of this contact person next to your description of each form.

Debriefing

Corporations often provide retirement and investment options to their employees. These plans are an important way to increase your net worth. One of the best methods of saving is to contribute to a retirement account. There are many retirement plans, and some provide the advantage of tax sheltering; that is, you gain interest on money you would have paid in taxes. Many countries allow you to save for retirement in this manner. In the United States, these options are called 401(k) and 403(b) accounts. IRAs, or Individual Retirement Accounts, also fit into this category. In Canada, there are programs that offer similar benefits.

You might think that you are many, many years from retirement; however, it is never too early to start saving. Do you want to be a millionaire? By putting $167 per month in a retirement account starting at age 21, you will have more than $1 million in savings at age 65 (based on a 9-percent rate of return on your investments and a projected 3-percent rate of inflation).

Think and write about the following:

Do some research on the Web or in your local library to learn more about 401(k) plans.

1. In brief terms, what is a 401(k) plan?

   _____

2. When do you (ideally) pay taxes on the contributions you make to the 401(k) and on the earnings?

   _____

3. What is the age for withdrawing funds from your 401(k) without a penalty?

   _____

4. What is the highest amount per year that you may legally contribute to a 401(k)?

_____

5. Who, besides you, might contribute to your 401(k) plan?

_____

SIC and NAICS Codes

SIC (Standard Industrial Classification) codes are assigned by the government. When a corporation files its taxes with the **IRS (Internal Revenue Service)**, it needs to list a SIC code. SIC codes are also used by other government agencies and by corporations to classify and compare businesses in similar categories.

NAICS (North American Industry Classification System) codes were created to replace SIC codes as a result of the North American Free Trade Agreement (NAFTA) in the 1990s. Developed by Mexico, Canada, and the United States, these codes represent a more international way of looking at industries and industry classifications. Here are some examples:

11111	Soybean Farming
11231	Chicken Egg Production
22111	Electric Power Generation
31132	Chocolate Manufacturing
4482	Shoe Stores

North American Industry Classification System (NAICS). *U.S. Census Bureau.* Online. Available: **www.census.gov/epcd/www/naics.html**. March 4, 1998.

Figure 8-5
The NAICS classifies industries in North America.

Activity 8-3   *Reviewing a Quarterly Report Summary*

Now it is time to look at Corporate View's performance for the last few quarters. Here is what the president and CEO of Corporate View, Madeline Tucker, said in a press release the day the report was released.

*This is one multinational corporation that is never shy about posting its **EPS (earnings per share)** or its quarterly reports. Profitability is on the rise. The future of the corporation looks great, never better. As we invest, we will have a few ups and downs, but the general trend and health of this corporation is secure for the next decade.*

So says Madeline Tucker. But it's time to look at the record for yourself and answer a few questions. Is all this great stuff you've been hearing about Corporate View real? Does it show up on the bottom line?

Figure 8-6
The SEC watches stocks, protecting investors from fraud.

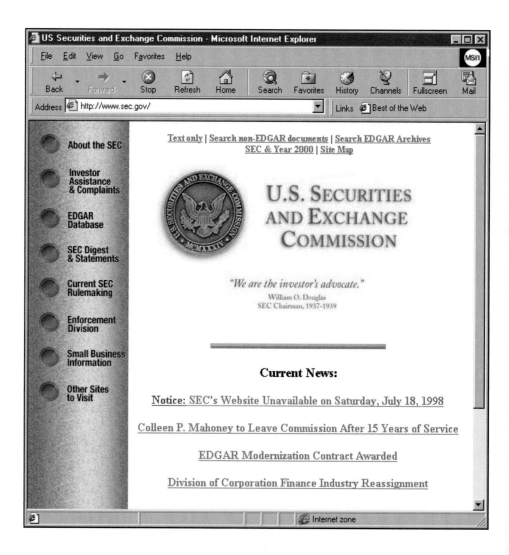

The Third Quarter

Actually, the business year consists of four quarters. Corporations report their quarterly earnings while an anxious Wall Street (home of the NYSE, but used in this case to mean influential company shareholders and stock market analysts) waits for the results. If earnings are high, the price per share usually goes up following the good news. If earnings are poor, the price often goes down, reflecting the poor performance. If a corporation posts a big loss, the bad news could send the company's stock price plummeting, weakening its ability to raise the capital (or resources) it needs to stay competitive.

Quarterly financial statements are the responsibility of the Finance and Accounting function of a corporation. An *earnings statement* is often validated by independent auditors to make sure the corporation is reporting its earnings accurately, which the company is legally obligated to do. The *SEC (Securities and Exchange Commission)* monitors corporate stock reports and protects investors from stock fraud.

Just-in-Time Training

Look at the Quarterly Report

1. Access the local Intranet or the Corporate View Web site.

2. Select the ***Finance & Accounting*** link.

3. Click the ***Quarterly Report Summary*** link.

Look up the following general information about Corporate View. If you don't know what some of the terms mean, visit the ***ShopTalk*** link on the Intranet for help.

4. In which state does Corporate View have its headquarters?

_____

5. What stock exchange trades Corporate View stock, and what is its ticker?

_____

6. What is the SIC code for Corporate View? What is Corporate View's NAICS code?

_____

7. How many shares does Corporate View have outstanding?

_____

8. How many shareholders does Corporate View have? How many shares does the average shareholder own? (Get out your calculator to solve this question.)

_____

9. Give a brief description of Corporate View's primary business activities as stated in the quarterly report summary:

_____

_____

_____

_____

10. Currently, Corporate View's stock is going (circle one): Up – Down – Same

11. The recent trend for Corporate View's stock has been (circle one): Up – Down – Same

12. The long-term trend for Corporate View's stock has been (circle one): Up – Down – Same

13. When does Corporate View's *fiscal year* end? Why do you think Corporate View's fiscal or financial year doesn't end in December?

_____

_____

14. How many cents were paid per share as a dividend?

_____

15. What does EPS stand for? What is Corporate View's EPS?

_____

Debriefing

Financial analysts examine many things when evaluating the health of a company. One indicator is how much money is earned per employee. When the quarterly summary was compiled, Corporate View listed its net sales per employee as $193,141. Does this seem high or low? Let's compare this and other figures with several other corporations.

Think and write about the following:

1. Use the Web to find information about the corporations listed below. Access the **Stock Watcher Links** on the **Regular Features**

page. Select a link and find the current stock quote for a company from the list below. Then look for links that provide additional details or profiles of the company. Try to find the net sales per employee, EPS, and annual dividend for each company and record the information below.

Corporation	Net Sales/Employee	EPS	Annual Dividend
MSFT	_____	_____	_____
HWP	_____	_____	_____
T	_____	_____	_____
FON	_____	_____	_____

2. How does Corporate View compare in each category with the corporations listed above?

   _____

   _____

3. Which of these companies would you like to own stock in and why?

   _____

   _____

Activity 8-4 — *The Major Accounting Firms Online*

Business Milestones

The Major Accounting Firms

To be recognized as one of the finest accounting firms in the world is a major achievement for any company. You will get a chance to visit these companies on the Web in Activity 8-4. The big hitters include

- Arthur Andersen & Co.
- PricewaterhouseCoopers
- Deloitte & Touche
- Ernst & Young
- KPMG

These firms and many similar smaller ones can help a company organize and maintain an effective accounting system.

Legendary firms in the accounting field are not hard to find. Several firms carry the industry designation of "major players." Working for one of these megafirms can help aspiring CPAs establish themselves in their careers.

In this activity, you will need a connection to the Web to visit several major accounting firms online. After your visit, you will write a white paper recommending one of these major firms as a potential partner that can help Corporate View with its tax accounting responsibilities. Then you will list reasons why Corporate View can benefit by outsourcing some of this work to experts.

Just-in-Time Training

Visiting Accounting and Consulting Firms

1. Access the Corporate View Web site.
2. Click on the ***Finance & Accounting*** link.
3. Select the ***Major Accounting Firms*** link.
4. Visit each major accounting firm listed on the Intranet page. Take notes on each. Specifically, search for reasons why Corporate View may improve its tax situation by employing one of these major accounting and consulting firms.
5. Write a white paper recommending one of these firms to help streamline Corporate View's tax accounting system. Which corporation, in your view, should Corporate View employ? If you would like to review how to write a white paper, look over the white paper you prepared for The Corporate Inbox in Chapter 7.

Save As:

WP2

In your white paper, you focused on tax issues only. What other things have you learned about the major accounting and consulting firms and the services they offer? In what other areas can these firms help Corporate View improve its corporate performance?

Think and write about the following:

Choose one of the major accounting firms. In a word processing file, identify five specific services this firm can provide for Corporate View, explaining each briefly and how each can be of benefit.

Save As:

CVConslt

The **Least** You **Should** Know **About...**

Stock Options

Want one of the best deals in the working world? Work for a corporation that gives ***stock options*** to its employees. Once upon a time, stock options were available only to company executives like CEOs, presidents, and vice presidents. Today, stock options are increasingly available to the rank-and-file workers in a corporation.

Stock options are awarded to employees as incentives. Employees are able to lock into the corporation's stock at a predetermined price—say, 100 shares at $30 per share. Then they can purchase the stock. They don't have to buy, but if they do and the stock goes up to $50 per share, the employee has just made an extra $2,000. Not a bad deal. The employees become shareholders in the corporation, with the rights and privileges other stockholders have.

Stockholders don't have to sell stock to make money. Successful companies pay dividends to each shareholder if the company makes a profit. Stockholders wait with anticipation for the quarterly reports so that they can get a sense of their EPS and anticipate the dividends, or payments, they will receive. If each of your 100 shares earns a dividend of $1, then you have earned $100.

Most corporations think that stock options make employees feel better about the company they work for and thus they are more interested in its success. Stock options provide an incentive for employees to work efficiently to make things better because they have a share in the success of the corporation. Also, employees tend to hold on to their stock longer than outside investors. This is considered a plus for the corporation's stability.

Executive Summary

Finance and Accounting is one of the most vital functions in any corporation. The goal of Finance is to make long- and short-term gains on investments. Managing money is an essential activity that requires research, strategy, and hard work.

To manage money in a large corporation, a small army of accountants and assistants is required, including controllers, analysts, auditors, bookkeepers, clerks, and account managers. A Finance and Accounting Department contains many functions, including Payroll, Accounts Payable, Accounts Receivable, taxes, and insurance, to name a few. Other departments, such as Purchasing and Marketing and Sales, interface closely with the accounting team. In fact, all departments have ties to Finance and Accounting.

The CPA designation is earned by accountants with college degrees and experience in the accounting field. To become a CPA, a candidate must pass a certification test prepared by the American Institute of Certified Public Accountants (AICPA). The AICPA sets standards for accounting. The GAAP, a set of generally accepted accounting principles, is maintained by the AICPA Financial Accounting Standards Board and the Governmental Accounting Standards Board.

Corporations rely on other corporations for financial and market research data. Dun & Bradstreet, Primark, McGraw-Hill, J.D. Power and Associates, and the major accounting firms are just a few examples of corporations whose business is helping other businesses stay in touch with their bottom line.

Employees can often invest a portion of their earnings in stock options and retirement plans. With the right kind of investments made through their corporations, they can accumulate a significant portfolio for retirement.

The three kinds of businesses are: single proprietorships owned by individuals, partnerships owned by more than one individual, and corporations owned by shareholders and incorporated under the laws of a particular state.

All businesses, large or small, need accurate accounting to make decisions, pay taxes, report earnings to shareholders, organize their work, pay bills, award benefits, manage insurance programs, and track profits. Successful businesses are solvent, are profitable, and maintain the cash flow they need to conduct their daily business activities.

Technical Communications

White papers are a means to express ideas or present options in a business setting. Financial statements are issued by businesses and can provide a wealth of information regarding the company's assets, liabilities, and overall financial position. Travel budgets and expense reimbursement forms are used to record projected and actual expenses for a business trip.

The Corporate Inbox

Here are some messages that need to be answered by someone in Finance and Accounting. Answer them with the help of the Corporate Intranet and your own best judgment. If you need help preparing documents, access the **Style Guide** under the **Corporate Communications** link.

TO: Intern
FROM: *smalone@corpview.com*
SUBJECT: Finance and Accounting Terms
MESSAGE:

We received this inquiry from Al Howard over in the MediView division.

Please send a response via email to *ahoward@corpview.com*. I would do it, but I have to finish this quarterly report.

Thanks,
Spence

<<<<<<<<Forwarded by Spence Malone>>>>>>>>>>

I have been working at MediView for two weeks now, and I am a bit confused. Corporate View has CEOs, CFOs, CIOs, COOs, presidents, and a chairperson of the board. Who is in charge? Also, the following terms keep showing up on the Intranet: EPS, GAAP, NAICS, and SIC. What do they mean, and are they related in any way?

Save As:

Inbox8A

18 Overbrook Avenue
Beverly, MA 01915-2846

Current Date

Corporate View
One Corporate View Drive
Boulder, CO 80303-0103

Ladies and Gentlemen:

Your company has come to my attention as a possible investment opportunity.
I heard that Corporate View is a partnership. Is that true? I am thinking about
buying 100 shares of Corporate View stock. Can you prove to me that Corporate View is profitable and solvent? How can I be assured of a return on my
investment?

Sincerely yours,

Christy Turrin

(Ms.) Christy Turrin

Dear Intern:

Please prepare a reply letter for my review and signature.

This letter is somewhat disorganized and hard to follow. Be professional in the reply. You will want to anticipate questions that are not asked about our corporation. We can use all the investors we can get.

Thanks,
Spence

Save As:

Inbox8B

TO: Intern
FROM: *rmills@corpview.com*
SUBJECT: Career Opportunities in Finance
and Accounting
MESSAGE:

We just received a letter of inquiry in HR
concerning employment at Corporate View. George
Hanks writes:

A rapidly growing company like Corporate View
requires the services of talented, committed
accountants. As the enclosed resume indicates, I
just completed my CPA and finished a six-month
internship at Arthur Andersen & Co., one of the
major accounting firms. What career
opportunities are available for me at Corporate
View?

We get a lot of inquiries like this. Can you
prepare a white paper explaining career
opportunities in Finance and Accounting? We plan
to use your paper as a training tool to brief our
HR recruitment specialists on how to answer this
type of question. Please focus on two aspects:

1. The background and on-the-job experience that
   many of our employees currently have.
2. The types of jobs we have here at Corporate
   View in Finance and Accounting.

Thanks,
Robin

Hi, this is Spence. We need your help in preparing a survey that will help us identify potential investors for Corporate View stock. Basically, we need ten questions that will tell us whether a person knows about Corporate View, whether she or he is in the habit of investing, what kinds of corporations the person invests in, and whether she or he would be interested in investing in Corporate View. You can put in questions to see what the person knows about our business units, whether she or he has a favorable impression of our products—that sort of thing.

Please send me your survey questions in an email message. Thanks. Bye.

Save As:

Inbox8D

Online Business Trends

Access the Corporate View Web site. Use the **_Stock Watcher Links_** on the **_Regular Features_** page to identify the following ticker symbols and learn how each of these companies did in the stock market today.

Current Date _____

Note:

Many major accounting firms, whose business it is to audit and account for other's performance, do not trade their company's stock on the open market for fear of creating conflicts of interest between themselves and their clients.

Ticker	Exchange	Company Name	Current Price
DNB	NYSE	_____	_____
PMK	NYSE	_____	_____
MHP	NYSE	_____	_____

When a Few Words Will Do

According to what you have read in this chapter or on the Corporate View Intranet, answer the following questions in a word processing document.

1. What is a CPA, and how does someone become one? Are they necessary in business?

2. How can stock options be of benefit to an employee and to a corporation?

3. Why would large corporations use a company like Dun & Bradstreet or one of the major accounting firms?

4. How can a quarterly report help you determine the health of a corporation?

5. What valuable service does the AICPA provide to the corporate world?

Save As:

Online8

Working in an Online World

One budget item many people in a corporation get involved with is the travel budget. Planning a business trip and reporting the expenses can take some time, but the work has to be done or the corporation cannot claim the costs as a business expense on its tax return.

A series of workshops and conferences is open to you as part of the TeleView Finance and Accounting team. Choose one of the conferences from the ***Conferences for Finance and Accounting Staff*** link on the ***Finance & Accounting*** page. Prepare a budget showing how much it will cost you to get there, participate in the conference, and get home again.

Use the Corporate View Travel Planning and Reimbursement Form to help you plan. To access the form, select ***Employee Travel Links*** on the ***Regular Features*** page. Scroll to the bottom of the page and select the appropriate link to download the form as a spreadsheet file. Or select the ***View Sample Form*** link to see a sample completed form.

You can also check airline, car rental, and hotel rates by accessing the ***Employee Travel Links*** on the ***Regular Features*** page.

Save As:

Pfolio8

Now that you have had some experience planning a trip for yourself, how about planning one for a group? The controller of TeleView has just come to your group and said, to everyone's surprise, "I am taking the entire team to the Spring Assurance Conference in San Diego. Get together and get us there in a reasonable fashion without shooting the entire travel budget for the year. Oh, by the way, this trip hasn't been approved yet by the CFO. Someone prepare a memo explaining why I need to take all of you to San Diego for three days so that you can do your jobs better."

1. Form a team with several other employees.

2. Divide up the workload. One person can write the memo, another can check on airline tickets, another on hotels, and so on. You will need a live Web connection to complete your travel plans. Use the ***Employee Travel Links*** on the corporate Intranet's ***Regular Features*** page.

3. Make your travel plans using the Travel Planning and Reimbursement Form. To access the form, select ***Employee Travel Links*** on the ***Regular Features*** page. Scroll to the bottom of the page and select the

appropriate link to download the form as a spreadsheet file. Or select the **_View Sample Form_** link to see a sample completed form.

4. If you need help formatting your memo, access the **_Style Guide_** under the **_Corporate Communications_** link. Have the form and memo on the controller's desk by morning.

Thinking and Writing About Your Business

Finance and Accounting is critical to the success of the corporation. More than probably any other function, it interfaces and interacts with each department, group, team, and individual in the corporation. Brainstorm some kinds of things an accountant can do for the following departments or individuals.

1. Human Resources
2. Research and Development
3. Corporate Communications
4. Manufacturing
5. Marketing
6. Sales
7. Legal Services
8. Information Technology

9. Individual employees
10. The Corporate View Board of Directors

Overtime

Tax Support Online

The U.S. Internal Revenue Service (IRS) posts all its forms and advice for businesses online. Visit the IRS and see what help businesses can get from the biggest tax collector of them all.

1. Access the Corporate View Web site. (You will need a live Web connection to complete this activity.)

2. Click on the **_Tax Information/IRS_** link on the **_Finance & Accounting_** Web page.

3. Review the IRS site. Prepare a white paper listing the types of support and forms available at this site for small and large businesses and for individual taxpayers.

Small businesses usually can't afford one of the major accounting and consulting firms to help them improve their financial performance. Small accountancy firms are in every town, however, and may be quite affordable for a small business.

Think and write about the following:

Locate three firms in your area that employ CPAs. See whether they have Web sites, or interview someone from each firm.

1. Name the firms.

2. Are these businesses single proprietorships, partnerships, or corporations?

3. How can these accounting firms help other small businesses? What kinds of services can they provide a small business entrepreneur?

4. Do you think you might ever use the services of a CPA?

Save As:

ASB8

Online Evaluation

Access the Corporate View Web site and take the Online Evaluation for this chapter.

1. Click on the ***Employee Training and Evaluations*** link on the ***Regular Features*** page.

2. Select the ***Online Tests*** link. (You must be a registered user to access the online tests. If you are not a registered user, click the ***Register*** link and follow the instructions on the screen. Then click the ***Online Tests*** link to return to the Online Tests page.)

3. Choose the ***Chapter 8 A View from Finance and Accounting*** link on the Online Tests page.

4. Enter the username and password you selected when you registered.

5. Take the test. Click the **First**, **Back**, **Next**, and **Last** buttons to navigate through the questions. Click the **Finish** button to submit your test for grading. If you wish to close the test without submitting it for grading, click the **Cancel** button. Any answers you have entered will be lost if you cancel the test.

Chapter 9

A View from Legal Services

CHAPTER OBJECTIVES

1. Explore the legal function in a business
2. Examine differences between civil and criminal law
3. Distinguish among copyrights, trade names, trademarks, and patents
4. Discuss the incorporation process
5. Describe how the law affects each mission-critical function

Technical Communications

- Simplify legal language into technical communications that are easy to understand
- Choose search terms to refine and narrow searches for relevant results
- Explain why obsolete, inaccurate, or misleading information should be purged from Web and Intranet sites

A Suitable Profession

"Hello. My name is Charles Cooper. Please, call me Coop. I'm the corporate counsel assigned by Legal Services to the TeleView division. This is my third year in this position.

"Melissa sent me an email saying you are interested in learning a little about the work Legal Services does for TeleView. I could start by referring you to the law books in our library because everything we do here is contained in them. But I don't think you would find that approach very useful.

"The fact that you often find so many legal books and case files around a legal office provides a clue to the kind of work lawyers spend most of their time doing. Lawyers work with laws, and laws take the form of written documents.

"I spend the majority of my workday writing and doing legal research. This isn't the stuff of an exciting episode of a television law show, nor is it the kind of material usually featured in novels. Nevertheless, the success of TeleView depends on exacting compliance to established laws.

"I don't need to tell you that we live in a time of great legal congestion. You would never believe some of the cases in the courts these days. My job as head counsel is to make sure TeleView has as little to do with the courts as possible. I'm here to see that everything TeleView says or does is in line with the written law. This is a major way TeleView and its parent company, Corporate View, protect their legal interests.

"As a corporation in the business of manufacturing products, one of our key concerns is that the products we produce and sell are safe for consumers. TeleView must adhere to many laws pertaining to product testing and product safety standards.

"Some of this may sound obvious, but our products must be made in such a way that they won't harm or endanger anyone who is using them properly. We can't sell phones with batteries that blow up in people's faces or shock folks when they try to make calls in a rainstorm. They can't be made of little pieces that fall off easily and that babies can swallow, and they shouldn't have volume controls that might cause permanent damage to someone's inner ear. This principle is true for all Corporate View products. We can't sell a dangerous medical device or a shirt whose dye comes off and causes a rash.

Figure 9-1
Products must be carefully made to not endanger consumers.

"If there is any reasonable possibility for harm or danger, however remote, appropriate warnings must be included in our product documentation. Obviously, we work closely with R&D, Marketing and Sales, and Corporate Communications to make sure the right kinds of product warnings are included with all our products.

"Some product statements mean exactly what they say. 'If an unauthorized person tries to fix the phone, the warrantee is void.' Other statements are implied, meaning they are subject to reasonable interpretation but cover a broader scope of possibilities. 'TeleView is in no way responsible for the unlawful use of any of its products or services.' We could never list every possible illegal use of a telephone, so we imply that TeleView is not responsible for any kind of misuse.

"We review TeleView's product literature and advertising to make sure they contain no misleading statements or violations of **trademark** or **copyright** laws. And we have a team responsible for following up on unauthorized use of our corporate trademarks and copyrighted material. Lately we've had a problem with the TeleView name showing up on some imitation, or bootleg, products from over-

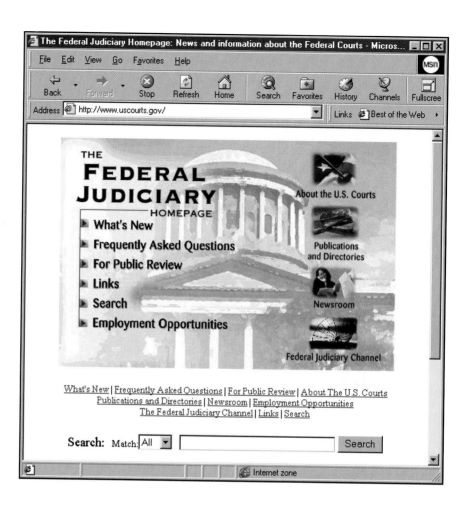

The **Least** You
Should Know
About...

Civil and Criminal Law

The violation of **criminal laws** dominates our news and our television screens. Criminal laws identify acts of aggression against the public that are punishable by imprisonment, fines, or both. Murder, assault, theft, and bank robbery are violations of criminal law. Criminal law places the public, represented by government attorneys, against the accused violator.

Civil laws are very different. Civil cases attempt to resolve disputes or **torts** between people, corporations, and other entities. For example, a dispute between two neighbors over the placement of a fence between their properties is a civil dispute. If you buy a CD player that breaks, and the company claims the breakage is

not covered under the existing warrantee, you can go to small-claims court to get your money back. In this case, you are in civil **litigation**. If you are in a car accident on the way home from work involving a driver who doesn't have car insurance, you may take civil action to recover damages.

Most litigation (lawsuits) against corporations occurs in civil court, not criminal court. If a corporation deliberately and knowingly dumps toxic waste into a river, killing fish and birds, criminal charges can be filed against individuals in the corporation or the corporation itself. But this is rare. It is more likely that a civil case will result. Read more about civil cases in the Business Milestones IBM's ViaVoice and Dragon's NaturallySpeaking on page 266.

seas. It's not an easy thing to stop, but we're doing our best to prevent these imitations from being imported.

"You know that TeleView outsources many services to independent contractors. In every instance, we insist on a signed contract stating the terms of the service provided. Some employees are under contract, particularly those dealing with sensitive materials from the R&D and Information Technology departments. We have to keep our trade secrets secret.

"Part of our job is to draft or review contracts before anyone signs them. You can imagine the time involved in reviewing all these documents. We do it to protect the legal interests of Corporate View and the staff of TeleView.

"We have legal teams that handle corporate communications and publications, which include service and work contracts. Product issues are also handled, and these include warrantees, product liability, and compliance with regulatory laws of the FCC and other federal and state regulatory agencies.

"We retain two large law firms that handle other legal matters. One firm manages compliance with tax laws, fair trade statutes, and other financial matters. The other firm goes to bat for us whenever we need to be represented in court. It handles our defense in class action suits, which are rare; liability suits, which are less rare; and suits claiming unfair business practices, which unfortunately are common. If our in-house legal staff does its job, these suits never carry enough weight to make it to court. I'm proud of our track record.

"From my vantage point, the best lawyer is always the one who knows the most about the law. I make my living from what I know about the law. Then I apply what I know to protect this company legally, and along with it, the livelihood of every person who works here. In that sense, Legal Services is the key to this whole operation."

Activity Overviews

Corporations are created according to state and federal laws. All states have laws that govern the creation and maintenance of corporations and other businesses. These laws affect every aspect of a business and influence the actions of employees in every business function.

Corporations establish *trade names* and trademarks by which they do business. These trademarks represent the brand names people associate with products and corporations. Such names are registered so that they can be used only by a specific corporation. Trademarks like Coca-Cola, Pepsi, and Snapple are examples in the beverage industry. Trademarks are protected under state, federal, and international laws.

Laws govern the manufacture and sale of products. Agencies have even been created to police corporations to make sure they are selling safe products. For example, all the prescription drugs developed by MediView, Corporate View's medical and pharmaceutical division, are tested and approved by the Food and Drug Administration, an agency of the U.S. government, before they can be sold in the United States.

Corporations pay taxes. Tax laws affect everything from an employee's paycheck to sales tax collected from customers. Import duties or taxes on supplies, parts, and finished products can be levied (charged) for Corporate View's overseas operations.

In these activities, you will see how laws affect every corporation, mission-critical function, and employee within the corporation.

Activity 9-1 Incorporation will explore how and why corporations are formed. You will use excerpts from state constitutions to study the roots of corporate law, rules that the states impose on corporations, and the kinds of corporations that states allow.

Activity 9-2 Copyrights, Trademarks, Trade Names, and Patents will discuss the ways products are protected so that corporations can maintain a competitive edge with their brand names and new creations.

Activity 9-3 The Complexity of It All will explore the law as it affects the critical departments and functions of Corporate View. This will help you see the complexity of corporate law and its many specialties.

Activity 9-4 Legal Translations will allow you to read excerpts from the United States **Code of Federal Regulations (CFR)**, those relating to **patents**. After you study some of the language, you will get a chance to "translate" a few passages and answer questions about trademarks.

" *Corporate* ShopTalk "

Understanding the meanings of these terms will help you learn the concepts and develop the skills related to law and the Legal Services Department covered in the chapter. In preparation for completing the chapter activities, access the Intranet and find the definition for each of these terms by clicking the ***ShopTalk*** link on the ***Regular Features*** page.

- Charters
- Civil Laws
- Code
- Code of Federal Regulations (CFR)
- Copyright
- Criminal Law
- Domain Name
- Eminent Domain
- Incorporation
- Intellectual Property Rights
- Litigation
- Patent Pending
- Patents
- Registered Trademark
- Servicemark
- Torts
- Trade Names
- Trademark
- United States Code (USC)

Figure 9-3
*Contracts help businesses
to work together.*

Business
Milestones

Contracts

A contract is an agreement between two parties. It spells out what each party is responsible for in the agreement. Contracts have been widely used since ancient times. Early Mesopotamians wrote contracts on mud tables in cuneiform, an ancient alphabet written using the ends of marsh reeds.

Contracts are binding and are enforced by law. Penalties are usually assessed when the terms of the contract are not fulfilled. Contracts make it possible for individuals and corporations to work together with an assurance that each party will hold up its end of the bargain.

For example, if TeleView is building a new phone, it might contract with a supplier to provide 100,000 plastic phone cases in an assortment of colors. TeleView agrees to pay 10¢ per case. The contract legally binds Corporate View to buy the phone cases at the stated price and the supplier to provide them.

Contracts often include a penalty for late work. The contract might state that if the plastic phone cases arrive at TeleView a month late, $1,000 may be deducted from the price. If TeleView fails to pay the full amount, the supplier can seek payment in court on the basis of the contract.

Without contracts, it would be very difficult for corporations to work together. Contracts are certainly one of the most significant inventions of the business world.

Activity 9-1   *Incorporation*

To gain a corporate view of the business world, you need to investigate how and why corporations are created in the first place. The process of creating a corporation is called ***incorporation***. As you will see, incorporation protects corporate officers and stockholders.

Corporations are very important legal entities created by individuals wishing to organize the affairs of business in accordance with the law. As you learned in Chapter 8, a business can also be organized as a sole proprietorship or a partnership. A corporation, however, provides the corporate founders and stockholders with greater legal protection than these other alternatives.

For example, if a sole proprietor is sued for $1,000,000 and loses, he or she must pay the money out of business or personal assets. Partners in a partnership are also responsible for debts of the business. In these kinds of businesses, the individuals are responsible for the company's debts, which can result in business owners declaring personal bankruptcy.

Business Milestones

IBM's ViaVoice and Dragon's NaturallySpeaking

In late 1996, Digital Equipment Corporation (NYSE:DEC), a leader in the computer industry, lost a major civil lawsuit. Three women were awarded a $6 million jury verdict against Digital because they had suffered from repetitive strain injuries (RSI) as a result of using one of its keyboards. This was the first major legal award of its kind for carpal tunnel-type injuries. (Carpal tunnel is a serious injury to the nerves in the wrist that can leave the victim unable to use one or both hands.)

Many computer manufacturers and corporations that depended on keyboard data entry were worried. With more than 800,000 new cases of these kinds of injuries being reported every year, HR insurance benefits managers began to look for ways to protect their companies from litigation.

Often, lawsuits like this can spur innovation and the acceptance of new methods of doing things. Less than a year after the famous DEC decision, in the spring of 1997, International Business Machines Corporation (IBM) (NYSE:IBM) announced the release of SimplySpeaking, and a short time later, its ViaVoice products. These products allow people to dictate, or speak to their computers, instead of typing.

When the computer and software are properly trained, speech-recognition technology can double an employee's typing speed. All employees need to do is speak into the computer's microphone and let the computer record the words. More important, using this technology results in fewer RSI injuries because employees are using the keyboard less.

IBM's main early competitor was Dragon Corporation, which had already created and released a similar product, called NaturallySpeaking. ViaVoice and NaturallySpeaking went head to head to capture the market for this technology. NaturallySpeaking eventually found its way into the suite of desktop software applications by COREL Systems (NASDAQ: COSFF) and has been designed to work with the WordPerfect word processing program.

In a corporation, only the assets of the corporation are available to make payments in lawsuits. In this way, personal assets of the stockholders are protected. Incorporation offers protection, but also imposes additional responsibilities. For example, most corporations have special record keeping and reporting requirements for tax and earning statements and stock transactions.

In the United States, rules for corporations are established by individual states. Many states declare in their state constitutions the right to issue corporate **charters** and regulate corporations. A corporate charter grants a corporation the right to exist under the laws of the state in which the charter is granted. Different states grant different rights. In this activity, you will explore portions of a few state constitutions that relate to corporations. You will also explore the different types of corporations that can be created in Corporate View's home state of Colorado. Similar variations exist in nearly every state in the United States.

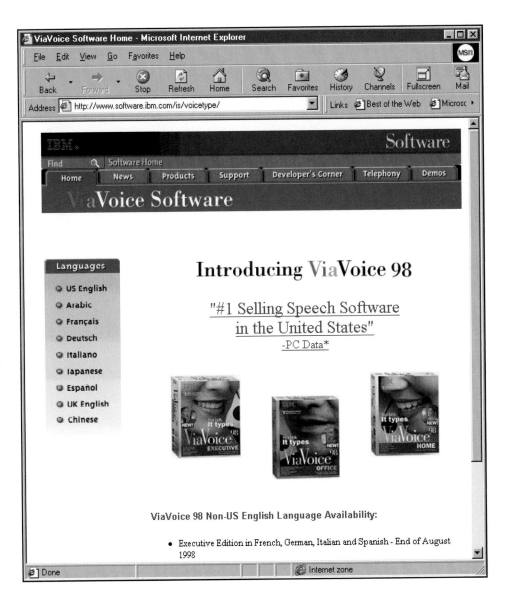

Figure 9-4
Products like IBM's ViaVoice bring relief to many RSI sufferers.

Save As:

Act9-1

1. Access the local Intranet or the Corporate View Web site.

2. Select the **Legal Services** link from the Corporate View Intranet Home page.

3. Select the **About Legal Services** link. Read the description of Legal Services.

Record your answers for questions 4 through 18 in a word processing file.

4. Write a 25- to 50-word description in your own words of what Legal Services is all about.

5. Select **Incorporation: Selected State Constitutions** and choose **Texas**. According to this brief excerpt from the Texas Constitution, what justification does Texas give for making general laws about the creation of corporations in the state of Texas?

6. Return to the **Legal Services** page and select **Kentucky**. According to the excerpt from Section 193 of the Kentucky Constitution, what must corporations know before they can issue stock without getting into trouble?

7. Explain in your own words the rule defined in the excerpt from Section 194 of the Kentucky Constitution.

8. Explain Kentucky's right of **eminent domain** as far as corporations are concerned. (See the excerpt from Section 195 of the Kentucky Constitution.)

9. Return to the **Legal Services** page and select **Delaware**. According to the rules laid out in the excerpt from Article IX, Section 1, of the Delaware Constitution, what conditions allow the Attorney General, on behalf of the General Assembly, to revoke corporate charters?

10. Compare the excerpt from Section 3 of Article IX of the Delaware Constitution with the excerpt from Section 193 of the Kentucky Constitution. Describe the similarities.

11. Explain the rule concerning foreign corporations as defined in the excerpt from Section 5 of Article IX of the Delaware Constitution.

12. What is Delaware's position on the taxation of stock from corporations created under the laws of Delaware held by stockholders living outside Delaware, as defined in the excerpt from Section 6, Article IX, of the Delaware Constitution?

13. Corporate View's international headquarters is in Colorado. Return to the **_Legal Services_** page and select the **_Colorado_** link.

14. According to the excerpt from Section 3 of Article XV of the Colorado Constitution, who has the power to revoke a charter of incorporation, and what are the conditions under which a charter may be revoked?

15. According to the excerpt from Section 8 of Article XV of the Colorado Constitution, how does Colorado's power of eminent domain affect franchises and corporations?

16. The excerpt from Article XV, Section 9, of the Colorado Constitution is similar to excerpts from sections of other state constitutions. List one excerpt from another state constitution that is similar to this excerpt from the Colorado Constitution.

17. Return to the **_Legal Services_** page. Select **_Colorado Incorporation Resources_** and choose **_How Do I Know Which Type of Business Is Best For Me?_**.

18. Briefly describe and explain corporations, limited partnerships, and limited liability companies, listing the advantages and disadvantages of each as explained on the Intranet page.

Debriefing

Incorporation is the creation of legal entities under the laws of a state. States have created different kinds of corporations to encourage the growth of new businesses. Corporate lawyers are needed to ensure that all the proper steps in incorporation are taken and that full compliance with the laws governing corporations is achieved.

Incorporation involves organizing corporate officers and filing the proper forms with the state in which you are creating your corporation. Once you file incorporation papers, you are subject to the rules and regulations of that state, as well as federal laws and international laws of the countries in which you do business. Corporate taxes are usually paid quarterly, and the results of shareholders' meetings must be filed with the state annually.

Colorado has prepared a checklist to help new corporations. Examine this checklist and see whether any incorporation troubles can be avoided by following the proper steps.

1. Access the local Intranet or the Corporate View Web site.

2. Select the **_Legal Services_** link from the Corporate View Intranet Home page.

3. Click **_Colorado Incorporation Resources_**, followed by **_Conducting Business in the State of Colorado (A Checklist for New Businesses)_**.

4. Under the "Incorporation" heading, there are ten items that need to be considered immediately after incorporation. Summarize each in your own words.

_____

_____

_____

_____

_____

_____

_____

_____

_____

_____

In the Debriefing for the previous activity, you summarized ten steps that Colorado recommends new corporations follow as they begin their operations. The seventh step reads:

> *Protect your ideas - Contact the Office of the Secretary of State and the U.S. Patent and Trademark Office for information on state and federal trademarks and copyright.*

This is good advice. Corporations like Corporate View create and make innovations on thousands of products. Protection of new ideas was first granted by the United States Constitution. This excerpt from Article I, Section 8, asserts the power of Congress to create laws to protect copyrights, patents, and trademarks:

> *The Congress shall have Power... To promote the Progress of Science and useful Arts, by securing for limited Times to Authors and Inventors the exclusive Right to their respective Writings and Discoveries...*

Congress created the U.S. Patent and Trademark Office (PTO) and passed laws to preserve ***intellectual property rights***. Intellectual property rights grant certain privileges to individuals and corporations that create something new, different, useful, and potentially profitable.

To protect intellectual property, the PTO can issue a patent giving exclusive rights to an invention, in many cases for up to 17 years. This is considered enough time for a corporation or individual inventor to recoup the costs of research and development.

When R&D researchers at Corporate View come up with a marketable new invention, the Patent and Copyright Team from Legal Services is brought in to see whether the company should apply for a patent. Once the paperwork for a patent has begun, the creator can use the term ***patent pending*** to deter competitors from applying for a similar patent and to let customers know the new invention is truly unique and worth investigating.

A trademark is another essential business tool. Often invented by marketing teams, trademarks are distinctive names or mottoes used to differentiate products for consumers. Pepsi is the ***registered trademark*** of a soft drink. So is Coca-Cola. Other companies can't use these trademarks. Dr. Pepper, Slice, 7UP, Sprite, and Crush are all very different soft drinks. Because each is registered, each can carry the registered trademark symbol ®. Because these product names are protected, other soft drinks like Mr. Pibb, Diet Coke, Fresca, and Barq's root beer cannot use them. Thus each of these products remains unique and differentiated from all others in the marketplace.

When a marketing team decides upon the name of a new product, that is called *branding*—inventing a new brand name. A clever brand name must be trademarked to protect it from other corporations that might want to use the same name.

Slightly different from a trademark is a trade name. International Business Machines Corporation (IBM), Microsoft Corporation, Corporate View, American Telephone and Telegraph Corporation (AT&T), Ford Motor Company, General Motors Corporation (GM), and Wal-Mart Stores, Inc. are all examples of trade names. A trade name is the name of a business that may have many trademarked products.

Trade names and trademarks are used to help customers distinguish a company's products from those of the competition. Only Ford can advertise and sell cars using the names Mustang and Taurus. Other car companies must invent their own unique product names.

Copyrights are given to original written or performance works like books, articles, music, plays, movie scripts, and artwork. Similarly, software is often covered under copyright law. Legally copyrighted materials can carry the © symbol.

Protecting trademarks, trade names, patents, and copyrights is a full-time job. Corporate View has an entire team that works on nothing else.

The **Least** You **Should** Know About...

Torts

A tort sounds like something you might eat with jam or jelly. Torts started with the Romans. In Latin, the word for "wrong" is *tortus*. In the Middle Ages, the French began to use the term to define a wrongdoing or an injustice. Today, a tort is a wrong or an injury for which the injured party has the right to sue in court for a remedy. A person who is wronged can sue for damages, usually compensation in the form of a cash award. The wrongdoing may be intentional or an act of negligence. In a tort there must be some evidence of pain or suffering directly related to the wrongdoing.

Corporations that knowingly sell defective or dangerous products that injure their buyers are open to tort lawsuits. One of the more famous torts was a series of suits brought by individuals against corporations that sell cigarettes. In a 1987 case, flight attendants won a suit against major tobacco companies because they claimed harmful health effects due to secondhand smoke.

At times, corporations are sued frivolously. *Frivolous* means silly or, in legal terms, lacking in merit or substance. Frivolous lawsuits are often brought against corporations that have *deep pockets*. This simply means they have lots of money and other assets. Have you heard of any frivolous lawsuits?

Just-in-Time Training

Product Protection

1. Access the local Intranet or the Corporate View Web site.

2. Select the **_Legal Services_** link from the Corporate View Intranet Home page.

3. Click the **_Patent, Trademark, and Copyright Resources_** link. Select the **_Copyright Basics_** link. Use this document to answer questions 4 through 8.

Key your answers to questions 4 through 12 in a word processing file.

4. What is a copyright, and who can claim a copyright?

5. Define a "work made for hire."

6. List the eight categories of work protected under copyright law.

7. What is not protected under copyright law?

8. Read the **_How to Secure Copyright_** section of **_Copyright Basics_** and explain the statement "Copyright is secured *automatically* when the work is created."

9. Patents are handled in a manner different from copyrights. Return to the **_Patent, Trademark, and Copyright Resources_** list on the **_Legal Services_** page, and select the **_Functions of the Patent and Trademark Office_** link. Briefly describe the PTO and explain its functions.

10. Return to the **_Patent, Trademark, and Copyright Resources_** list and click the **_What Is a Patent?_** link. How does the PTO define a patent for an invention?

11. How does the PTO define a copyright? A trademark or **_servicemark_**?

12. Return to the **_Patent, Trademark, and Copyright Resources_** list and click the **_What Can Be Patented_** link. In your own words, explain what can be patented. Are there any things that cannot be patented? Explain.

Act9-2

Debriefing

As you can imagine, the PTO receives lots of questions every working day. To help alleviate having to answer repetitively some of the more frequently asked questions, the PTO has created a FAQs page.

Return to the **_Patent, Trademark, and Copyright Resources_** list on the **_Legal Services_** page and click the **_Answers to Questions Frequently Asked_** link. Use the information found there to answer the questions for this Debriefing.

Think and write about the following:

1. Do inventors need to worry that others might learn about their inventions from their patent applications at the PTO before the patents are granted? Why or why not?

_____

_____

2. Who will receive the patent when two or more people work on an invention, both providing ideas for the invention?

_____

3. Who will receive the patent when one person provides the ideas for the invention and another provides the money for building and testing the invention?

_____

4. What is the PTO policy on assisting inventors in marketing their inventions?

_____

Learning the law is a labor-intensive experience. Law libraries are full of books outlining every significant case since the Laws of Hammurabi (circa 1750 BC) were written in Mesopotamia. As the supreme ruler, Hammurabi had all 282 clauses of his laws carved on a black stone more than eight feet high so that all could see the laws by which they lived.

Many laws dealt specifically with commercial activity, debt, and product liability. For example, if a man built a house poorly and the owner was killed by the roof caving in, the builder would be put to death. Most offenses in Hammurabi's *code* were capital offenses—that is, punishable by death.

Oh, for the days when knowing all the laws was so simple! In Hammurabi's day, you could read all the laws on a big black public rock. Today, you must chip away on tens of thousands of books in miles and miles of law libraries full of cases, decisions, law reviews, contracts, and legislation.

Laws passed by legislatures are written into books called *codes*. For instance, the ***United States Code (USC)*** contains all the laws passed by Congress that are currently in effect. But there are other sources of laws that affect business beyond legislative codes. Laws that affect business come from several sources:

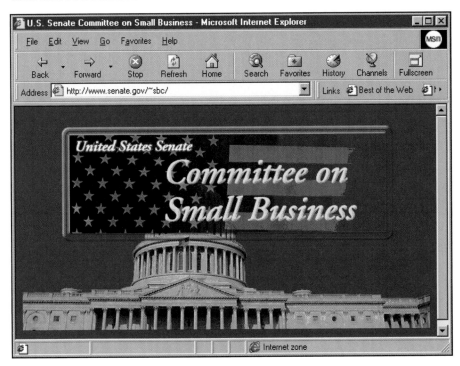

F i g u r e   9 - 6
The Senate Committee on Small Business reviews laws to help small businesses.

- State and federal constitutions
- Government agency rulings and policies
- Treaties
- Contracts
- Custom and tradition
- Court cases and judicial rulings

Today, we live in an age where the law is, to say the least, confusing and complicated. The many levels of the law include

- International law
- Federal law
- State law
- Local law

Laws that govern corporate behavior are everywhere. In Human Resources, for example, the law affects

- The hiring of talented employees
- The promotion process within a corporation
- The way conflicts among employees are resolved
- The fair and equitable treatment of employees
- The orderly dismissal of employees

And this is just Human Resources. Many other rules and government agencies influence the way business is conducted in each mission-critical function.

The Intranet and the Web can help people stay informed about laws and the interpretations of laws. You will use these tools in this activity to help bring some understanding to how the law affects each mission-critical function at Corporate View and the employees who work there.

Just-in-Time Training

Corporate Law and Mission-Critical Functions

In this activity, you will think and write about ways the law affects Corporate View mission-critical functions. You can get ideas from the Intranet, the chapter material, or by searching the Web. The Legal Services Intranet page is a good place to start.

1. Access the local Intranet or the Corporate View Web site.
2. Select the **_Legal Services_** link from the Corporate View Intranet Home page.

3. Select ***Colorado Incorporation Resources*** and then ***Conducting Business in the State of Colorado (A Checklist for New Businesses)***.

4. In the Activity 9-1 Debriefing, you read the Incorporation section of this checklist. Now take some time to read the rest of the Intranet page. It may help you in the steps that follow.

   Record the answers to questions 5 and 6 in a word processing file.

5. Choose four of the mission-critical functions below. Describe briefly three examples of how the law affects each of the functions (12 examples total). For example, Human Resources would be affected by laws concerning equal opportunity employment.

   - Human Resources
   - Research and Development
   - Marketing, Sales, and Customer Support
   - Finance and Accounting
   - Legal Services
   - Information Technology
   - Corporate Communications

Save As:

Act9-3

6. Compare your list of 12 examples with the list of specialty areas of law practice found in The Least You Should Know About… Specialty Areas in Business and Corporate Law below. Identify at least five business and corporate law specialties that would deal with the legal issues in the list you just created. For example, the employee and union relations specialty would address many HR concerns and questions. Create a table, spreadsheet, or chart to organize your answers.

The **Least** You **Should** Know **About…**

Specialty Areas in Business and Corporate Law

Business and corporate law contains many specialties. Here are a few examples:
- Banking
- Bankruptcy
- Business ethics
- Contracts
- Employee and union relations
- Employee benefits, relocations, and health care
- Finance and accounting

- Franchises
- Incorporation and dissolution of corporations
- International business
- Liabilities
- Liquidations
- Mergers and acquisitions
- Partnerships
- Patents
- Securities and investments
- Tax

Believe it or not, this is a short list of specialties that can be found in corporate law. In fact, there are more legal specialties today than the total number of laws in Hammurabi's code.

Figure 9 - 7
*Corporate law today has
many legal specialties.*

Debriefing

The Web provides an opportunity to keep abreast of the law as it
relates to the mission-critical functions of a business. Search tools,
like those provided by Yahoo, Excite, and Lycos, scour the Web,
looking for Web pages containing words that match your request.
Thinking carefully about your search words is important for getting
usable search results.

Think and write about the following:

Think of search terms that will return names of Web pages on the
law and the mission-critical functions at Corporate View. For example, the search terms *human resources law* and *employment law*
are good choices for finding legal information on the HR function.
Advertising law will return resources that could affect Corporate
Communications, as well as Marketing.

List search terms below that would help you locate legal information for each of the mission-critical functions. Try your search terms
to see whether they bring you the information you are looking for.

1. Human Resources _____

2. Research and Development _____

3. Marketing, Sales, and Customer Support _____

4. Finance and Accounting _____

5. Legal Services _____

6. Information Technology _____

7. Corporate Communications _____

Searching Successfully

Finding the information you need is often one of the most difficult and time-consuming parts of preparing a document. Search tools (often called search engines) are widely used to help locate information on the Web.

When using search engines on the Web, try more than one search engine or search tool. You will find that some search engines are superior to others at finding information about certain topics.

Be careful to spell search terms correctly to get the results you are looking for. Some newer search engines are speech driven and allow you to search with your voice, which prevents some spelling errors but introduces others. Double-check your spelling before you hit the **Search** button.

When selecting a search term, think through your choice of words. For example, if you use the search word *animals*, you will probably get some results that are not animal-related. For example, you could get an article containing a paragraph about a football team that played like "a bunch of animals" on its way to a championship. More specific search phrases like the following examples may give you more accurate, pinpointed results:

- Zoo animals
- Lions and tigers and bears
- African mammals
- Marsupials North America

Special search operators, such as *AND* and *OR*, can help narrow a search. These two operators are easy to use. For example, *cats AND dogs* returns a list of sites having information about both cats and dogs. Substitute the OR operator, *cats OR dogs*, and you will get an increased number of sources that talk about just dogs, or just cats, or both dogs and cats. Other operators and options are available with most search engines to help you refine and narrow your searches. For example, some search engines allow you to limit search results to those in a particular language, such as English or French. Access the Search Help feature of the search engine you use to learn about other operators or options.

In Hammurabi's day, the laws were much simpler. A series of "thou shalt not" codes made understanding the law easy. The penalties were easy to understand too. "Off with his head" was often considered a justifiable penalty in a culture that believed in an "eye-for-an-eye and a tooth-for-a-tooth" punishment system.

Today, the laws are more complicated. Lawyers spend a great deal of their time interpreting and explaining complicated laws to their clients in technical communications. Technical communications often require reading, understanding, translating, and simplifying information. Here is a classic example from Title 37 of the Code of Federal Regulations (Patents, Trademarks, and Copyrights).

Trademark correspondence. All correspondence concerning trademark matters, except for trademark-related documents sent to the Assignment Division for recordation and requests for certified and uncertified copies of trademark application and registration documents, should be addressed to "Assistant Commissioner for Trademarks, 2900 Crystal Drive, Arlington, Virginia 22202-3513." This includes correspondence intended for the Trademark Trial and Appeal Board.

This style of writing is designed to be very specific and accurate. When this passage is interpreted by a court or by employees working at the PTO, there should be no doubt as to its meaning. However, the passage breaks nearly every rule of online technical communications. Read it aloud. Don't take a breath until you reach a period. Can you make it?

Rewriting this passage for better readability will take some doing. Let's see whether this is easier to read and understand.

Trademark Correspondence

Most correspondence concerning trademark matters should be addressed to the Assistant Commissioner for Trademarks, 2900 Crystal Drive, Arlington, VA 22202-3513. This includes correspondence intended for the Trademark Trial and Appeal Board.

Do not send the Assistant Commissioner

- trademark-related documents to be recorded (send them to the Assignment Division)

- requests for certified and uncertified copies of trademark application and registration documents

The original passage had some problems. For instance, two ideas were merged into one long sentence, making it difficult to follow. Breaking up that sentence makes it easier to understand. Bulleted items help organize additional information. Notice that the title is now set off to attract the reader's attention to the topic. The space between paragraphs also makes the passage easier to read.

In this activity, you will have a chance to simplify some legal language. You might have to read and think about the passages several times before you will be able to see how they can be rewritten. In rewriting the passages, use relatively short sentences and state ideas in short, concise terms. Break a process into a list of steps where possible. Cut out unnecessary words, but be careful not to change the meaning with your revision.

Technical
Communications

Deleting Outdated Web Information

Deleting outdated information from Internet and Intranet sites is essential from a legal and liability perspective. One of the most exciting aspects of corporate Intranet and Web sites is the massive amount of information available to consumers and employees on a wide variety of topics. Corporations must be careful, however, to update and correct their online sites regularly.

Court cases have been filed because corporations have failed to remove obsolete information from Web sites. In one case, information regarding the beneficial effects of a combination of prescription drugs was proven false. Still, months after the discovery of problems with these prescription drugs, many Web sites still had the erroneous information posted. Web surfers using search engines continued to encounter this erroneous information, and because the information was posted by reputable companies, many people still believed this combination of drugs was beneficial.

Technical communications involves more than simply presenting new information; it also means deleting old and erroneous information. Redundant information should also be deleted.

Responsible businesses must make sure their Internet and Web sites are, from time to time, purged of information that is misleading or erroneous. For example, suppose a company changes its medical leave policy but fails to remove information concerning the old policy. What kinds of problems could arise? If an employee reads that a certain set of medical benefits or procedures is not covered and acts accordingly, the erroneous information may cause injury or deprive the employee of needed benefits. A tort could result. This situation could trigger a civil lawsuit.

1. Access the local Intranet or the Corporate View Web site.

2. Select the **_Legal Services_** link from the Corporate View Intranet Home page.

3. Click the **_Patent, Trademark, and Copyright Resources_** link.

4. Select the link for **_Patent Rules (Title 37)_**.

5. Scroll down the index of headings and select a few links. Read portions of the document for 10 to 15 minutes.

6. What do you think of the style of writing used in this document? Is it clear or difficult to follow? Did you understand what you read, or was it all a blur?

   _____

   _____

   _____

7. Select the links listed below on the Patent Rules index and read each passage. You may wish to copy these passages into a word processing file and print them for further study.

   Section 1.42 When the inventor is dead.

   Section 1.47 Filing when an inventor refuses to sign or cannot be reached. Paragraph (a)

   Section 1.47 Filing when an inventor refuses to sign or cannot be reached. Paragraph (b)

   Section 1.311 Notice of Allowance. Paragraph (a)

8. In a word processing file, rewrite three of the four passages from the Patent Rules. Imagine your audience includes a group of your friends or colleagues. Your purpose is to explain your selected passages in a clear and easy-to-understand manner.

Save As:

Act9-4

Debriefing

A question commonly received by the PTO is whether an Internet *domain name* can also be registered as a trademark. A domain name is used on the Web to identify a Web site, such as **_www.corpview.com_**. Some people or companies would like their domain names protected legally, just like their trademarks.

Find out more by reading about this topic. Access the **_Legal Ser-_** **_vices_** page from the Corporate View Intranet Home page. Select **_Patent, Trademark, and Copyright Resources_** and then select **_Trade-_** **_mark Examination of Domain Names_**.

Think and write about the following:

1. When can an Internet domain name be registered as a trade-mark?

   _____

   _____

2. What must an applicant show to register a domain name as a trademark?

   _____

   _____

3. What three phrases does the PTO use to classify services pro-vided via the Internet?

   _____

   _____

Chapter Review

Executive Summary

Corporate legal representation is an essential function in business. Corporate lawyers spend a great deal of time researching the law and attempting to protect their clients. Contrary to common opinion, lawyers don't spend most of their day in court. To the contrary, lawyers spend most of their day trying to keep corporations out of court, working hard to prevent problems that could escalate into litigation. All employees need to know a little about the legal function and laws that apply to the specialty area they work in.

The process of incorporation, which creates a corporation, has many steps. Most states have Web sites that provide information to help new businesses incorporate successfully. When a business incorporates, it becomes a legal entity subject to the rules and regulations of the state in which it incorporated and the states and countries in which it does business.

Most legal difficulties for corporations result in civil rather than criminal problems. A lawyer must watch all aspects of the law as it relates to the business activities of the corporations he or she represents.

Many rules and laws protect corporations and their ideas. Some of the most important include copyright, trademark, trade name, and patent laws. Many government regulatory entities provide this protection and ensure that businesses comply with laws and rules governing their business activities. For example, everyone knows the Internal Revenue Service collects taxes. A less-known federal entity is the Patent and Trademark Office (PTO). The PTO is a bureau that registers and protects inventions and new ideas under the Constitution of the United States. Its mission is outlined in the United States Code, which consists of those laws approved by Congress that are currently in effect.

Rules and regulations regarding copyright can be obtained over the Web. These rules make it very clear what can be protected under copyright law. Copyrighting concerns the preservation of intellectual property or the creation of something new, different, useful, and unique. Written and recorded works are considered under copyright law, as is computer software.

Patents protect inventions and innovations that are new, unique, and useful. A patent allows the inventor or corporation to profit exclusively from that invention for a specific amount of time.

Trademark protection is often sought for brand names created to identify company products in the marketplace. Once a brand name is registered as a trademark, no other corporation can use it. To register a brand name as a trademark, a corporation must demonstrate to the PTO that the name is not being used by another company for a similar type of product.

A trade name is the name the corporation itself is known by. For example, Ford Motor Company is a trade name, whereas Ford Taurus is the name of one of Ford's products. Taurus, then, is the trademarked name for a specific Ford automobile.

Technical Communications

Legal language is sometimes very difficult to understand. One main job of the Legal Services Department is to translate difficult-to-understand legal documents into plain English the employees can understand. Methods of simplifying a document include breaking up long sentences, using bullets and lists, and eliminating repetitive words. When simplifying a legal document, you must make sure the legal meaning is maintained. Simplified legal documents can never replace the legislation itself. Such translations are only meant to help explain aspects of the law.

Information on a corporate Intranet or Web site should be constantly updated, and incorrect or outdated information should be removed to avoid misinformation and possible exposure to litigation.

The Corporate Inbox

Legal Services receives questions from both inside and outside the corporation. These questions are distributed among the Legal Services team members. Some easier questions are given to interns. Here are some messages that need to be answered by someone in Legal Services. Answer them with the help of the Intranet and your own best judgment.

If you need help preparing documents, access the **_Style Guide_** under the **_Corporate Communications_** link. Access the **_Basic Facts About Registering A Trademark_** and **_The Registration Process_** links under **_Patent, Trademark, and Copyright Resources_** on the **_Legal Services_** page for help with writing the email to Alan Bean.

CORPORATE VIEW

From the Desk of Jake Milton...

Dear Legal:

I am trying to look up some information on the Web about medical benefit and employment law, but my searches are yielding a lot of Web sites and documents that aren't relevant. Do you have any ideas on how I can narrow my search? If so, please email them to me.

Thanks!
Jake Milton
HR Benefits Specialist
jmilton@corpview.com

TO: Intern
FROM: *ccooper@corpview.com*
SUBJECT: Trademark Design
MESSAGE:

Please answer Mr. Bean's questions by email. His email address is *abean@corpview.com*. Thanks.

<<From Alan Bean, Forwarded by Charles Cooper>>

I have been at TeleView for a few weeks. My workgroup is designing a trademark for a new wireless phone for which we'll soon be seeking registration. We'd like to forestall any problems by finding out what reasons, if any, the federal government has for not approving a trademark. We know, of course, that our trademark can't look like anyone else's. Can you give us any other advice about what to avoid?

Thanks,
Alan Bean
Marketing Manager

Hi. This is Xu Zingshi here in Legal Services. We need to develop a policy statement about deleting obsolete information from our Intranet. Please prepare a memo to Charles Cooper, describing the problems that can result from maintaining outdated information on the Intranet. We will use your memo to start the ball rolling on a policy statement. I'd like to see a draft by the end of the day if possible. Thanks.

Save As:

Inbox9C

TO: Intern
FROM: *ccooper@corpview.com*
SUBJECT: White Paper on Patent Applications
MESSAGE:

Please help me out by preparing a white paper for R&D workgroups on how to prepare applications for patents. Explain exactly how the applications should be formatted and organized.

Refer to Title 37 of the Code of Federal Regulations—specifically, Section 1.52, governing the form of an application. Summarize what this application needs to look like. These R&D folks are too busy inventing stuff to take time out to read the Patent Rules. You will need to translate the instructions into simple English.

Thanks,
Charles

Save As:

Inbox9D

Access the Corporate View Web site. Use the **_Stock Watcher Links_** on the **_Regular Features_** page to identify the following ticker symbols and learn how each of these companies did in the stock market today.

Current Date _____

Ticker	Exchange	Company Name	Current Price
KO	NYSE	_____	_____
PEP	NYSE	_____	_____
MSFT	NASDAQ	_____	_____
IBM	NYSE	_____	_____
T	NYSE	_____	_____
F	NYSE	_____	_____
GM	NYSE	_____	_____
WMT	NYSE	_____	_____

When a Few Words Will Do

According to what you have read in this chapter or on the Corporate View Intranet, answer the following questions in a word processing document.

1. Explain the difference between civil and criminal law. Which of these affects corporations more?

2. Why was the Digital Equipment Corporation keyboard case so important? What new technology arose that can help protect employees on the job and corporations from similar lawsuits?

3. Select three specialties in law that would be very important for a corporation like Corporate View to keep up on. Explain your three choices.

4. Why is it a bad idea for corporations to leave outdated or incorrect information on their Web sites?

5. What is a tort, and why should corporations try to avoid torts?

6. Why are contracts important legal tools for corporations?

Save As:

Online9

Portfolio-Building Project

Aspects of Corporate Law

Prepare a white paper discussing an aspect of corporate law that you think is important for employees to know about. Choose a topic from the Intranet, such as patents, trademarks, copyrights, or incorporation. To get ideas, use Web links and URLs you found using search words in Activity 9-3 Debriefing. Prepare your white paper on one aspect of the law that relates to one of Corporate View's mission-critical functions. Refer to Activity 9-3 for ideas. Your white paper should be 300 to 500 words in length.

Save As:

Pfolio9

High-Performance Workgroup Project

The technical communications theme for this chapter is simplification—making difficult language readable. Consider the white paper you prepared for the Portfolio-Building Project. How readable is it?

Form a team with three or four other interns. Read each other's white papers and make revisions together to make your writing easier to understand and follow. Print a new, revised version of your white paper.

Save As:

HP9

Thinking and Writing About Your Business

According to what you have learned in this chapter, think and write about three of the following questions. Record your answers of 50 to 150 words in a word processing document.

1. Choose three legal terms not defined in the ShopTalk section that you think employees might need to refer to or might not understand. Research and write a definition of each term with one or more examples.

2. In this chapter, you used many legal resources available on the Corporate View Intranet. Which resources were the most and least helpful? In what ways?

3. Give two suggestions for topics or sources that could be added to the *Legal Services* page on the Intranet that would help employees. Explain why your suggestions should be integrated into the Intranet page.

4. Suppose you were to give a seminar for Legal Services personnel on how to simplify legal writing for Corporate View employees. Prepare a brief outline of the seminar. Include at least two strategies not suggested in the chapter for simplifying legal writing.

5. Suppose Legal Services is planning a series of five seminars for employees. List five important legal issues you think should be discussed in company-wide seminars or seminars for particular departments. Explain why these issues should be included in the seminar plan.

Think9

Overtime

State Incorporation Search

Write a white paper on incorporation in your state, province, or country. Search the Web or other sources and discover the rules of incorporation for your locale. For those living in Colorado, some of the information can be found on the Corporate View Intranet. Use what you have learned about search words and apply it to your research effort. Your white paper should be about 250 to 350 words in length.

Otime9

Applications to Small Business

Legal Resources

Small companies may not be able to afford a full-time legal staff like a large corporation. Use the Web or other resources to research and create a list of ten good resources a small company can rely on for legal information. Note the title and source of the information and a brief description of each resource. Include URLs for Web sites. For example:

Legal Information Institute

http://www.law.cornell.edu

Prepared by Cornell University's prestigious law school. The site provides excellent online legal resources in all areas of law, including corporate and business law.

ASB9

Access the Corporate View Web site and take the Online Evaluation for this chapter.

1. Click the ***Employee Training and Evaluations*** link on the ***Regular Features*** page.

2. Select the ***Online Tests*** link. (You must be a registered user to access the online tests. If you are not a registered user, click the ***Register*** link and follow the instructions on the screen. Then click the ***Online Tests*** link to return to the ***Online Tests*** page.)

3. Choose the ***Chapter 9 A View from Legal Services*** link on the ***Online Tests*** page.

4. Enter the username and password you selected when you registered.

5. Take the test. Click the **First**, **Back**, **Next**, and **Last** buttons to navigate through the questions. Click the **Finish** button to submit your test for grading. If you wish to close the test without submitting it for grading, click the **Cancel** button. Any answers you have entered will be lost if you cancel the test.

Chapter 10

A View from Information Technology

Of Bits and Bytes

"Hi! I'm Luis Delgado, and I'm the lead network engineer and **Webmaster** for the TeleView division. I stay very busy. We're always hopping, always moving on to the next task. I guess many feel that way at TeleView. But there's a difference. Everyone is completely dependent on us.

"Let me explain. If Human Resources is down for a week, a few people don't get hired. Still, Research and Development, Legal Services, and Corporate Communications can keep working. If our Intranet is down, however, this whole place shuts down. We're under a lot of pressure when the computer networks go down. Everybody depends on the Information Technology or IT Department to keep information flowing.

"On the other hand, it makes you feel good when somebody calls you in to fix a problem with a computer and you can solve it—sometimes in a matter of a few seconds. People are amazed. They think of us as some sort of Intranet wizards. The reward—besides the satisfaction of making the Intranet work—is how grateful people are. We tell them we're just doing our jobs, but they still thank us profusely.

"I guess the IT Department is like the heart of this company. We feel we're the common thread that links its different parts. We tie every department, every team, every person into a single unit. It all starts here, and it branches like veins through the network cabling, above the ceiling panels, into the cubicles, behind the desks, and into the computers.

"We also support many people who telecommute. We hook them up through phone or cable lines, and a few have wireless connections. We beam their work right to their homes.

"You've seen and used the corporate Intranet. That's our masterpiece. Of course, it's a work in progress. We work very closely with Corporate Communications on the Intranet. For the most part, we manage the technology and Corporate Communications manages the content.

"Intranets were created when the World Wide Web started getting big and companies began to say, 'Wouldn't it be nice if we could have a little Web just for our employees and workgroup teams?' It's such a great way to communicate and share information.

"What's amazing with a corporate Intranet is not what it is, but how it is used. At Corporate View, every message sent, every file read, every idea exchanged electronically travels through the Intranet. Every minute, thousands of events are taking place through our servers. Six different teams might be video conferencing with vendors in Japan, Bolivia, or Mongolia. A hundred different people may be sending email messages to coworkers or clients. Others might be checking the price of Corporate View stock.

"Of course, the main reason we have a corporate Intranet is to give everybody easy, open access to the shared information that helps employees make good decisions. Conditions change fast in this industry. If a department has to wait a week, a day, or even an hour to make a decision, it slows everything down and hinders Corporate View in responding to the market.

"Here's an example of what I mean. If I'm a team leader in Corporate Communications and need to know something about a project R&D is working on, I can wait around for someone in R&D to schedule time to gather the information I need and put it in my mailbox. Or I can pull up the information from the R&D site of the corporate Intranet and have the data I need in a matter of seconds.

The Information Technology Department

In many corporations, the Information Technology Department is called the Information Systems or Information Services Department, often abbreviated as *IS*. Some corporations add the word *Management* to the department name for Management of Information Systems/Services or *MIS*. Job titles include IT or IS manager, certified system engineer, and Webmaster. Whatever they are called, IT managers are essential to the survival of every corporation, large or small.

Webmasters are the guardians of the Intranet. They are the people who create, organize, and manage Intranet sites. Managing a top-quality Web site is a complex business. Some Webmasters focus on hardware, software, and Intranet (Web) protocols, while others focus on the content of Web pages. Both jobs require an understanding of technical communications and how it impacts Intranet users. As with other IT positions, the pay is often good, but the hours can be irregular because some of the work has to be done after the normal working day.

A wide variety of training is required for members of the IT team. They must be able to repair computers of all types, link them together into networks, and configure them to communicate with the Intranet. IT employees do backups of all critical data and restore services after computer crashes and power outages.

IT must know about all the latest equipment and industry trends. Like the friendly postal person, IT makes sure the email is delivered, but also posts Web pages, installs software upgrades, and shows people how to use new software. Every now and then, IT members get a chance to rest, but only for a short time—until the next emergency call comes in.

"We link parts of our Intranet to other companies that work for us or supply us with parts. These connections are called *Extranets*. We want our outsourcing partners to have just enough access to our Intranet to work effectively with us, but not so much that they know everything we are doing. Corporations that are our partners today could be working for our competitors tomorrow, so we limit their access to our critical information.

"I work closely with Robin Mills, the TeleView HR director, to make sure everyone who comes to work for the TeleView division is trained to function effectively in our information-intensive environment. New employees must learn to find important information on the Intranet— that's obviously critical—and they must effectively use the applications and utilities we provide to publish their own information and keep it up to date. If they don't know how to do this, we must train them.

"Enjoy the Intranet. The more you know about it, the more effectively you will use it. If you have any questions about it, email us."

Activity Overviews

As in many corporations, the IT Department at Corporate View spends a great deal of its time managing the corporate Intranet. As a Corporate View Intranet user, you have had plenty of practice sending email, selecting hyperlinks, and finding information on the Intranet. The activities in this chapter will show you the Intranet from a different perspective and will teach you the basics of creating simple Web pages.

To understand the Intranet, you need to learn a little about *Hypertext Markup Language (HTML)*, the language of the Intranet. It sounds technical, but it really isn't. You will learn just enough about HTML to understand how and why the Intranet works the way it does. This will help you in all your interactions with the corporate Intranet.

Activity 10-1 Web Talk will explain how simple HTML *tags* define the appearance of Web pages on Intranets and Web sites all over the world.

Activity 10-2 Saving, Moving, and Converting Files will show you how to convert word processing documents to HTML files. You will convert your biography to a format that can be posted to the Intranet.

Activity 10-3 Picture It on the Intranet will show you how to use graphics to add pizzazz to Web pages.

Understanding the meanings of these terms will help you learn the concepts and develop the skills related to Information Technology covered in the chapter. In preparation for completing the chapter activities, access the Intranet and find the definition for each of these terms by clicking the **_ShopTalk_** link on the **_Regular Features_** page.

" Corporate ShopTalk "

- File Extensions
  .com
  .doc
  .edu
  .gif
  .gov
  .jpg (.jpeg)
  .mil
  .net
  .org
  .txt
  .wpd
- FTP (File Transfer Protocol)
- HTTP (Hypertext Transfer Protocol)
- IP (Internet Protocol) Number
- Protocol
- Tags
- Text Format
- Webmaster

The **Least** You **Should** Know About...

Understanding URLs

When you enter a URL (Uniform Resource Locator) in your Web browser, you are looking for a specific file located somewhere in cyberspace. This file may be on your local computer, on your corporate Intranet, or somewhere on the World Wide Web. To get to the file, you need to know the *path* contained in the URL or Web address. This path is the key to finding HTML files.

Consider this URL as an example: **_http://www.corpview.com/teleview/products/productinfo.html_**.

Let's see what this means by breaking down the sample URL shown above into its discrete parts.

http:// In some URLs, you might see the letters *http* followed by a colon and two slashes. *HTTP (Hypertext Transfer Protocol)* tells your network how to transfer or move the file you are requesting. A *protocol* is a communications system used to transfer data over networks. It is like a digital language that both Web and Intranet computers use to communicate. HTTP is one kind of protocol, *FTP (File Transfer Protocol)* is another, and there are many more.

www.corpview.com The second part of the address contains the name of the computer that hosts the Web or Intranet site. The *www* stands for *World Wide Web* and tells you this computer uses Web technology. In this case, *corpview* is short for *Corporate View*. The *.com* says this is a commercial or business site. Here are some examples of *file extensions* you might see in a server name:

.com	company
.edu	educational institution
.gov	government site
.mil	military site
.net	network gateway or host
.org	private organization

/teleview/products/ The slashes and names in this part of the URL represent folders or directories on the host computer. If you want to find a file on a computer, you need to know the path through the many possible folders to the one that contains the file.

productinfo.html You can often see the name of a file at the end of a URL. Look at the end of our sample URL. Productinfo is the name of the file. The .html extension tells you this is an HTML file and that Web browsers can read it.

HTML is a document description language. It defines how an HTML document, commonly called a Web page, should look. A variety of software programs, such as Netscape Navigator and Communicator, Microsoft's Internet Explorer, word processors, and applications in office suite software, can display HTML documents. If you know a little bit about HTML, you will be able to use the corporate Intranet more effectively.

HTML uses tags to format Web pages. These tags are enclosed by angle brackets and look like this:

```
<HTML>
<TITLE></TITLE>
<BODY>
<CENTER><H1></H1></CENTER>
```

You might use the Web your entire life and never see HTML tags. However, HTML tags carry a lot of meaning for a Web browser. These tags work behind the scenes, making all the exciting Web pages you see on the WWW and the Intranet display properly in your browser.

Tags can be very complex. To see what HTML tags look like on a real Web page, try this experiment:

1. Launch your Web browser and navigate to a page you find interesting.

2. Click **Source** on the View menu in Internet Explorer, or click **Page Source** or **Document Source** from the View menu in Navigator/Communicator. Different browsers use slightly different words for this command, so you may need to hunt around, but the option will be there.

Figure 10-1
*In Explorer, click **Source** on the View menu to see the tags for a page.*

You will then see the tags that are normally hidden underneath. The tags will look something like Figure 10-2.

Figure 10-2
The tags you see here create a Web page.

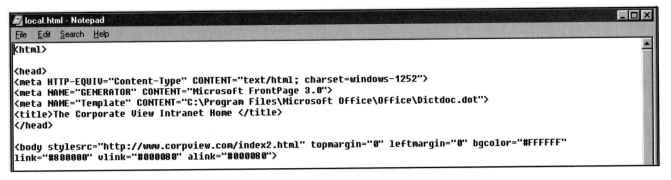

```
local.html - Notepad
File  Edit  Search  Help
<html>

<head>
<meta HTTP-EQUIV="Content-Type" CONTENT="text/html; charset=windows-1252">
<meta NAME="GENERATOR" CONTENT="Microsoft FrontPage 3.0">
<meta NAME="Template" CONTENT="C:\Program Files\Microsoft Office\Office\Dictdoc.dot">
<title>The Corporate View Intranet Home </title>
</head>

<body stylesrc="http://www.corpview.com/index2.html" topmargin="0" leftmargin="0" bgcolor="#FFFFFF"
link="#800080" vlink="#000080" alink="#000080">
```

3. Use Table 10-1 to uncover the meaning of a few selected tags.

Deciphering HTML

Table 10-1

HTML Tag	Function
<HTML></HTML>	Tells the browser that this is the beginning and the end of an HTML file.
<HEAD></HEAD>	Includes information about a Web page. However, this information isn't displayed to the user.
<TITLE></TITLE>	Identifies the title of the Web page that appears in the title bar.
<BODY></BODY>	Marks the main portion of the Web page that is displayed in the browser window.
<CENTER></CENTER>	Marks text that should be centered in the Web browser window.
<H1></H1>	Marks a level 1 heading. Heading numbers indicate the level of importance for marked headings, with 1 being the most prominent and 6 being the least prominent.
<P></P>	Creates a paragraph break or a double-space.
<UL></UL>	Starts a bulleted list or unordered list.
<LI></LI>	Marks items to be listed.

How HTML Tags Work

HTML tags pass instructions to the Web browser to make Web pages. Tags can appear in uppercase <CENTER></CENTER> or lowercase <center></center>. HTML tags usually appear in pairs containing an *open* tag and a *close* tag. A close tag has a slash in it. The open tag starts a process and the close tag stops the process. For example, this string <center>Corporate View</center> will center the words *Corporate View* horizontally on the page.

You don't need any special tools to create HTML tags. In Windows, you can use Notepad or Wordpad; on a Macintosh, SimpleText works just fine. These programs are called text editors. You can also use most word processors, such as Microsoft Word, WordPerfect, or WordPro, but saving the files in the correct format can be tricky.

Saving HTML Files

The filename extension describes the kind of file you have created. For example, *.doc* in *letter.doc* identifies a Word document, and *.wpd* in *memo.wpd* signals a WordPerfect document. Another important filename extension is *.txt* for *text*.

Text format is the simplest kind of document format. HTML uses text format, but replaces the .txt extension with its own .htm or .html extension as in *webpage.html.*

In this activity, you will learn to save files in a format that can be displayed by your browser.

Just-in-Time Training

Using HTML Tags

1. Access the local Intranet or the Corporate View Web site.

2. Select the **_Information Technology_** link from the Corporate View Intranet Home page. Select and read **_About Information Technology_**.

3. Write your own brief description of IT. You will use this description in a later step.

   _____

   _____

   _____

   _____

4. Launch Notepad, Wordpad, or SimpleText. (This exercise provides instructions for creating simple HTML files using a text editor. You will explore using other programs, such as your word processor, to create HTML files in a later exercise.)

5. Enter these tags exactly as shown. Be careful not to leave out an angle bracket, letter, or slash.

```
<HTML>
<TITLE></TITLE>
<BODY>
<CENTER><H1></H1></CENTER>
<P></P>
<UL>
<LI></LI>
<LI></LI>
<LI></LI>
</UL>
</BODY>
</HTML>
```

6. Key the requested information between the HTML tags as shown below.

```
<HTML>
<TITLE>Information Technology Report</
TITLE>
<BODY>
<CENTER><H1>The Function of Information
Technology</H1></CENTER>
<P>Key your description of the function
of IT between these tags.</P>
<UL>
<LI>List one important function of IT
between these tags. </LI>
<LI>List another important function of IT
between these tags. </LI>
<LI>List another important function of IT
between these tags. </LI>
</UL>
</BODY>
</HTML>
```

7. Click **Save As** on the File menu.

8. From the Save As dialog box, create a new folder to save your HTML work in. (If you need help doing this, see ***Regular Features***, ***Intranet FAQs***, and ***Creating Saving Folders*** on the Intranet.) *MyFiles* or *My HTML Files* would be a good name for this new folder.

9. Save your file in text format using the filename *One.html*. The filename extension may be truncated, or shortened, to .htm. Wordpad, Notepad, and SimpleText automatically save documents in the desired text format. If you are using some other program, be sure to select a text format when saving the file. Figure 10-3 shows Notepad's Save As dialog box.

Note:

Create a new folder just for your HTML documents. This will make it much easier to locate your files when you need them.

Save As:

One.html or *One.htm*

Figure 10-3
Saving files in Notepad

10. Viewing your HTML page in your Web browser is easy. Launch your Web browser. Browse to the folder you created for your HTML documents, such as *My HTML Files*. Select and open the *One.html* or *One.htm* file. Refer to the Just-in-Time Training for Activity 1-1 if you need help with opening files in your browser.

11. View your file. It should look similar to the one in Figure 10-4. If you need to make corrections, do so in your text editor, be sure to save again and then return to your browser to view the changes. (You can use the **Reload** or **Refresh** button or View menu option to view the updated pages.)

Figure 10-4
Your Web page should look similar to this example.

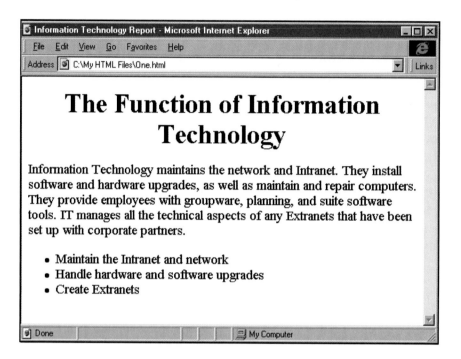

The **Least** You **Should** Know About...

Networks, Clients, and Servers

When two or more computers are connected together, a network is born. Large companies usually connect their computers to client-server networks. A *server* is a high-speed computer that stores information, programs, and data, which are shared with requesting clients. In a client-server Intranet, the software on the computer you use is called *client software*.

Client computers do not need to be expensive or run expensive software. For instance, during most of the short history of the Web, the main client browsers—Netscape Navigator and Internet Explorer—have been free to users. Prices for workstations capable of running client software have dropped dramatically every year in relation to their speed, performance, and efficiency.

Servers, however, run much more expensive software and cost a great deal more money to buy, configure, and install. They are connected to the Net with more expensive modems, switches, and routers—devices that allow servers to send information over the Web and the Intranets they serve.

For IT managers, the top priority must be the maintenance of the company's servers. If a server is down, the repairs to your client personal computer will have to wait!

The process of creating HTML documents becomes easier with each new release of Web site creation tools. Upgrades to software application programs continue to enhance and improve their Web editing tools, making it easier for employees throughout the company to create HTML documents. IT personnel often check Web sites maintained by software and hardware developers for the latest information on Web site creation tools and other software and hardware updates. Five links that might be helpful for IT personnel are listed below.

Microsoft Corporation	**www.microsoft.com**
Sun Microsystems	**www.sun.com**
IBM	**www.ibm.com**
Apple Computer, Inc.	**www.apple.com**
Netscape Communications Corporation	**www.netscape.com**

Think and write about the following:

Access the Web and visit all five of the recommended IT Web sites listed above. In a word processing file, list each Web site. Describe two or more features of (or types of information found on) the site that would be helpful to Webmasters or other IT employees.

Save As:

ITSites

Business
Milestones

Tim Berners-Lee Invents HTML

When Tim Berners-Lee invented Hypertext Markup Language in the late 1980s, he sparked a massive communications and commercial revolution. HTML's little tags, along with the Hypertext Transfer Protocol (HTTP), gave birth to the World Wide Web—a group of computers all over the world that speak HTML.

A new Web server is connected to the Web every few minutes. Since 1996, most of these Web servers have been set up by businesses for their corporate Intranets. The World Wide Web has no center. In fact, it can be said that wherever you are is the center of a growing Web of information. There is, however, a definite center to your corporate Intranet. Its center resides on your designated corporate Intranet server or servers, and is managed by the Webmaster.

Corporate Webmasters are taking Tim Berners-Lee's invention and turning it into an economic force in the business world. From direct sales and marketing to customer support, from HR to legal services, HTML and the Web have become vital parts of the information-oriented business environment.

Activity 10-2 *Saving, Moving, and Converting Files*

Moving files from place to place over the Intranet and your local network can be a bit confusing. There are so many places to save things. For example, you can save to:

- A floppy disk
- Your hard disk
- A Zip disk or compressed drive
- Your local network server's hard disk
- Your corporate Internet or Web server's hard disk

Every time you save a document, you are making and moving a copy of the information from your computer's short-term memory to a more permanent storage place for safekeeping. To do this, you use the **Save** command. You can save copies of your document anywhere your computer system allows you to. It is important that you save multiple copies of all important files. That way, if one copy goes bad, you always have another. This is called *backing up* files.

File transfer allows you to back up files on different computers and servers. With file transfer, you can copy files from one place to another. Before information can be displayed on an Intranet, however, a file must be transferred from your client computer to a special Intranet or Web server. Intranet and Web servers are designed to share Web and Intranet (HTML) documents with requesting clients. Your work must be saved in the proper format (usually HTML) and put in the right place. Your IT engineers must tell you exactly where this place (usually a folder or directory) is located. In the Just-in-Time Training for this activity, you will save a file created earlier in HTML format suitable for viewing with a browser or posting on an Intranet.

You may need to use a tool called *FTP (File Transfer Protocol)* software to save information to the Web or to the corporate Intranet. FTP is a program that allows you to transfer files from your computer to an Intranet or Web server. In the past, to use FTP, you had to learn a lot of complicated text commands. Today, using FTP is as easy as selecting **Save As** and the **FTP** option in many of your software applications. You can also use FTP with Web browsers like Internet Explorer or Netscape Navigator. Special FTP clients, like FTP Explorer, can be downloaded over the Net. These FTP clients make complicated FTP transfers a snap!

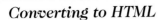

Converting to HTML

Now that you have a basic understanding of how HTML tags work, you will open a file you created in a previous activity and convert it to an HTML document.

1. Open the word processing file *Mybio*, which you created in Activity 1-5.

2. Type tags in and around your text so that your document looks similar to the one you created in Activity 10-1. Begin creating your Web page by keying the open `<HTML>` tag at the top of the page. Go to the end of your document and key the close `</HTML>` tag.

3. Return to the top of the document. Near the top of your page, under the `<HTML>` tag, key `<HEAD><TITLE>My Online Biography</TITLE></HEAD>`.

4. Key the open `<BODY>` tag before the body text you want to display in your Web browser. Key the close `</BODY>` tag after the last word you want to display. Place the close `</BODY>` tag before the close `<HTML>` tag.

5. Key `<H1></H1>` or `<H2></H2>` tags around headings or main topics in your Web document.

6. Center your main headings by keying the `<CENTER></CENTER>` tags.

7. Key paragraph tags `<P></P>` around each paragraph in your bio.

8. If you list information about yourself, like skills you have or things you like to do, key the `<UL><LI>Your text here</LI></UL>` list tags.

9. Save your new file as explained in Activity 10-1 with the name *Mybio.html* or *Mybio.htm*. Saving is the most important step.

10. View your work and see how it turned out! Make any needed corrections and save the file again. Print a hard copy of your final document from the browser.

Save As:

Mybio.html or *Mybio.htm*

Debriefing

Ideally, every employee would attend IT training seminars before undertaking a new task like Web site design. The reality is, however, that in a large and busy company like Corporate View, IT has so many demands on its time that training can't always be provided when it is needed. Companies often expect their employees to have a certain amount of self-sufficiency. Online help systems, print manuals, other employees, and online product support are some resources for corporate workers who must teach themselves how to use software to complete a timely assignment.

Think and write about the following:

1. Describe two methods the IT Department can use to assist employees with software questions when IT doesn't have time to train them.

   _____

   _____

   _____

   _____

2. Considering what you know about Web page creation, do you think most employees should be expected to create and post documents to an Intranet? Why or why not?

   _____

   _____

3. Choose two job positions from any Corporate View mission-critical function. Access the ***Current Job Openings @ TeleView*** under the ***Human Resources & Management*** link on the Intranet if you need help thinking of jobs. For each job, give an example of a document that someone in this position might need to create or convert to HTML format for posting on the Intranet.

   _____

   _____

   _____

   _____

Hyperlinks

One of the most important aspects of HTML is its ability to hyperlink to other HTML documents located around the World Wide Web and the Intranet. Just like everything else in HTML, hyperlinks are created with tags. Hyperlinking tags are often called *anchor tags* and look like this:

```
<A HREF="http://www.corpview.com">
Corporate View</A>
```

An anchor tag links Web pages as an anchor chain links a boat to its mooring. The above link will appear as ***Corporate View*** in Web page text. Clicking on the link will take you to the Corporate View Web site.

In the anchor tag above, the A stands for *anchor*. The A signals your browser to search for the desired Web site: ***http://www.corpview.com***. The words *Corporate View* are underlined to show it is a hyperlink. The close tag < / A > ends the hypertext linking anchor command and is where the underlining stops.

H R E F is short for *hypertext reference*. The reference equals (=) the name of the Corporate View computer.

Activity 10-3   *Picture It on the Intranet*

Two common formats are used for pictures, or graphics, on the Web. One is *.gif* (pronounced *gif* as in *gift*, or *jif* as in *jiffy*, depending on which part of the world you live in). The other is *.jpeg* or *.jpg*, which is short for *Joint Photographic Expert Group* format. Both .gif and .jpg (or .jpeg) files are small and compact; they zip along all the modems and routers, transferring graphics files from Web servers to their requesting clients.

If you have a digital camera, you can take a picture of yourself, save it as a .gif or a .jpg file, and put it into your Web page bio. To practice inserting graphics, you will download the Corporate View logo from the Intranet and put it into your HTML file.

Just-in-Time Training

Downloading a Picture from the Intranet

1. Access the local Intranet or the Corporate View Web site.

2. Choose the ***Intranet FAQs*** link on the ***Regular Features*** page and select ***Copying and Pasting Information from the Web and the Intranet***.

3. Learn how to download pictures from the Intranet by clicking on the ***Copy Pictures or Graphics*** link and reading the information provided.

4. Return to the ***Regular Features*** page.

5. Download/save the Corporate View logo to the same folder where your *One.html* and *Mybio.html* files are stored.

6. After you have downloaded the picture, open your *One.html* file in the text editor you used to create the file.

7. Add the following HTML tag to insert the Corporate View logo. Place it directly after the open `<BODY>` tag so that the image will be near the top of the page.

   ```
   <CENTER><IMG SRC="CV_logo.gif" HEIGHT=100
   WIDTH=125></CENTER>
   ```

Save As:

Two.html or *Two.htm*

8. Save your file as you did in Activity 10-1 with the name *Two.html* or *Two.htm*.

9. Open your new *Two.html* or *Two.htm* file in your Web browser. The image should appear centered near the top of the page as shown in Figure 10-5. If it doesn't, double-check the tags in your HTML file. If the image appears distorted—too short, tall, wide, or narrow—experiment with the height and width settings to correct the problem.

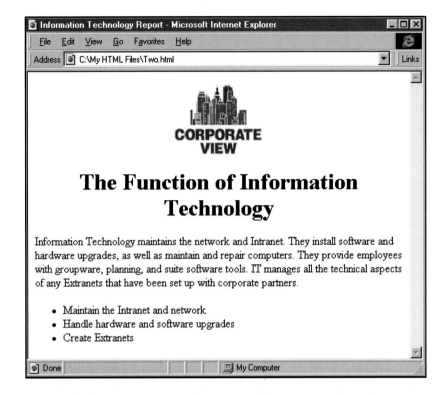

Figure 10-5
Images add interest to Web pages.

*Domain Names and IP
Numbers Foster New
Business Opportunities*

One big new element in corporate advertising is the emergence of domain names. A domain name is an address, like the address of your house or apartment. The URLs **www.microsoft.com**, **www.netscape.com**, **www.ibm.com**, **www.apple.com**, and **www.sun.com** are all examples. These domain names are centers of business activity in the new online commercial world. Billions of dollars are now being made by companies with their own domain names. Online commerce cannot be conducted without them.

When you key a URL or click a hyperlink, a computer called a DNS or Domain Name System server looks up the domain name and finds the corresponding computer number that you are looking for. This is how clients find information and how servers know how to send it back to a specific requesting client.

Just as citizens of the USA have Social Security numbers, every computer on the World Wide Web and the corporate Intranet has an *IP (Internet Protocol) number*. The numbers look something like this: 158.90.74.88 or 6.178.46.1. Special DNS computers look up the domain name (**corpview.com**), convert it to a number (187.57.123.7), and put the request back out over the Net to search for the exact piece of information you are looking for on that specific server.

So, never forget the power of numbers! IP numbers, that is. You can't get online without them.

Technical
Communications

Web Page Design

Intranet and Web pages must be organized, interesting, well written, and geared to the attention span of a busy corporate audience. With a Web page, you only have about three seconds to attract the reader's attention before he or she will lose interest, click a hyperlink, and zoom off to a new page. Web page designers also face two other challenges.

One challenge concerns *window real estate*. This term defines the area within a Web browser window that is visible to the reader. To understand the limitations of Web window real estate, compare the size and shape of a sheet of 8 1/2 by 11-inch paper or a page from a magazine to the average Web page on your screen. The Web page in your browser is much smaller, and so, you must use the limited space or real estate you have to maximize reader interest.

The second challenge is keeping your readers' attention. Features such as graphics, animation, sound, and video are often used to heighten interest in Web pages. Such features help with the three-second rule. Beware, however. Not only must your site attract attention, but it must also have something of value if a visitor is to return again. If your site is poorly organized or written, users may not come back. Too much glitz and glitter and not enough substance will make a site unappealing.

Pictures play an important role in technical communications. Think about the biographies you have accessed on the Intranet. Suppose the bios did not include pictures. After reading a bio, you might think that you know a little bit about the person. With a picture, however, you are able to match a face to the facts you read. A picture makes it easier to feel as if you know someone.

Pictures enhance written text. Soft colors can give viewers a feeling of warmth. Animated or moving graphics add interest and encourage people to look further into the Web site. Diagrams, charts, and graphs present information in graphic form, making it easier to understand.

Think and write about the following:

1. Pick your favorite Web site from those you visited in Activity 10-2. List the URL for your selection:

   _____

2. How do graphics add to the image of the Web site you chose?

   _____
   _____
   _____

3. Are any pictures on this Web site unnecessary or distracting? Explain.

   _____
   _____
   _____

4. How would you change the graphics on the Web site you selected?

   _____
   _____
   _____

Figure 10-6
Vice President Al Gore played a major role in the growth of the Internet.

Business
Milestones

Albert Gore and the Information Superhighway

In the early days of the Net, Al Gore, then a U.S. Senator from Tennessee, coined the term *Information Superhighway* to describe all the lines, wires, cables, fiber optic lines, satellites, and wireless connections that carry information over the Internet and World Wide Web.

Gore's Information Superhighway has become very crowded since the birth of the World Wide Web. In 1995, so many new businesses had come online that many feared the Web would become overcrowded. Industry invested billions in the Web's infrastructure or communications system, though, and the Web has continued to function effectively despite its rapid growth.

On April 14, 1998, Al Gore, Vice President of the United States, announced a joint initiative with business partners to create an Internet expressway—in other words, a second-generation Information Superhighway. This new highway is designed to ship information 1,000 times faster than earlier information roadways. Priority on the new expressway is to be given to medical and emergency services. For example, an x-ray that needs to be analyzed by a specialist at the Mayo Clinic would be sent before an order for 100 copies of the latest Web client software.

The role Al Gore has played in the growth of the Internet has been enormous. Gore believes in the Internet as a means of economic growth and job creation. Much of the current economic prosperity in the United States is a result of the growth of the Information Superhighway.*

Networks for People: Clinton-Gore and the Information Superhighway. Online. Available: **www1.whitehouse.gov/WH/New/Starbright/Network.html. July 26, 1998.*

Executive Summary

The Information Technology Department is critical to the smooth functioning of a corporation. IT personnel maintain the corporate Web site and Intranet. They purchase and install computer equipment and fix everything from your PC's printer to the Internet and Web connections that allow the corporate Intranet to function smoothly. IT maintains the security of the corporate Intranet and creates Extranet connections to other companies. Without IT, a huge investment in technology would be wasted.

IT goes by other names in other companies. Many use the acronym *IS* for Information Services or Information Systems. Other companies use *MIS* for Management of Information Services or Systems. Whatever its name, the IT function is vital if information is to be shared electronically by employees in a corporation.

HTML is the language of the World Wide Web and the corporate Intranet. HTML is a document description language that uses tags to describe how Web pages should appear in Web browsers like Netscape Navigator or Internet Explorer. Using HTML tags, you can create Web pages. It is even easier to create Web pages using Web page creation software, newer versions of word processors (like Word or WordPerfect), and other newer office suite software programs.

Hyperlinks are important features of HTML documents, allowing you to move easily to other documents on the World Wide Web or Intranet. This is accomplished by placing the exact path to the particular file inside special hypertext reference anchor tags. This path will lead you from server to server, and folder to folder, to the exact HTML file your are looking for.

Web pages are stored on special Web and Intranet servers. Web client software, like Netscape Navigator or Internet Explorer, allows you to access these HTML pages.

Technical Communications

Pictures or graphics add interest and warmth to a Web page and can convey important information. Graphics also attract viewers. On the Web or the corporate Intranet, you only have about three seconds to attract someone's attention before he or she loses interest and moves on to another Web page.

After your visitor has read your Web page, will he or she return? The answer depends on the page's content. For readers to make subsequent visits to a Web page, the information must be well organized and well written.

Managing your Web page window's real estate can help you attract attention, engage your reader, and organize your information in a way that keeps visitors coming back.

The Corporate Inbox

Here are some messages that need to be answered by someone in Information Technology. Answer them with the help of the Intranet and your own best judgment. If you need help preparing documents, access the **_Style Guide_** under the **_Corporate Communications_** link.

In his voice mail message, Karl Stockton suggests posting a card on the Intranet. Your instructor will indicate the path/folder where you should save the HTML and graphic files if this option is available to you.

TO: Intern
FROM: **_ldelgado@corpview.com_**
SUBJECT: Addition to Intranet FAQs
MESSAGE:

We have had a great deal of interest in adding to our Intranet FAQs on how to convert word processing files into HTML. Let's be honest, many employees are either too busy or too intimidated by the technology to look up how to do this in their software's help files. Please write a response that we can post on the Intranet that will explain this process. Look at a few of the Intranet FAQs to see how we write them. Here is the question:

"How do I convert my word processing files into HTML documents for the Intranet?"

Have a draft on my desk by the end of the day if you possibly can.

Thanks.
Luis

Save As:

Inbox10A

Hi, this is Cory Thomas. Here in Corporate Communications, we have two employees who plan to telecommute part-time working from their home offices. Both employees have indicated that their home office computer systems are old and need to be updated before they begin telecommuting. We're not sure, however, what equipment they should purchase to access the Corporate View Intranet and run the current office suite programs.

I think they should purchase fairly high-end systems that will not become outdated too quickly. Please email me with your hardware and operating system recommendations for these employees as soon as possible at ___cthomas@corpview.com___*. If you could indicate reasonable prices for the various pieces of equipment, that would be helpful too.*

Thanks. Bye.

Save As:

Inbox10B

Hi, this is Karl Stockton in HR. Melissa Kim is having a birthday tomorrow. She was born in 1976. We thought it would be fun to have a birthday card for her using her picture from her online bio. If you have the time, can you take care of this for us? The card could be in hard copy or in the form of a Web page with the HTML and graphic files to be posted on the Intranet.

Thanks!

Save As:

Inbox10C

From the Desk of Luis Delgado...

Dear Intern

We are opening up a new IT position for our TeleView business unit. We have so much going on that we have outgrown our current resources, so we are adding another full-time Webmaster to work directly with Maria Bravo's team in Corporate Communications. This person will need to be a good proofreader and understand technical communications. He or she will also need to know HTML. Good people and organizational skills are essential. Please prepare a job description that we can pass along to Robin Mills over in HR.

Luis

Save As:

Inbox10D

Online Business Trends

Access the Corporate View Web site. Use the **Stock Watcher Links** on the **Regular Features** page to identify the following ticker symbols and learn how each of these companies did in the stock market today.

Current Date _____

Ticker	Exchange	Company Name	Current Price
SUNW	NASDAQ	_____	_____
IBM	NYSE	_____	_____
MSFT	NASDAQ	_____	_____
AAPL	NASDAQ	_____	_____
NSCP	NASDAQ	_____	_____

When a Few Words Will Do

According to what you have read in this chapter or on the Corporate View Intranet, answer the following questions in a word processing document.

1. What are IP numbers and domain names, and why are they important?

2. Why has Tim Berners-Lee's invention of HTML given birth to entire new industries, new markets, and expanded business opportunities?

3. What do Webmasters do?

4. What is a server computer or program, and how is it different from a client computer or program?

5. Why and where should you back up your important files?

Save As:

Online10

Portfolio-Building Project

Updating Your Bio

In Activity 1-5, you composed a biography in a word processing file, telling a bit about yourself and describing your skills and abilities. In Activity 10-2, you converted this word processing document into an HTML document. In this project, you will update the content of your bio HTML file and add a graphic to make it more appealing.

1. Review the content of your bio. You have worked in several departments and gained new skills and knowledge since you composed the original document. You probably also have a better idea of which mission-critical function or area you might like to work in at Corporate View or another company once your internship is over. Revise your bio to reflect these changes and updates.

2. Search the Web or other sources to find an appropriate graphic image and add it to your document. Search terms such as *free clipart* will return good sources. You might choose an image related to the function or area in which you wish to work, your hobbies or personal interests mentioned in the bio, or any business-related image that seems appropriate and that will enhance the page. If you have trouble finding a suitable image, use one from the Corporate View Intranet, such as the company logo.

3. Save your HTML file and view it in your browser. Make any needed corrections or adjustments to the file and save it again.

4. Print your HTML bio page from your browser and add it to your portfolio.

5. Post your bio on the Intranet for others to view. (Your instructor will indicate the path/folder where you should save the HTML and graphic files if this option is available to you.)

Save As:

Mybio2.html or *Mybio2.htm*

Lots of powerful tools for Web page development are available. They include FrontPage by Microsoft, FileMaker's Home Page, Macromedia's Dreamweaver, and Adobe's PageMill.

Besides these high-end Web page creation and management tools, all the newer major word processors and office suite software have HTML capabilities. If you are using such a program created after 1997, you probably have the capability to create Web pages as easily as you would any other documents. You can take existing documents and convert them easily into Web pages. New versions of these programs will work well for this task:

- Microsoft Word
- Microsoft PowerPoint
- Microsoft Excel
- COREL WordPerfect
- Lotus WordPro

1. Form a workgroup with other employees. Consider the software you have at hand, and figure out the easiest way to convert a document into an HTML file. Your software's help system and print manual are two good resources. If your software does not have HTML capabilities, you can create your Web pages with tags as you did earlier in this chapter.

Save As:

Press1.html or *Press1.htm*

2. Convert *Press1,* the first press release you created in Activity 5-4, to a Web page. You can work together as a group or assign tasks to different members.

3. Convert a few other documents, such as your remaining press releases from Activity 5-4 or your usability study from Activity 6-4, to Web pages to thoroughly familiarize yourself with the process.

4. View the documents you have converted in your Web browser to see how they display.

5. Choose the converted HTML document that represents the group's best efforts and print a hard copy from your Web browser.

6. Post your document on the Intranet for others to view. (Your instructor will indicate where you should save the HTML and graphic files if this option is available to you.)

Information Technology managers keep the information society and its economy thriving. Think and write about this digital world by answering the following questions:

1. How important are Web sites to a modern business?

2. What kinds of businesses don't need Web sites for their customers?

3. What kinds of businesses depend on Intranets the most, and why?

4. Where do you think the Web ranks in terms of the greatest inventions of the 20th century? Can you name five inventions that are more significant?

5. What do you think are the five most important characteristics that should be listed in a job description for an IT Webmaster?

Save As:

Think10

Overtime

Create an Index Page

Wouldn't it be great to access from one location every key report, white paper, press release, or other assignment you have written so far in this course? You can. With the few skills you have learned in this chapter, you can convert these documents to HTML files and create a simple index page that lists them as hyperlinks.

1. Decide where you will save your index and HTML documents. They must all be in the same folder. You may wish to use your *CVFolder* or create a new folder.

2. Choose your key assignments and convert them into HTML documents as you learned to do in Activity 10-1 and 10-2 or in the High-Performance Workgroup Project.

3. Create an index page that lists the files you have converted to HTML. In the sample below, *"press1.html"* represents the file you wish to link to. *Press Release 1* represents the link name you want to appear on the index page. Refer to The Least You Should Know About... Hyperlinks to review anchor tags.

Sample index file:

```
<HTML>
<HEAD><TITLE>My Index</TITLE><HEAD>
<BODY>
<H1>Index of Assignments</H1>
<UL>
<LI><A HREF="press1.html">Press Release 1
</A></LI>
<LI><A HREF="press2.html">Press Release 2
</A></LI>
<LI>[Your Turn]</LI>
</UL>
</BODY>
</HTML>
```

Save As:

MyIndex.html or MyIndex.htm

4. Save your index file as *MyIndex.html* or *MyIndex.htm*.

5. Open your index in your browser and try to access your HTML assignment Web pages. If any of the links do not work correctly, make corrections in the HTML index file and save it again.

6. Print a hard copy of the index file from your browser.

Applications to Small Business

Designing an Intranet

Even though a small business may not be able to afford a large Information Technology staff, finding economical ways to implement an Intranet can improve efficiency and help employees communicate effectively.

One way a small business can save money when implementing an Intranet is to complete much of the design work in-house. Pretend you work for or run a small business and design an Intranet for the company. You can do this on sheets of paper, with index cards, or by creating Web pages as a working model.

1. Begin by choosing a business you are interested in. You might choose a small business in your community or use a hypothetical business.

2. Give the name of the business (real or fictitious) and a brief description of the company—its size, location, and product or service line.

3. List and describe in a logical order the pages, links, content, page design, and graphics to be included on the Intranet. Design all the parts and elements needed for the successful implementation of the Intranet. Remember to plan pages and access for outsourcers, suppliers, and telecommuters.

Save As:

ASB10

Access the Corporate View Web site and take the Online Evaluation for this chapter.

1. Click the ***Employee Training and Evaluations*** link on the ***Regular Features*** page.

2. Select the ***Online Tests*** link. (You must be a registered user to access the online tests. If you are not a registered user, click the ***Register*** link and follow the instructions on the screen. Then click the ***Online Tests*** link to return to the Online Tests page.)

3. Choose the ***Chapter 10 A View from Information Technology*** link on the Online Tests page.

4. Enter the username and password you selected when you registered.

5. Take the test. Click the **First**, **Back**, **Next**, and **Last** buttons to navigate through the questions. Click the **Finish** button to submit your test for grading. If you wish to close the test without submitting it for grading, click the **Cancel** button. Any answers you have entered will be lost if you cancel the test.

Section 3

Moving Up

The future looks bright and promising, and the time to prepare for it is today. Imagine what wonderful new challenges and adventures await you at the start of the new century, what marvelous new technologies will be available.

As you consider what you might experience in the next century, think back to someone born at the dawn of the last century, in the horse-and-buggy age. A person born in 1899 and living today would have experienced the first automobiles, airplanes, televisions, computers, artificial satellites, moon landings, digital phones, and even the World Wide Web. When you consider that progress in this new century will happen at a faster rate, the possibilities are exciting.

In large part, you will shape your own future career. Because of the rapidly changing needs of society and technology, you will likely make several job changes in your lifetime. It's important to be prepared for change and to look constantly toward the future. You must be dynamic and flexible.

As an intern, you looked at the mission-critical functions of a corporation. In this section, you will focus on a specific area in which you are interested. You will explore how to prepare for a career in this field by using resources available on the Internet and the World Wide Web.

Chapter 11

A View of Change

CHAPTER OBJECTIVES

1. Explain the purpose of a job placement center
2. Explore how economic and job-market change can affect employment
3. Think and write about how technological change affects modern office work
4. Examine jobs in a business by mission-critical functions
5. Compare jobs in the military with those in businesses
6. Explore job-market risks
7. Investigate information sources that discuss technological change
8. Explore the impact of multimedia on the high-tech office
9. Examine the role of government agencies related to employment
10. Examine the rights and benefits of eligible displaced workers

Technical Communications

- Reinforce skills by writing action plans, memos, and white papers

Welcome to the Placement Center

"Hi! My name's Raj Syal. I'm an employment specialist in HR's *Placement Center*. At our center, we help employees, as well as interns, find jobs both inside and outside Corporate View.

"One of HR's missions is to retain the best people. Whenever we can, we promote from within—keeping employees with proven track records. It makes good business sense. This, of course, gives Corporate View employees the chance to move up or transfer to other Corporate View jobs they think might be more interesting or enjoyable.

"As you'd guess, this does present a coordination problem. In a company as large as Corporate View, many job opportunities open and close daily. It's often difficult for employees to learn about all the various employment opportunities—which is where the Placement Center comes in. If a qualified employee wants to move up the corporate ladder or to change jobs, either to a higher salary range or to expand his or her professional skills, it's in our best interest to help that employee. We coordinate this process.

"There are other reasons for a placement center too. Economic conditions are always changing, which affects corporations and profitability. A few years ago, we were forced to shut down our Ohio manufacturing plant. We had to downsize to compete with cheaper products being produced abroad. More than 2,000 people had to find new places to work. During this shutdown, the placement center idea was born.

"A recruitment specialist in HR read a white paper on the Web about how other corporations set up placement centers in the wake of devastating cuts in their workforces. She proposed the idea, and the

PC was created. The HR Placement Center was charged with helping our Ohio employees. We relocated, found new jobs for, or retrained as many employees as we could.

Figure 11-1
The Corporate View Placement Center

"The center was a huge success from the start. We worked closely with state and federal government employment departments and covered health benefits for the displaced workers through the **COBRA** program. After the Corporate View positions were filled, the PC actively helped employees find new jobs at other companies. Training was a big part of our Placement Center effort. About 20 percent of the employees took advantage of our retraining program and learned new skills so that they could move into other kinds of jobs. Our training and seminar programs really made a difference.

"After the Ohio difficulties, the center continued helping employees. By the way, as interns, you have access to Corporate View's HR Placement Center. Naturally, we give our full-timers first priority on our services, but we can also help interns find jobs.

"After completing your rounds of the various departments and mission-critical functions, it's time to apply what you have learned to your future. It's your future and you are the one who shapes it, but technological and socioeconomic forces can also change your future.

"Take Linda's career, for example. Linda started out as a keypunch operator, punching cards and feeding them into mainframe-computer card readers in the 1960s. In the 1970s, she used a terminal with a keyboard for the same purpose. In the 1980s she came to Corporate View and learned to use a DOS-based word processor, which required that she memorize numerous combinations of keystrokes. By the end of the decade, she was into Windows and Macintosh GUIs, or graphical user interfaces. With GUI software, she began clicking on user-friendly icons and buttons to get the job done. Printing became as easy as clicking on a button.

"Just before Linda retired, she was one of our first employees to enter data with speech-recognition technology. Using a speech-recognition program, she found she could enter data more efficiently by speaking into a microphone connected to her computer. Now, printing can be as easy as saying 'print' to the computer.

"Linda's career spanned four decades and more than 35 years. Each decade brought considerable change. Her story is typical and illustrates the pace of change faced by most people in the workforce today. The one big difference between what we face and what Linda faced is that the rate of change is increasing.

"We start every placement center session by looking at changes in three areas: the economy, the job scene, and workplace technology.

"In our seminars, we always say, 'Keep your skills up to date and your resume handy. You never know when you will need to make a move.' Hopefully, this will be a move up, a move for the better."

Figure 11-2
The U.S. Department of Commerce online

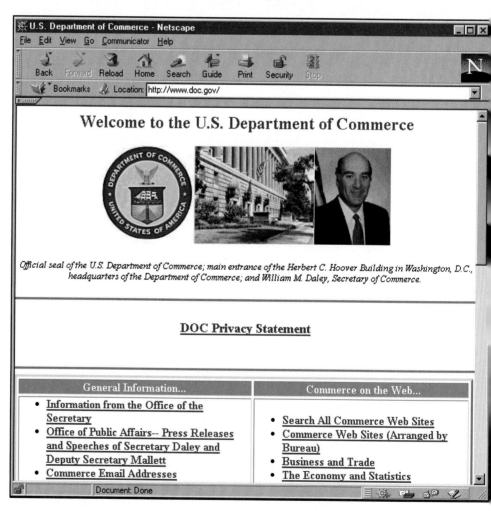

The U.S. Department of Commerce

The U.S. Department of Commerce (DOC) was created in 1903. Within five months it had acquired 10,000 employees located in Washington, DC and throughout the United States. The DOC often served as a repository for various new, small agencies like the Federal Aviation Administration (FAA) and the Federal Communications Commission (FCC).

The Department of Commerce was established to help American businesses and to encourage trade. It seeks to expand U.S. exports and develop new technologies that will help the economy. It gathers statistics and other data to measure economic growth, grants patents and trademarks through its Patent and Trademark Office, promotes entrepreneurship, and fosters economic growth and the creation of new jobs.

As of 1997, 33,000 employees worked at the DOC, managing a budget of nearly $5 billion. The Census Bureau is one of the important branches of the DOC.

Many smaller agencies are part of the Department of Commerce. For example, it is home to agencies charged with oceanographic research and forecasting the weather. Believe it or not, the weather does affect business. The effects of El Niño, La Niña, and other weather-related phenomena can shape the economy in the short term.

Because the DOC collects data related to the performance of the economy, it is a good place to visit if you are searching for business data.

Activity Overviews

When people are looking for work, they often experience stress unnecessarily. It usually isn't a matter of finding *a job* (there's always a job out there). Rather, it's finding the *right* job. Many people do not see how good their situation really can be—which is why many employment seminars start by looking at the "big picture."

Great jobs often come at a price. You might have to move, retrain, or even start over at the bottom of the ladder, but the job could be worth the effort in the long run. The job world is, at best, a risky place. Every fluctuation in the economy affects the job market. Taking calculated risks is just part of the job improvement process. You can't avoid risks, but you can manage them.

For the adventurous, there is always entrepreneurship—that is, risking it all on a start-up business. This is an option only for the strong-hearted or for those willing to work harder than they have ever worked before. Still, the rewards of owning your own business can be very satisfying.

Before you change jobs or start a business of your own, however, it is important to see whether your plans make sense. You have to do a fair amount of homework to manage the risks. Fortunately, you can look up much of what you need to know in cyberspace. In the activities in this chapter, you will review employment conditions in today's economy and consider how they might affect your future.

Activity 11-1 The Changing Economy will explore domestic and international economic and business trends through online government sources. These public sources can help corporations and individuals gain a perspective on their financial futures.

Activity 11-2 The Changing Job Scene explores ways to stay on top of the changing job market. In this activity, you will search the Web for both public and commercial job sites.

Activity 11-3 Changing Technologies on the Job lets you search the Web for information that will help you cope with the pace of change and the newest technologies you might need to use. You will also learn how multimedia technologies are changing the workplace.

Corporate ShopTalk

Understanding the meanings of these terms will help you learn the concepts and develop the skills related to change covered in the chapter. In preparation for completing the chapter activities, access the Intranet and find the definition for each of these terms by clicking the ***ShopTalk*** link on the ***Regular Features*** page.

- Acceptable Use Policy (AUP)
- COBRA
- Machinist
- Occupational Therapist

- Placement Center
- Private Sector
- Public Domain
- Public Sector
- Recession
- Reduction-in-Force (RIF)

- Severance Pay
- Unemployment Compensation
- Webcasting
- Workers' Compensation

The Changing Economy — Activity 11-1

Most of today's jobs didn't even exist ten years ago. How do we know this? The U.S. government and other bodies around the world keep track of such things. This information is available to the public through various sources, including the Department of Labor, the Bureau of Labor Statistics, the Department of Commerce, the Congressional Budget Office, the Census Bureau, the Small Business Administration, and other sources. All of these U. S. Government statistics are in the **public domain**, which means they may be used freely.

Other governments and agencies also track important economic and employment trends. Locating these data is as easy as visiting a few Web sites. For example, technology is one of the fastest-growing employment areas. In the next few years, thousands of high-paying technology-related jobs will go unfilled. This trend means good employment opportunities for workers with the necessary technical skills and training.

To find the latest economic and employment statistics, visit a few places that track these data. Knowing this information can help you plan a career, and it can help businesses identify new growth areas and launch new strategic business units. These kinds of data can help corporations anticipate new markets and emerging industries.

Business Milestones

The U.S. Department of Labor

The U.S. Department of Labor (DOL) is charged with helping every American learn the skills he or she needs to hold a good job, moving people from welfare to work, securing and protecting retirement and pension programs, and guaranteeing a safe, equal-opportunity workplace.

Rules and regulations that the DOL enforces affect well over 100 million workers and 10 million employers.

The DOL is involved in many areas, including overseeing massive layoffs and plant closings, monitoring labor statistics, establishing occupational safety standards, and implementing other protective measures. For instance, the DOL oversees the Fair Labor Standards Act, which establishes a minimum wage. Overtime work is also controlled by the DOL. The DOL works with miners to help prevent black lung disease and ensure mine safety. As you can probably guess, the DOL Web site is a good place to start searching for information concerning your rights as an employee.

One of the most important divisions of the DOL is the Bureau of Labor Statistics (BLS), which compiles and interprets statistics about the nation's workers.

Figure 11-3
The U.S. Department of Labor online

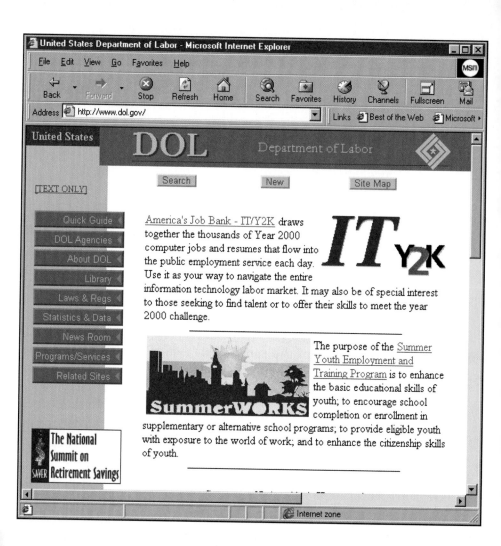

Just-in-Time Training

Locating Economic Trends Online

1. Access the Corporate View Web site.

2. Select the ***Human Resources & Management*** link from the Corporate View Intranet Home page.

3. Click the ***Other Government Employment and Economic Links*** and access three of the sites listed there. In a word processing file, key the following information for each of the three sites you selected:

   - The site name and URL

   - A list or description of the information available there

   - A description of anything new you learned at this site about economic or employment trends

4. Which of the three sites you visited was the most interesting?

Save As:

Trends

5. Which site had the most valuable information?

_____

6. Which site was the easiest to navigate? What made it easy to navigate?

_____

_____

Debriefing

The economy is a complex thing. Regional and local factors can have part of the country booming and another part suffering from a _recession_ or economic downturn. Nevertheless, the regional economies all interact. The economy is global. No country or region is immune from a banking crisis in Asia or the impact of fluctuations in the Euro, the new currency of Europe.

Return to the **_Human Resources & Management_** page and click **_International Employment and Economic Links_**. Select the **_International Statistics_** link and explore a few international economic sites.

Think and write about the following:

1. Choose one of the sites you visited. What is the name and URL of the site?

_____

2. Are you investigating a specific country?

_____

3. List or describe the kind of information available at this site.

_____

_____

4. What new information did you learn at this site about economic or employment trends?

_____

_____

_____

Activity 11-2 *The Changing Job Scene*

When you think of the various mission-critical functions in a company, jobs available in some departments are obvious. For instance, you would probably expect to find an attorney in the Legal Services Department or a recruitment specialist in the Human Resources Department.

Other great jobs hide in unusual places. For example:

- An Information Technology engineer could be relocated to a Sales group to help sell high-tech products and solutions to high-tech corporate clients.

- A medically trained **occupational therapist** might be found on an HR team working to solve employee injury problems by implementing a new safety training program.

The **Least** You **Should** Know About...

Unemployment

It is rarely pleasant to have to leave a job. Many terms are used to describe the process of laying off workers. *Downsizing* and **reduction-in-force (RIF)** are popular terms. Federal and state governments have enacted legislation to minimize the negative impact of being out of work. This legislation relates to workers' compensation, unemployment benefits, and health care insurance.

Workers' compensation is somewhat like an insurance program. If you experience a life- or limb-threatening injury while on the job and must leave work for a long period of time, you could qualify for workers' compensation. State and federal laws require corporations to supply this insurance to their employees.

Unemployment compensation is meant to provide a safety net for people who are temporarily out of work. If you lose your job through no fault of your own and meet certain eligibility requirements, you are entitled to monetary payments for a certain period of time. The program is paid for by taxes collected from workers.

The Consolidated Omnibus Budget Reconciliation Act (COBRA) and the Health Insurance Portability and Accountability Act (HIPAA) were designed to help displaced workers cope with changes in health insurance coverage when changing jobs. One of the biggest problems when leaving a job can be losing your health coverage benefits. COBRA allows you to purchase insurance at your employer's group rates for 18 months or more after you leave the company if certain criteria are met. HIPAA expanded this protection by ensuring that people cannot be denied health insurance for preexisting medical conditions and other reasons. Your HR representative and government agencies will help you understand all these benefits.

Many employers offer **severance pay** to employees affected by RIFs. Severance pay packages usually include cash payments that match a certain number of weeks, months, or years of salary. Some people will only work for a corporation that offers severance packages and makes such packages part of the initial employment contract.

- A photographer or video editor could become a critical member of a Corporate Communications *Webcasting* workgroup.

- A *machinist* could become part of an R&D team making parts for product prototypes.

Corporations hire employees based on their business needs. Those needs can create some very interesting occupations in some very unlikely places. In this activity, you will visit various repositories of job information online.

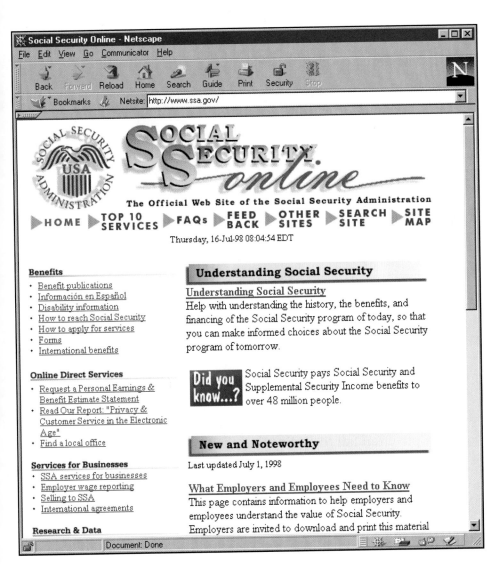

Figure 11-4
Social Security online

Just-in-Time Training

1. Access the Corporate View Web site.
2. Select the **Human Resources & Management** link from the Corporate View Intranet Home page.
3. Click **Placement Center Job Links**.
4. Select three of the sites to investigate. In a word processing file, key the following information about each site:

   - Site name and URL
   - Purpose of the site
   - Type of information available at the site
   - Description of who might benefit from the site

5. Of the three sites you have visited, which site would you recommend to a friend who is seeking a job in one of the mission-critical functions like HR, R&D, or Marketing and Sales? Why?

_____

_____

_____

Save As:

Jobsite

Debriefing

Public service jobs, government jobs, college jobs, and jobs in education often require the same skills that are needed in corporations. People often fail to realize that the military also requires many of the same mission-critical functions and jobs that businesses require. For example, military recruitment divisions are similar to corporate HR Departments because they, too, seek to find the best possible employees or recruits. The military has its own equivalent of a Corporate Communications function because it has its own television and radio stations, Web sites, and email.

Look for some other examples of military jobs that parallel those found in businesses. Access military Web sites, visit recruitment offices, interview your local ROTC instructor, or research military publications. (Links to military Web sites can be found under **Human Resources & Management**, **Military Sites**.)

Think and write about the following:

After reading or hearing about military jobs, choose two military jobs that would most closely match each critical function and list them below.

1. Human Resources and Management

   _____

2. Corporate Communications

   _____

3. Research and Development

   _____

4. Marketing, Sales, and Customer Support

   _____

5. Legal Services

   _____

6. Finance and Accounting

   _____

7. Information Technology

   _____

Remember Linda, the punch-card operator in the 1960s, who used a mainframe terminal in the 1970s, DOS in the 1980s, Windows in the 1990s, and before she retired, entered data by using her voice? When she started working, the Internet was nothing more than a small government project called the Advanced Research Projects Agency Network (ARPANET). ARPANET was established for military and scientific research. Many of the technologies developed for ARPANET are still used in today's Internet.

While Linda was learning her first DOS applications in the '80s, the National Science Foundation (NSF) funded a network of super-computers around the United States. It created a high-speed telecommunications backbone between these centers, and the National Science Foundation Network (NSFNET) was born. The NSFNET

Figure 11-5
The Small Business Administration online

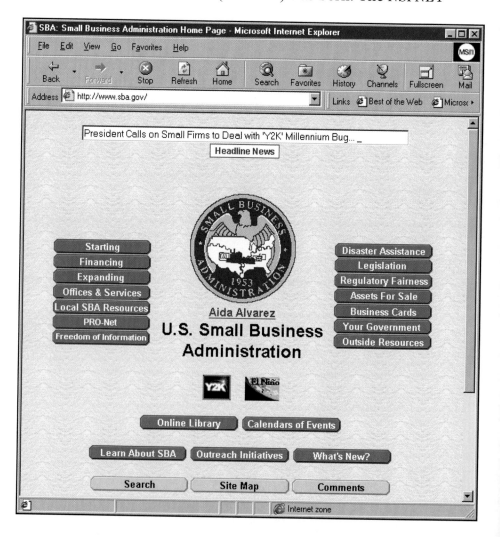

allowed researchers and academics from all over the world remote access to high-speed supercomputers. The idea of an Information Superhighway began to take shape. At this time, Linda downloaded her first file from the Internet, as people had started to call it.

The Internet before 1994 was a noncommercial zone. Business was discouraged, even forbidden, by some who considered the Net an academic playground. *Acceptable Use Policies (AUPs)* from the universities that hosted the Net of the '80s and early '90s directly discouraged commercial activity on the public Internet.

The early Net was a character-based environment. Thankfully, unwieldy commands were replaced by the wonderful graphical icons, buttons, and menus of the World Wide Web. Then Netscape came along and business discovered the visually rich, multimedia environment of the Web. Corporations quickly adapted their business practices to this new economic opportunity. A few years later, most of the activity of the Information Superhighway was commercial in nature.

Toward the end of her career, Linda was Web surfing with the best of them. She always said how much she loved the Web because finding what she needed was finally easy.

Business Milestones

The Small Business Administration

It might seem as if large corporations get all the breaks in obtaining government contracts, subsidies, and tax breaks. Whether or not that is true is up to the politicians. To help make sure small businesses get a chance to compete, Congress has organized several government agencies specifically to look out for small businesses. This makes good sense because more people work for corporations with fewer than 500 employees than for corporations with more than 500 employees. In many ways, small businesses are the backbone of the North American economy.

The Small Business Administration (SBA) is assigned the task of looking out for small-business interests. A small business, by legal definition, is independently owned and operated and not dominant in its field. If small businesses meet certain criteria, they can get loans through the SBA.

The SBA has answers for small business. Here are a few of the most frequently asked questions listed on the SBA FAQs page. These questions help point out the concerns of small business owners. (You can link to the SBA site from the Corporate View Web site.)

1. Do I have what it takes to own/manage a small business?
2. What business should I choose?
3. What is a business plan and why do I need one?
4. Why do I need to define my business in detail?
5. What legal aspects do I need to consider?
6. What do I need to succeed in a business?
7. Would a partner(s) make it easier to be successful?
8. How can I find qualified employees?
9. How do I set wage levels?
10. What other financial responsibilities do I have for employees?

Frequently Asked Questions. *U.S. Small Business Administration.* Online. Available: ***www.sba.gov/starting/faqs/***. April 25, 1998.

The rate of change in Linda's 35 years at work was slow, however, compared with the current rate of change. The knowledge available to us today doubles every few years. The speed and power of computers also doubles at a similar rate. The bandwidth of our Web connections continually improves.

The way we work with our office technology changes every year. Printers and input devices get better, databases on the Intranet get bigger, and access to information gets easier. In this information age, it is important to keep track of the latest office technologies. The computer industry drives continuous change in the way we work. In this activity, you will discover how to learn about the latest and greatest Intranet and Web technologies.

Just-in-Time Training

Locating Technology Trends Online

1. Access the Corporate View Web site.
2. Select the **_Information Technology_** link from the Corporate View Intranet Home page.
3. Click the **_IT Research Sites_** link.
4. Select one site from each of these three categories: Software, Hardware, Technology Webzines.
5. In a word processing file, key this information about each site.

   - The site name and URL

   - Main theme or topic of the site

   - Description or summary of how information on this site would be helpful to an IT manager trying to improve the effectiveness of the corporation's office technology systems

Save As:

Offtech1

In a word processing file, key your answers to questions 6–8.

6. List several new innovations affecting business that were not available to Linda when she retired in May of 1998.
7. How can the sites you visited in this activity help the average employee keep up with the changes in technology on the job?
8. Where do you see the biggest changes in office technology occurring in the future? Explain the kinds of changes you see and their impact on employees.

Save As:

Offtech2

In the early days of Intranets, most information was available in text format. Although the written word will always be important in business, for obvious reasons, this trend is changing as more video, audio, and multimedia devices are made available every day.

The RealPlayer became available on the Net in the mid-1990s. This piece of software brought realistic sound to personal computers over the Net. PointCast was another pioneer, unleashing push technology on an unsuspecting Web. PointCast software allows news and other types of information to be sent automatically to Web users.

Many other multimedia options are available. To learn about a few, access the Corporate View Web site and select the **_Information Technology_** link from the Corporate View Intranet Home page. Click on the **_IT Multimedia Web Sites_** link and explore a few of the sites.

Think and write about the following:

1. What kind of information was presented at the sites you visited?

   _____

2. What types of information do you think can be presented most effectively in text form?

   _____

3. What types of information can be presented most effectively in multimedia form?

   _____

4. How can multimedia help improve the technology of the office and the Intranet's performance?

   _____

Chapter Review

Executive Summary

Some corporations establish placement centers to help employees find new jobs within the corporation or to help displaced workers find work elsewhere when a reduction in force is necessary. Placement centers can also help employees or former employees continue their health care plans and collect other benefits, such as unemployment compensation or workers' compensation.

The job market is constantly changing. New technologies, competition from other corporations, changes in the employment picture, and economic downturns or recessions can alter career paths. Many public and commercial Web sites specialize in helping people keep up with the changing economy.

Stress is often a problem for people who are looking for work. Analyzing economic data and studying various job-related opportunities can help a job seeker reduce stress by providing a better understanding of the overall employment picture and implementing strategies for changing careers.

Federal and state governments have enacted legislation to minimize the negative impact of being out of work. Workers' compensation provides benefits to eligible workers who are injured on the job. Unemployment insurance provides benefits to eligible workers who lose their jobs through no fault of their own. COBRA and HIPAA legislation ensures that workers can continue to purchase their health care insurance for a period of time after leaving a job and that they cannot be denied health care insurance due to preexisting medical conditions.

Many of today's jobs did not exist ten years ago. Various government agencies in nations around the world keep labor statistics that help track employment trends. In the United States, agencies such as the Bureau of Labor Statistics, the Department of Commerce, the Congressional Budget Office, the Census Bureau, and the Department of Labor all track employment trends and the economy.

Technological change is driving many of the changes in the office workplace. You can follow these trends by searching Webzines and sites for software developers, hardware manufacturers, and other creators of office technologies.

The military offers many career opportunities and positions that parallel the mission-critical functions found in corporations.

Here are some messages that need to be answered by someone in the Human Resources Placement Center. Compose an answer for each of these questions with the help of the Intranet and your own best judgment.

Hi, this is Raj Syal. We have had a great deal of interest in what you have been doing out on the Web—locating economic and employment resources. Would you please help the placement center by writing a white paper on how to find and use public-domain Web sites to identify economic and employment trends. Perhaps your findings will help others make the most of the Web when looking at economic change.

Thanks for your help with this report. Let me know if you have any questions. Bye.

Save As:

Inbox11A

CORPORATE VIEW

From the Desk of Maria Bravo...

Dear Intern

Corporate Communications needs a press release showing how Corporate View is keeping up with technology trends. We need to reassure shareholders that we are keeping our eye on economic and technological change. Please write a press release that talks about changes in the technology industry and how the TeleView division can take advantage of these trends and make a profit. It doesn't need to be long—200 to 400 words should do it.

Thanks
Maria

Save As:

Inbox11B

TO: Intern
FROM: *rmills@corpview.com*
SUBJECT: Employment Inquiry
MESSAGE:

We just received an email from a Navy veteran who is about to retire. Please read this message and write a reply.

Thanks,
Robin

<<<<<Message forwarded from **Stephen.Hillfigger@navy.mil**>>>>>

Dear Corporate View:

Your company has been recommended to me as one I should investigate for possible employment. I am retiring from the military after 20 years of service. I most recently served as a communications specialist for the Navy's Shore Patrol. What options may be open to me at Corporate View?

Lieutenant Stephen Hillfigger, USN

Save As:

Inbox11C

Save As:

Inbox11D

TO: Intern
FROM: *mkim@corpview.com*
SUBJECT: New Position—Online Research Specialist
MESSAGE:

We are creating a new position that will support all the strategic business units. The position is called online research specialist. The job will involve researching topics on business and economic trends for the various marketing teams. The person holding this job will need to be very good at collecting information from the Web. Many other corporations have entire teams that do nothing but this kind of research. This is our first effort. This person will need to be prepared to build an entire workgroup team.

The online research specialist will need to be a good technical communicator too. Good interpersonal and organizational skills are also essential. Please prepare a job description that we can pass along to Robin Mills in HR for this job.

Thank you,
Melissa

Perhaps you have taken an interest in the stock performance of some corporations you have learned about. Checking a stock price at regular intervals, such as once a week for a month or every day for four days, and graphing the prices can give you a better picture of the stock's performance.

Consider Microsoft, for instance. How is Microsoft's stock doing today? Look up the stock price and enter it below.

Current Date _____

Ticker	Exchange	Company Name	Current Price
MSFT	NASDAQ	_____	_____

You were also asked to look up Microsoft's stock price in Chapters 1, 4, and 9. Look back and see what you recorded for the stock prices then. How have the prices changed? Prepare a graph or chart that shows the changes in the stock price.

When a Few Words Will Do

According to what you have read in this chapter or on the Corporate View Intranet, answer the following questions in a word processing document.

1. What is the role of the DOL in helping businesses succeed?

2. How does the DOC help evaluate the economy?

3. How did the U.S. Government influence the development of the Internet, the Web, and modern-day Intranets?

4. How are the COBRA and HIPAA programs designed to help workers?

5. What is a RIF, and why is it sometimes necessary?

Save As:

Online11

Portfolio-Building Project

Finding Work in an Online World

Suppose you have been working for Corporate View for five years, making cellular phone technology in the Ohio manufacturing plant. Then suddenly the market shifts to digital phones, and the company is shutting down your division. You have just become part of a RIF. What are you going to do?

Create an agenda for action outlining your plans. Review The Least You Should Know About... Planning Through Problems in Chapter 2, page 57. You have many options. What are you going to do? What steps should you take to get back into the job market?

High-Performance Workgroup Project

Everything seems easier when a team is involved, even finding a new job. Placement centers often have displaced workers organize teams and discussion groups. These teams share ideas and plans for the future. And, as the saying goes, "Many hands make light work."

Many sources of information about jobs are available online. You can use the Intranet, the Web, and Web search tools to find sites describing *private sector* jobs, *public sector* jobs, and corporate job descriptions or postings.

In a group of three, discuss the kinds of jobs each of you would like to apply for. Then have each team member complete one of the job-seeker research tasks listed below. Combine your findings so that each team member has a copy of the links you find.

Search for private-sector jobs:

One team member should search for private-sector jobs using the WWW. Private-sector jobs are those found in industry or in privately owned businesses. Start by using the Intranet's **Placement Center Job Links** on the **Human Resources & Management** page. Then use search words to find other listings. Prepare a list of ten Web job sources and their addresses that other team members can use to visit these same sources.

Search for public-sector jobs:

One team member should search for public-sector jobs that are similar to the jobs team members have selected. Public-sector jobs are found in government and education. Start by searching various government Web sites, such as the U.S. Department of Labor, military sites, and other government economy-related Web sites. Start with the various government links found on the Intranet. Use search words to find other sites. Prepare a list of ten government or education job-related links that other team members might find valuable.

Search for job descriptions from major corporations:

One team member should list ten major corporations highlighted in the Business Milestones reports in this text. Then find ten corporate Web sites and see how many of them post corporate job descriptions online. Search the corporate job descriptions for employment opportunities that match the jobs team members have discussed. The **_Placement Center Job Links_** on the **_Human Resources & Management_** Intranet page is a good place to start. Use search engines to find other sites. Prepare a list of Web addresses that team members can use to find these job descriptions quickly.

Save As:

HP11

Thinking and Writing About Your Business

Based on what you have learned in this chapter, answer seven of the following questions in your own words. Key your answers in a word processing document.

1. How does government contribute to business success?

2. How can government interfere in the success of certain businesses?

3. Do you think government should be involved in business? If yes, how and to what extent?

4. How easy do you think it would be to make a move from the military to the corporate world?

5. What kinds of businesses will not be around in ten years?

6. What kinds of new businesses will grow rapidly in the next ten years?

7. What big changes do you see in the software industry that could affect the office workplace?

8. What big changes do you see in the computer hardware industry that could affect the office workplace?

9. Since the government funded the early Internet, is it right for businesses to take advantage of it today? Explain.

10. What is the FLSA, and who administers it?

11. In your view, what is the most important government-sponsored benefit program a RIFed employee can take advantage of?

Save As:

Think11

Overtime

Comparing Strategic Business Units

Corporations must make lots of tough decisions. So must investors who are investing their money in these corporations. Imagine that Corporate View needs to bounce back from a business decline. Management is considering the possibility that one or more of the business units should be sold and the money used to shore up other, more profitable business activities.

Investigate the future potential of Corporate View's strategic business units. Using the online searching skills you learned in this chapter, research the market potential of each Corporate View SBU. Which are on the way up and why? Which are on the way down and why?

Save As:

Otime11

Document your sources as you do your research. In a short white paper, make a case for selling one of the SBUs. Who goes and who stays: TeleView, RetailView, MoneyView, MediView, PublishView, or TravelView?

Applications to Small Business

Starting a Business

The Business Milestones report concerning the Small Business Administration presented several questions the agency has been asked over and over again. Review the list and select the five questions you think are the most important from the perspective of someone starting a small business for the first time. List the five questions in a word processing file.

Save As:

ASB11

Select one of the questions and prepare your own answer to it. Research the Intranet and the Web for answers to your question. You can link to the Small Business Administration, other agencies, or businesses to help you construct a good answer. Keep your answer between 100 and 150 words.

Access the Corporate View Web site and take the Online Evaluation for this chapter.

1. Click the ***Employee Training and Evaluations*** link on the ***Regular Features*** page.

2. Select the ***Online Tests*** link. (You must be a registered user to access the online tests. If you are not a registered user, click the ***Register*** link and follow the instructions on the screen. Then click the ***Online Tests*** link to return to the ***Online Tests*** page.)

3. Choose the ***Chapter 11 A View of Change*** link on the ***Online Tests*** page.

4. Enter the username and password you selected when you registered.

5. Take the test. Click the **First**, **Back**, **Next**, and **Last** buttons to navigate through the questions. Click the **Finish** button to submit your test for grading. If you wish to close the test without submitting it for grading, click the **Cancel** button. Any answers you have entered will be lost if you cancel the test.

Chapter 12

Researching a Specialty

CHAPTER OBJECTIVES

1. Review the mission-critical functions
2. Choose a mission-critical function and research it in detail
3. Select mission-critical corporate careers you would consider
4. Define your personal criteria for accepting a job
5. Explore vital corporate functions and careers
6. Distinguish between public- and private-sector careers
7. Research and catalog a variety of Web resources
8. Identify growth markets in new industries based on economic data
9. Search for jobs using the *Occupational Outlook Handbook*

Technical Communications

- Prepare mailing list messages, white papers, and email messages

Who Is at the Heart of the Corporation, Anyway?

"As we start our final session, let me say that every function at Corporate View is vital. It appears that we can't live without any of them. Do you remember the quotes? It seems that each vital function sees itself as the heart of the corporation. Here, let's look at a few:

"From Human Resources: 'Our job at HR is to manage the services and benefits that will attract, motivate, and retain a highly talented, committed, and diverse workforce for TeleView.'

Robin Mills, HR Director

"From Corporate Communications: 'Corporate Communications is the heart of the company, if you think about it. Corporations like Corporate View depend on information to survive and remain competitive.'

Maria Bravo, Communications Coordinator

"From Research and Development: 'In one sense, Research and Development is the heart of Corporate View. Without exciting, innovative products continually being introduced to the market, Corporate View would soon wither and die.'

David Wu, Assistant Director of R&D

"From Marketing, Sales, and Customer Support: 'Marketing, Sales, and Customer Support teams are the very heart of Corporate View and all its business units. None of this would be here if it weren't for us—neither the buildings nor the Corporate View Research Park— and all the people would be working somewhere else.'

Casey Jones, Director of Marketing and Sales

"From Finance and Accounting: 'Finance and Accounting is the heart of any business, and money is the blood. As long as we keep the blood circulating at the right pace, TeleView will continue to do well. If we do well, that helps all of Corporate View do well, Corporate View stock goes up, and more investment money will be available for new corporate ventures.'

Spencer Malone, Certified Public Accountant

"From Legal Services: 'From my vantage point, the best lawyer is always the one who knows the most about the law. I make my living from what I know about the law. Then I apply what I know to protect this company legally, and along with it, the livelihood of every person who works here. In that sense, Legal Services is the key to this whole operation.'

Charles Cooper, Corporate Attorney

"From Information Technology: 'I guess the IT department is like the heart of this company. We feel we're the common thread that links its different parts. We tie every department, every team, every person into a single unit. It all starts here, and it branches like veins through the network cabling, above the ceiling panels, into the cubicles, behind the desks, and into the computers.'

Luis Delgado, Intranet Webmaster

"So, who's right? Who's at the 'heart' of the corporation, anyway? Either we're all myopic and somewhat self-absorbed, or we're collectively making an important point: A corporation is a pretty complex system. As you've no doubt guessed, each mission-critical function must work in concert with the others. It takes a well-oiled team to make the corporation perform efficiently.

"Consider some scenarios.

"Where would the greatest R&D Department be without the Marketing and Sales Department? Without money coming in, the research team would be hired away to better-paying jobs at other corporations.

"Imagine the world's greatest Information Technology team building the finest-looking corporate Intranet in the world. It would lack the needed content without Corporate Communications' researching, writing, and editing. A great-looking Intranet devoid of content would be worthless.

"Imagine selling products without supporting them. How long would customers stay loyal to the products? Sales can generate a huge cash flow, but without a team of accountants managing the money, the corporation would go bankrupt before long.

"And what about all those patents and trademarks? Without a legal team, they could be stolen and the corporation's competitive advantage would be lost.

F i g u r e   1 2 - 1
Customer Support is vital to continued sales success.

Figure 12-2
The Occupational Outlook Handbook *is only one of many valuable labor- and employment-related publications maintained by the BLS.*

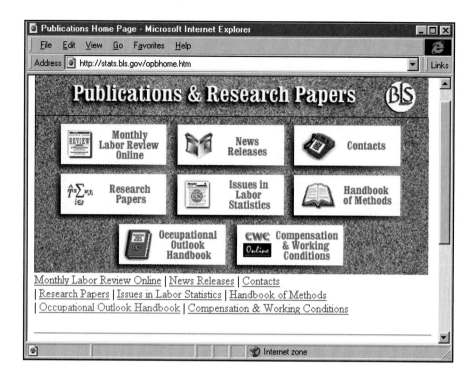

Business
Milestones

The Bureau of Labor Statistics

One branch of the U.S. Department of Labor (DOL) catalogs jobs—from accountants, auditors, and able seamen to zoologists and zookeepers. It is called the ***Bureau of Labor Statistics (BLS)*** and is a research arm of the Department of Labor.

The BLS keeps economic statistics, manages employment surveys and special programs, and disseminates publications and research papers on labor issues. It shares its job information in a valuable biannual publication called the ***Occupational Outlook Handbook (OOH)***. The *OOH* provides forecasts in *Tomorrow's Jobs*, lists sources of career information, gives advice on how to find a job, and tells how to evaluate a job offer.

Here are a few trends the BLS predicts for the decade from 1996 to 2006.

- Service-providing industries will increase faster than the average with a growth rate of over 30 percent.

- Within the service industry arena, business, health, and education services will account for 70 percent of the growth. Over 1.2 million new teachers will be needed.

- The health care industry will increase 30 percent and account for 3.1 million new jobs, the largest numeric increase of any industry.

- Computer and data processing services will add over 1.3 million jobs, a 108 percent increase due to technological advances. This will increase the need for highly skilled workers in this area. This area should be the fastest-growing area percentage-wise during the decade.

These predictions can be helpful in choosing a career or specialty area.

Occupational Outlook Handbook. *Bureau of Labor Statistics.*
Online. Available: ***http://stats.bls.gov/oco/oco2003.htm***.
April 25, 1998.

"Finally, how long would a corporation last without HR finding quality employees and managing excellent benefits packages to keep its employees happy?

"One person, one department, one division... can't do everything. We're in this together, and we have to work as a team. That doesn't mean we don't disagree—we sometimes do. We must realize, however, that we are dependent on each other. Each function needs the others.

"When you go to work for a corporation, you have to decide which of these vital functions you are the most comfortable with. In other words, which one would you like to work in?

"In your final training session, let's take a closer look at a specialty area that interests you the most . . . and learn about it in more detail. In other words, where would you be happy working in the corporate world?

"For you, where's the heart of the company?"

Activity Overviews

Most business people specialize. In other words, they become experts in performing certain functions or jobs crucial to the success of the corporation. In this series of activities, you will select a mission-critical function to explore in greater detail.

As you think about the functions you are interested in, keep an open mind. Don't narrow your options too quickly. You can always change your mind later if you want to. For example:

A young lawyer became the manager of a huge Customer Support team almost by accident. He found that he liked working with people more than working with the law. He went on to transform his support staff into the best in the industry. His legal background came in handy as he trained his support operators in what they could and couldn't say to customers over the phone, in email, and in support FAQs on the Web.

Consider the draftsperson, expert in *CAD (Computer-Aided Design) software*. She went to work for the Buildings and Grounds Department, drafting landscape and office designs. Her plans directed the work of teams of gardeners, carpenters, and electricians as they created a comfortable corporate environment. Demonstrating management ability, she began to lead the entire department. Eventually, she became the vice president of Buildings and Grounds.

Many great careers and great opportunities are waiting for you. Whatever you choose, make your specialty "the heart" of your company.

Figure 12-3
Many business people choose to specialize within their field.

Activity 12-1 Careers at the Heart of the Corporation will explore a mission-critical function you would like to learn more about.

Activity 12-2 Other Critical Functions Not to Be Forgotten examines additional functions essential to a healthy corporate environment. These jobs provide many opportunities for well-trained employees in the ***Security***, ***Manufacturing***, ***Warehousing***, and ***Buildings and Grounds*** Departments.

Activity 12-3 Mission-Critical Resources on the Web lets you explore the Net, searching for virtual support centers for the career specialty area you have selected.

"*Corporate* ShopTalk"

Understanding the meanings of these terms will help you learn the concepts and develop the skills covered in the chapter. In preparation for completing the chapter activities, access the Intranet and find the definition for each of these terms by clicking the ***ShopTalk*** link on the ***Regular Features*** page.

- Buildings and Grounds
- Bureau of Labor Statistics (BLS)
- CAD (Computer-Aided Design) Software

- Mailing List
- Manufacturing
- Market Sector
- Newsgroup
- *Occupational Outlook Handbook* (*OOH*)

- Security
- USENET
- Warehousing

The corporate world is specialized, with different people performing different functions for the good of the enterprise. At some point, you might have to answer this question, "What career do I want to specialize in?"

Some people take jobs they have spent only a few hours thinking about. They graduate, visit a recruitment fair, an employment office or placement center, or a career site on the Web; find an interesting job; and apply. Maybe they apply for dozens of jobs on the same day. Then they wait and see what happens. A few interviews later, "presto," a new career. Some great careers may evolve "accidentally," but for most of us it is important to think seriously about our careers.

Other people took the jobs they have because they knew people working at their places of employment. Sometimes "who you know" helps a great deal in finding a job. When you are looking for work, a helping hand from a friend can be useful. Taking a job allows you to earn some money, learn a few new skills, and add a new employer to your resume.

Be warned, however. Taking a job because your friend works at the same company might not be a good idea if it's a job you don't like or it turns out to be a "dead-end" job. If you find yourself in a job with less-than-desirable future prospects, think about changing positions or even careers.

Take some time to ask yourself a few questions:

- Am I qualified for this job?

- Is this a job I want?

- Is this job in a department or mission-critical function that will allow me to expand my skills? Can I grow in this job?

- Would I enjoy it? Is it challenging?

- Does it pay enough money?

- Will I be able to live where I want to live?

These are tough questions.

There was a time when many employees worked at one company for their entire careers. It was possible to find a great job at a great corporation and work there for 25, 30, or even 40 years and retire.

These "cradle-to-grave" jobs are now rare, however. Most people will change jobs, departments, companies, or even careers many times before they retire. You may have heard, "The only constant in

Figure 12-4
Hewlett-Packard's URL is easy to guess. The company simply uses its acronym, HP, in the name ***www.hp.com****.*

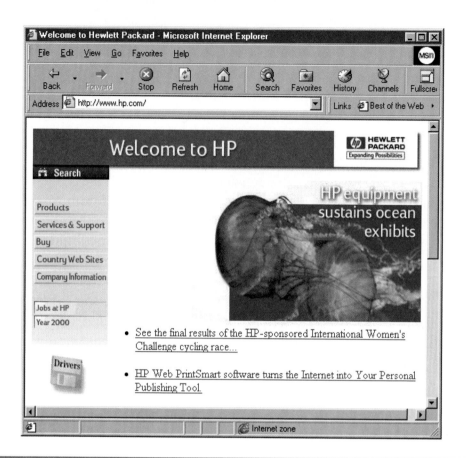

The **Least** You **Should** Know About...

Locating Corporate URLs

Locating corporate Web addresses, or URLs, isn't difficult. You can use a few tricks to make finding them even easier:

- *Guess.* Nearly all corporate URLs start with *www* and end with *.com*. Because most corporations try to obtain domain names that are close to their corporate trade names, you can guess many business URLs. Microsoft's **www.microsoft.com** is easy to remember. Hewlett-Packard's **www.hp.com** is also very easy to figure out. You can guess the URLs for many major corporations.

- *Use a search engine.* If you can't guess a URL, try entering the name of the corporation into a search engine and see if the company's site comes up. You might find some sites that concern the desired corporation, and they might have links to the Web site you are looking for.

- *Check stock market ticker sites.* Most of these sites have links that allow you to search corporations by name, some providing brief summaries of each corporation listed. From there, you may be able to find the URL you are looking for.

- *Check job-related Web sites.* Some of these sites, like America's Job Bank, list participating corporations in alphabetical order.

- *Try Webzines.* Many Webzines, or online magazines, link to corporations that are discussed in their articles.

Try these five tricks to find the Web sites for corporations you wish to locate.

the universe is change." Change is inevitable. Change can be good or bad, depending on how you approach it. If you possess something special, such as valuable skills or experience, the likelihood of landing a better job will be good.

Perhaps the best advice is not to worry about change, because it is inevitable, but to try to manage change for your benefit. Keep your resume handy and be on the lookout for that special opportunity that change could bring your way.

Just-in-Time Training

Corporate Jobs

1. People are naturally attracted to certain careers. In Activity 4-1, you were asked to look at **_Current Job Openings @ TeleView_** under the **_Human Resources & Management_** link. The jobs are organized according to mission-critical function. Do you remember the mission-critical function you clicked first? At the beginning of this course, which mission-critical function or department did you consider the most interesting at that time? Circle it here:

   Human Resources and Management

   Corporate Communications

   Research and Development

   Marketing, Sales, and Customer Support

   Finance and Accounting

   Legal Services

   Information Technology

2. Has your perception changed about which of these functions you would find the most interesting? If you had to make a choice at this moment, in which area would you like to work?

   _____

3. Explain why you are currently attracted to your choice.

   _____

   _____

   Answer questions 4 through 10 in a word processing file.

4. Make a list of ten corporations that interest you. Then, find the Web sites and list the URLs for those corporations. (See The Least You Should Know About... Locating Corporate URLs feature box.)

5. Search the corporate Web sites you have selected and see if they have an HR link with pages that list current job openings or a link that takes you to corporate Jobs or Careers. Among the corporations you have selected, which have jobs available in the mission-critical function you selected in step 2? Find ten jobs for the mission-critical function you selected. (You may use several related jobs at a single corporation.) List the name of the corporation and the job description/title.

6. Of all the jobs you listed, which one seems most interesting? Why is this a job you might want?

7. Do you think this is a job in a department or mission-critical function that will allow you to expand your skills? How will you be able to grow professionally in this job?

8. Do you think this job would be enjoyable and challenging? Why?

9. Does this job description state a salary range? What is the pay, and do you think it is adequate for the job?

10. Where is the job located? Where would you have to live if you were to take this job?

Save As:

Act12-1

Debriefing

In the United States, the terms *private sector* and *public sector* have curious meanings. As far as employment goes, the public sector includes government careers; the private sector includes business or corporate careers.

Use a search engine to find government careers in an area of interest to you. This might be easier than you think. (Do not include military careers because you already looked at those in a previous activity.) Search for careers in the U.S. Federal Government or other national level governments, state or provincial governments, or local governments.

Think and write about the following:

1. Before you start your search, think of five search words or terms that could lead you to these careers. List your search words or terms.

_____

_____

2. Use a search engine on the Web. Locate three public-sector jobs that are similar to jobs in the private sector.

Name of Government Agency _____

Job Title _____

URL _____

Name of Government Agency _____

Job Title _____

URL _____

Name of Government Agency _____

Job Title _____

URL _____

Activity 12-2 *Other Critical Functions Not to Be Forgotten*

Corporations are complex creations of human invention. Some functions in a corporation encompass all the other functions. For example, Corporate Communications' mission is to keep employees in all the other mission-critical functions informed.

Security is another function that encompasses the corporation. Retail stores often employ Security teams to protect their goods from theft. But the Security function usually goes beyond that role in large corporations. In major technology corporations, the R&D Department needs to be protected from corporate espionage. The military knows all about this kind of security. In fact, many experienced ex-police or ex-military security personnel eventually work for corporations that seek to protect themselves from pilfering. Security also protects employees on the job, in the parking lots after hours, and from the occasional irate customer. At security-conscious corporations, employees carry identification cards that give them access to the buildings they work in. Every time employees enter or leave a building, perhaps even a section of a building, their movements are tracked.

F i g u r e 1 2 - 5
Employees use ID cards to gain access to secure parts of the workplace.

Buildings and Grounds (often called *Facilities and Grounds* or *Maintenance*) is a department that some take for granted, but no corporation would want to be without this vital function. Most employees will tell you they like working in clean, pleasant facilities where all the electrical, plumbing, heating, and cooling systems work. There is nothing worse than working in a building in the summer when the air conditioning goes out or in a cold room during the winter. A nice, clean office building surrounded by attractive grounds with super facilities and the latest technology attracts and keeps quality employees.

Keeping everything clean, beautiful, and working is not as easy as it first appears. Just handling cleaning chemicals safely in ways that avoid serious injury requires extensive training. Many people have sustained serious respiratory injury or nearly died by accidentally mixing two of the wrong cleaning agents.

Some corporations move employees around quite a bit. This is particularly true in corporations that are growing or shrinking rapidly. On moving day, perhaps after a restructuring, affected employees will need help moving. This isn't as easy as it sounds. Picture an entire division of 50 or more people being moved to another wing or to a building across town. Employees in every pod, cubicle, or office need workers to set up everything—making sure all the electrical outlets work; all the equipment arrives; chairs, tables, and desks are in place; and everything connects properly. Often the job must be done overnight so that no work is lost during regular working hours. This process takes extensive planning.

Just-in-Time Training

Job Opportunities

1. Which of these mission-critical functions do you find most interesting? Circle your choice.

   Security

   Buildings and Grounds

   Manufacturing

   Warehousing

2. What jobs do you think might be available in these mission-critical functions? Use your search skills to find three jobs available from corporations in each area listed in step 1. In a word processing file, list each mission-critical function. Under each function, list the company name, job title, and URL for each job. You might want to revisit the ten business URLs you located in Activity 12-1, step 4.

Save As:

Act12-2

In the last few activities, you have looked at employment opportunities from a variety of perspectives, including careers in the mission-critical functions, as well as private- and public-sector employment. Another way to think about employment is from the perspective of the strategic business units.

SBUs are often organized around what marketing people call *market segments* or *market niches.* Another popular term is **market sector.** A market sector focuses on one industry from its beginning stages in R&D, into marketing and sales, through final customer support.

TeleView is an SBU that focuses on the electronics sector. The electronics industry could be considered an industry sector. For instance, we might say, "The electronics sector rebounded today on Wall Street," or, "The telecommunications sector united behind a new set of technology standards."

There are other industry sectors or market niches. Corporate View has several business units that seek to make a profit in these various sectors:

- RetailView, Corporate View's sporting goods and sports apparel business unit, goes after the billions of dollars in the sports industry.

- MoneyView, Corporate View's banking, insurance, and financial business unit, goes after billions in potential profits in the banking and finance industries.

- MediView, Corporate View's medical and pharmaceutical business unit, tries to carve out a market share in this highly profitable industry.

- PublishView, Corporate View's online publishing business unit, tries to make a name for itself in this highly competitive industry.

- TravelView, Corporate View's online travel and vacation business unit, manages to make a small profit in this huge industry.

Each SBU represents a different market, a distinct industry sector. This creates interesting career choices. For example, someone might take a job at RetailView because he or she likes sports, sports clothing, and sports equipment; but the person might be doing the job of an HR recruitment specialist. In fact, HR recruitment specialists work for each business unit listed above. An HR recruitment specialist for

MediView might need to learn a great deal about the medical profession. An HR recruitment specialist in PublishView will need to learn a great deal about the publishing industry.

It's the same with every mission-critical function. For example, a Corporate Communications technical writer may write copy for the Intranet on sports for RetailView, stock market trends for MoneyView, a new operating-room procedure for MediView, and a trip to Bermuda for TravelView. It is important to remember that mission-critical functions work across each industry segment or SBU.

In this debriefing, you will examine how job interview questions might change for the same position for different strategic business units. What kinds of questions would you want to ask? How might they differ, depending on the SBU? How might they be similar?

Think and write about the following:

1. If you were interviewing candidates for a sales representative position in TeleView, what two questions would you be sure to ask?

   _____

   _____

2. How would your interview questions change if you were now interviewing candidates for a sales representative position in the MediView SBU? What two questions would you be sure to ask?

   _____

   _____

3. List two new questions you would likely ask someone applying for a sales representative job selling sports equipment for RetailView.

   _____

   _____

4. If someone were applying for a sales representative position at MoneyView, what two things would you want to ask him or her?

   _____

   _____

5. A new candidate for a sales representative position at TravelView might have to answer what two questions?

   _____

   _____

6. Finally, how would you alter interview questions for someone applying for a sales representative job at PublishView?

   _____

   _____

Activity 12-3 *Mission-Critical Resources on the Web*

Conditions are constantly changing in each mission-critical function and in each strategic business unit. There are always new issues to consider, new problems to solve.

Professionals can keep track of changes in their fields in several ways. These include a variety of Web- and Internet-related sources. For example:

- Webzines are published on nearly every mission-critical function.
- Chat and **USENET newsgroups** exist for every mission-critical function. (See The Least You Should Know About... USENET Newsgroups.)
- Professional organizations for each mission-critical area sponsor conferences, publications, and electronic **mailing lists**. (See The Least You Should Know About... Electronic Mailing Lists.)
- Web pages about each mission-critical function are posted by thousands of interested people.
- Professional organizations often provide Webcasts to broadcast training and other career-advancement information to organization members.

In this activity, you will search for some of these resources. Choose one mission-critical function and concentrate on it for this activity.

- Human Resources
- Corporate Communications
- Research and Development
- Marketing, Sales, and Customer Support
- Finance and Accounting
- Legal Services
- Information Technology
- Security
- Manufacturing
- Buildings and Grounds
- Warehousing

In the Just-in-Time Training, you will use a combination of Web surfing and searching to locate resources that can keep you up to date in your selected area.

USENET Newsgroups

One of the most democratic areas of the Internet is USENET. USENET is short for *user network*. This huge system consists of tens of thousands of newsgroups covering nearly every topic you can imagine. USENET is not a news service. USENET newsgroups are more like discussion groups on topics of interest. When a USENET user becomes part of a newsgroup, she or he can join in the conversation, ask questions, make comments, and get answers. Newsgroups can be found on topics such as:

- Sports, including sports teams and notable players
- Business trends and mission-critical functions
- Books and authors
- Government and politics

- Computer hardware, software, and other technology issues
- Humor

Conversations follow *threads,* with each thread being a separate conversation. When you initiate a discussion, you start a thread. When someone replies to your thread, he or she keeps the thread going.

Newsgroup software looks and acts like email software with special threading capabilities. One difference is that with newsgroup software, the messages are usually intended for a larger group of readers.

Newsgroup addresses are different from Web URLs or email addresses. For example, ***alt.cad.autocad*** is a group discussing Computer-Aided Design software. The group ***alt.tv.friends*** discusses the television show "Friends."

Just-in-Time Training

Web Resources

You will need a live connection to the Web for this activity.

1. What specialty area or mission-critical function do you wish to explore?

2. Use your searching and surfing skills to find seven online resources that will keep you informed about changes and new trends in this mission-critical function. In a word processing file, list the name and URL of each source. Briefly describe the information found at each site.

Save As:

Act12-3

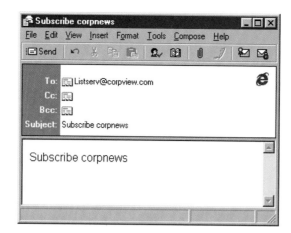

The **Least** You **Should** Know About...

Electronic Mailing Lists

Mailing lists use the power of email to generate messages to large numbers of people at a minimal cost. To participate in a mailing list, you first need to subscribe. This is as easy as typing SUBSCRIBE<NAME OF MAILING LIST> in an email message to a particular mailing list service. To stop receiving mail from a mailing list, you can use UNSUBSCRIBE <NAME OF MAILING LIST> or SIGNOFF<NAME OF MAILING LIST>.

Businesses use mailing lists to great advantage. When you visit certain Web sites, you can click a few buttons, provide your email address, and automatically subscribe to an electronic mailing list. When you buy and register a new product electronically, you might be placed on a mailing list so that you can automatically receive news about the product.

Corporations assign one or more Corporate Communications employees to prepare their mailing lists. A mailing list is like a press release sent to interested readers. Evaluating your audience, the purpose of the message, the length of the message (it should never be too long), and personality (which livens up the message) are as important in a mailing list message as in other email messages or press releases.

Debriefing

As you learned in this activity, a wealth of online information is available to help you keep current on the mission-critical function of your choice. In fact, sorting through the vast mass of information available can be overwhelming. How can you decide which sources are the best ones for you?

Think and write about the following:

1. Of all the online resources you located in this activity, which one seemed to be the easiest to use or understand? What makes this source more user-friendly than others you accessed?

_____

_____

2. Which resources would be helpful for accessing regular updates or news on the mission-critical function?

_____

_____

3. Which resources would be helpful for networking with others interested in your specialty area?

_____

_____

Newsgroups

Newsgroups are great places to practice your technical communications skills. You should follow accepted practices when communicating in newsgroups. General guidelines include:

- Stick to the topic under discussion. USENET users become annoyed when someone gets off the topic.
- Be brief. Lengthy messages are usually not well received.
- Be considerate. Newsgroup postings usually go to many people with a variety of backgrounds and beliefs.
- Spell correctly and use proper grammar to have your message taken seriously.
- Don't use "big words," trying to impress your readers. Use your vocabulary naturally in context.
- When you respond to a thread, mention what the topic is before you start your message so that it will be easier to follow.
- Give your name. People who use anonymous names can be considered shallow, uninformed, or unwilling to support what they say.

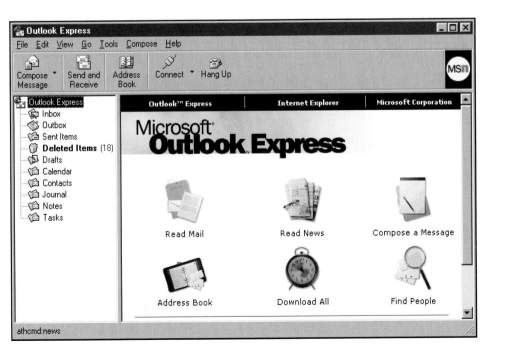

Figure 12-7
Microsoft Outlook allows you to read newsgroup postings, as well as email.

Chapter Review

Executive Summary

This chapter discusses how vital each mission-critical function is to the success of the corporation. Each function can be considered the heart of the corporation. The key is to select a function in which you would be comfortable working. Your choice should allow you professional growth, enjoyment, challenges, and income.

Very few business people spend their entire careers at one corporation. People can successfully change careers if their skills are constantly improving. One key to success is to specialize in a function you enjoy and are good at.

As you plan your career specialty, it pays to research careers available in corporations you find interesting. Establishing criteria for taking a job can also help direct your choice of a job and a career. Private- and public-sector career specialties are available for every mission-critical function.

Beyond the mission-critical functions presented in Section 2, desirable careers can be found in other vital functions, such as Security, Buildings and Grounds, Warehousing, and Manufacturing. These functions are found in most corporations to some extent. Additionally, each strategic business unit at Corporate View represents markets or industry sectors with differing career opportunities.

Keeping up with the changes in your career specialty is easier than ever before because of the Internet and the Web. Webzines, Webcasts, newsgroups, and electronic mailing lists can keep you informed about your mission-critical career specialty.

Government continues to gather statistics about the economy. The Bureau of Labor Statistics (BLS) compiles data and prepares the *Occupational Outlook Handbook*, a biannual report on employment trends.

Technical Communications

USENET newsgroups and electronic mailing lists provide ways to communicate information on business and a variety of other topics. As with other technical communications, consider your audience and the purpose, length, and personality of the message when preparing messages for mailing lists or newsgroups.

Here are some messages to be answered by someone familiar with how Corporate View works. Compose an answer for each of these questions with the help of the Intranet and your own best judgement.

TO: Intern
FROM: *mtucker@corpview.com*
SUBJECT: Employment Trends
MESSAGE:

Please help me prepare for an industry advisory panel I was asked to sit on. The panel is sponsored by the DOL's Bureau of Labor Statistics and will look at future employment trends at major corporations. I need you to research and prepare a white paper, something I can share with the panel, on the following:

- What kinds of jobs are likely to increase in number at Corporate View and in what SBU sector in the next five years?

- What jobs are likely to decrease in number over the next five years at Corporate View?

Give reasons for your conclusions.

Thanks for doing this for me. I have a big Board meeting next week and can't give it my time. Please email the report to me as soon as you finish it.

Madeline

Save As:

Inbox12A

*Hi. This is Jay Miller. I see that you have a job open for a computer operator/programmer in a Corporate View manufacturing and warehousing facility. I have always viewed work in manufacturing as involving low-tech assembly-line jobs. What kinds of things can I expect in this job? What's the job environment like? Please send some further information about these jobs to **Jmiller@myaddress.net**. Thanks. Goodbye.*

Save As:

Inbox12B

TO: Intern
FROM: *jbrown@corpview.com*
SUBJECT: Job Searches
MESSAGE:

We need an Acceptable Use Policy (AUP) statement on searching for positions at other corporations during regular working hours. The truth is, we don't have a policy on this. We have never tried to stop employees from looking for jobs they like better. My philosophy is that if employees aren't happy here, they should look for new jobs in other corporations. One of our managers in RetailView, however, says he has two employees who spend every daylight hour on the Web, looking for new jobs rather than doing their work. This isn't right either. Anyway, this has prompted a debate.

Please prepare a policy statement or Acceptable Use Policy on this issue. We don't want to limit their freedom or their options, but there is an appropriate time and place for everything.

Can you get us a draft of what you think the policy should look like? Do it in the form of a mailing list message, but send it to me first so that I can discuss it with the other corporate officers before we actually send it out.

Save As:

Inbox12C

Now that you have considerable experience viewing the stock performance of various companies, choose five corporations and pretend you are investing $10,000 in their stocks. Track the stock performance of each stock for a period of time (as indicated by your instructor) to see whether you gain or lose money.

Distribute the numbers of shares you buy among the five companies any way you like. The goal, of course, is to pick stocks that are going to increase in value. Invest up to $10,000, but not a penny more. Use the following form to help you track your stocks.

Stock Ticker	Corporation Name	Starting Price/Date	Number of Shares	Ending Price/Date	Gain or Loss

When A Few Words Will Do

According to what you have read in this chapter or on the Corporate View Intranet, answer the following questions in a word processing document.

1. What is the value of a mailing list to a corporation?

2. How does the Bureau of Labor Statistics help evaluate the economy?

3. Should business people subscribe to newsgroups? What topics would be important to follow?

4. Explain how to join and quit a newsgroup.

5. What are some methods you can use to find corporate Web sites?

Save As:

Online12

Portfolio-Building Project

Jobs Mailing List

So many people are asking about jobs at Corporate View that HR can't keep up with the requests for information, particularly for TeleView jobs. At last count, TeleView's HR records showed nearly 1,000 active applications.

Melissa has an idea to help improve this situation: a mailing list for interested people. One electronic mailing every day would inform every subscribing job seeker of the current openings.

During a weekly HR coordination meeting, the decision was made to go with the ***TVJobs@corpview.com*** mailing list. All applicants with email could subscribe. The first part of the message will be a little like a press release, announcing the purpose of the electronic mailing list and giving some positive information about Corporate View and TeleView so that readers will be interested in coming to work for TeleView. The email message should be relatively short and list the current job openings. A highlight feature at the end should go into more detail on one key job that Corporate View is eager to fill in the TeleView division.

You have been assigned to prepare the message for release tomorrow. You can find the current job openings by reviewing the Intranet's job listings. (Select ***Human Resources & Management***, followed by ***Current Job Openings @ TeleView***.) Write the rest of the message on your own.

Save As:

Pfolio12

Apply what you know about writing effective email and press releases to writing this mailing-list message. Put the two skills together and prepare the first ever mailing list for ***TVJobs@corpview.com***.

High-Performance Workgroup Project

You are sitting in the break room when your marketing research team leader comes in with a memo from President and CEO Madeline Tucker. Apparently, Madeline read a report in a business magazine that said, "According to the Bureau of Labor Statistics, service-providing industries are going to grow steadily in this decade."

At Madeline's request, your team has been asked to research business growth potential in the service-providing industry sectors for Corporate View. Instructions from the chief say to find out what these service-providing industries are and how Corporate View can capitalize on the growth in these industries to make a profit. The CEO is confident of your workgroup's abilities to explain this sector in more detail. Be sure to explain what the service-providing industries are and list some profitable products and services they include.

Using what you know about researching the Web, work with your team to find answers and prepare a three-page white paper suggesting a course of action. The potential of any one or all of Corporate View's strategic business units to capitalize on the growth opportunities should be discussed in your report.

Save As:

HP12

Thinking and Writing About Your Business

Who is at the heart of the corporation, anyway? Corporate View has had a great quarter and has the resources to increase seven department budgets between 1 and 7 percent based on the value each function has to the corporation.

Which function do you think matters most? Based on what you have learned in this book, choose one of the functions listed on page 360 and make a short case (25 to 50 words) for this function to receive a 7 percent increase in its budget. Then choose the second most important function and make a case for it receiving a 6 percent increase. Keep working your way down until you pick the seventh most important function and make a case for it receiving a 1 percent increase in its budget.

Save As:

Think12

Overtime

Web Resources

You have visited many public and private sources of information on the Web during your work here at Corporate View. Which were the most helpful and why? Can you easily access these sources again?

1. Create an HTML page listing the five most valuable job- and employment-related resources you have found. Explain why these Web sites are valuable to you. Create hyperlinks so that you can easily access these resources from this page. (If you need help creating a Web page with hyperlinks, refer to Chapter 10.) You might wish to include pictures or other multimedia options on your page to make it more interesting.

2. On the same page, create another list of the five most valuable resources relating to your favorite career specialty. For each resource, include the name of the Web site, the URL, and why the resource is worth visiting again. Create a hyperlink to each resource.

Save As:

Otime12.htm or
Otime12.html

Applications to Small Business

Employment Trends

The Bureau of Labor Statistics reported that computer and data processing services will add more than 1.3 million jobs, a 108 percent increase in the forecast period, because of technological advances. This will increase the need for highly skilled workers.

Think and write about the following:

Save As:

ASB12

1. Search the Web to find five computer-related occupations in this market sector that are going to become the hot jobs of the next century.

2. Would you want to specialize in any one of these jobs? If so, why? If not, why not?

3. Would your job choice be appropriate for a small business or a home-based consultant? Explain.

Online Evaluation

Access the Corporate View Web site and take the Online Evaluation for this chapter.

1. Click the **Employee Training and Evaluations** link on the **Regular Features** page.

2. Select the **Online Tests** link. (You must be a registered user to access the online tests. If you are not a registered user, click the **Register** link and follow the instructions on the screen. Then click the **Online Tests** link to return to the **Online Tests** page.)

3. Choose the **Chapter 12 Researching a Specialty** link on the **Online Tests** page.

4. Enter the username and password you selected when you registered.

5. Take the test. Click the **First**, **Back**, **Next**, and **Last** buttons to navigate through the questions. Click the **Finish** button to submit your test for grading. If you wish to close the test without submitting it for grading, click the **Cancel** button. Any answers you have entered will be lost if you cancel the test.

A

acceptable use policies (AUPs), 335
account manager, 231
accounting, 238-241
   generally accepted principles, 242
   major firms, 250
   for small businesses, 259
   visiting firms, 250-251
Accounts Payable and Receivable, 231
action, agenda, 55-59
actuary, 231
addressable advertising, 220
adjuster, 231
administrative assistants (AAs), 86
advertising, addressable, 220
affiliates, 178
after-market sales, 202
agenda for action, 55-59
America Online (AOL), 153
American Institute of Certified Public Accountants (AICPA), 238, 242
analyst, 231
annual report, 141
antitrust, 18
applications, desktop, 14
assets, 238
asynchronous, 25
AT&T, 18, 174
audience
   of flowchart, 88
   market, 205
   for press release, 153-156
   split, 155
   in writing, 34
auditor, 231

B

balance sheet, 238
benchmark, 114
benefits packages, 106, 122
beta testing, 171
biannual, 127
BLS, *see* Bureau of Labor Statistics
bonuses, 90
bookkeeper, 231
branding, 201, 272
Buildings and Grounds, 356
bundle, 48
Bureau of Labor Statistics (BLS), 327, 348

business, types of, 234-235

C

cash flow, 233
certifications, 120
certified public accountant (CPA), 238
channel, 201
charters, 267
civil law, 262
clerk, 231
client software, 300
communications
   corporate, 140-160
   small business, 166
comparative value testing, 171
compensation, 330
competencies, 127
competition
   comparing, 69-70, 165-166
   strategic business units and, 195-196
competitive advantage, 108
computer-aided design (CAD) software, 349
consumer quality testing, 171
Consumer Reports, 172, 185
consumer surveys, *see* surveys
contracts, 265
controller, 231
copyright, 261, 271-274
corporate
   culture, 11
   image, 152
   investment, 233-234
   jobs, 353
   vocabulary, 5
corporate communications, 140-160
corporation, 231
   multinational, 2
   state laws and, 268-269
   types, 235
criminal law, 262
critical path, 84
culture, corporate, 11
customer support, 202-204
customer surveys, *see* surveys

D

defaults, 22
Department of Commerce (DOC), 325

Department of Labor (DOL), 327, 348
desktop applications, 14
dividends, 233
domain name, 282, 308
downsizing, 43, 330
Dun & Bradstreet, 233, 235

E

earnings per share (EPS), 246
earnings statement, 247
economic trends, online, 328
email, 25-29
employee profiles, 30-35
employment
   finding, online, 341
   searching, 342-343
   trends, 332
   unemployment, 330
entrepreneurs, 43
equity, owner, 238
etiquette, *see* netiquette
evaluation, 126-128
extensions, filename, 9, 295
Extranet, 7

F

family benefits, 122
FAQs, *see* frequently asked questions
Federal Communications Commission (FCC), 170
feedback, 216, 218, 219
field study, 183-185
fieldwork, 181
file transfer protocol (FTP), 295, 302
filename extensions, 9, 295
files
   converting to HTML, 303
   moving, 302
   saving, 302
financial planning benefits, 122
fiscal year, 248
flexibility, 121
flowcharts, 73, 87-88, 95, 99
focus groups, 201
forms, 242-245
foundation skills, 127
Franklin Covey Co., 48, 79
frequently asked questions (FAQs), 16, 20
FTP, *see* file transfer protocol
functions, mission-critical, 1, 44-63

G

Gantt chart, 85
general ledger, 238
General Motors (GM), 45
generally accepted accounting
  principles (GAAP), 242

H

headhunter firms, 107
health benefits, 122
Health Insurance Portability and
  Accountability Act (HIPAA), 330
home page, 22
Human Resources (HR), 106
hyperlinks, 305
hypertext markup language (HTML),
  9, 294, 296-301
  converting files to, 303
  design, 308
  images in, 306
hypertext transfer protocol (HTTP),
  295

I

IBM, 188, 266
image, corporate, 152
images, computer, 306-310
incorporation, 266-270, 290
information
  managing flow of, 84-89
  superhighway, 310
Information Technology (IT), 292-311
in-house training programs, 90
Intel Corporation, 92
Internet, 6
Internet Protocol (IP) numbers, 308
Internet service provider (ISP), 153
interviews
  questions for, 121, 123-125
  rating scale, 129
Intranet, 3, 6-12, 14
  copying from, 53
  downloading images from, 306
  researching on, 91
  for small businesses, 318
investment, corporate, 233-234

J

job descriptions, 106, 110-120
  parts of, 132
  writing, 114-120, 132, 137
job environment, 124

L

law
  civil, 262
  complexity of, 275
  corporate, 276
  criminal, 262

specialty areas, 277
  state, 268
ledger, general, 238
legal
  language, 282
  translations, 280-283
Legal Services, 260-285
length, in writing, 35
liabilities, 238
Liquid Assets, 230
litigation, 262
localize, 141
logos, 199

M

mailing lists, electronic, 146, 360,
  362, 368
Management, 106
management by objectives (MBO),
  107
manager, role in evaluations, 126
Manpower Inc., 110
Manufacturing, 44
market, 198
  identifying, 227
  niche, 205, 207-209, 358
  research, 170
  sector, 358
  segment, 205, 358
  share, 18, 198
  strategic, 170, 174-176
Marketing, 199-201
McGraw-Hill, 233
memos, 67-68
merit awards, 122
mirror sites, 14
mission-critical functions, 1, 44-63
  corporate law and, 276-278
  resources on the Web, 360-362
mission statement, 3
monopoly, regulated, 18
multinational corporation, 2

N

NASDAQ, 12
netiquette, 21, 27
network, 300
New York Stock Exchange (NYSE),
  12
news release, 145
newsgroups, 360, 361, 363
niche, market, 205, 207-209, 358
notes, 181, 182

O

Occupational Outlook Handbook
  (OOH), 348
occupational therapist, 330
online
  finding work, 341

job descriptions, 115
major accounting firms, 250
press releases, 164
searching, 279
tax support, 258
testing, 17
trends, 328, 332, 336
usability reports, 194
writing, 35
operating system (OS), 25
options, stock, 251
outsourcing, 90, 138-139, 142
owner equity, 238

P

partnership, 234
patents, 264, 271-274
Payroll, 231
PCWeek Online, 146
peer evaluation, 128
performance
  awards, 122
  points, 90
  product, 50-51
  report, 52-54
  reviews, 107, 127-128
personal digital assistant (PDA), 78,
  83, 101
personal information management
  (PIM) software, 78, 80-81
personal planners, 78
personality, in writing, 34
personnel, 106
PERT chart, 85-86
Placement Center, 322
planning, 72-89, 99
  problems and, 57
portfolio, 40
press kit, 141
press release, 141, 145-159
  audience, 153-156
  evaluating, 147-149
  in online world, 164
  purpose, 153-156
  types, 147
  writing, 150-152, 157-159
price point, 205
private sector, 342
problem-solving workgroups, 58
problems
  formulating solutions for, 60-61
  planning through, 57
  small businesses and, 70
product
  designing, 175
  packaging, 228
  performance, 50-51
  performance report, 52-54
  protection, 273-274
  prototyping, 175
  research, 48-51